The Cuchulain Plays of W. B. Yeats:

A Study

Reg Skene

*Director of Theatre and Associate Professor of English
University of Winnipeg*

Columbia University Press
New York   1974

Published in Great Britain in 1974 by
THE MACMILLAN PRESS LTD

Printed in Great Britain

Library of Congress Cataloging in Publication Data

Skene, Reg
The Cuchulain plays of W. B. Yeats.

1. Yeats, William Butler, 1865-1939 — Criticism and
interpretation. I. Title.
PR5908.C8S55   821'.8   74-10725
ISBN 0 231 03930 1

TO ANNETTE

Contents

Introduction

W. B. Yeats wrote five plays about the Irish hero Cuchulain. The first written, *On Baile's Strand,* was completed in 1903 and was performed on the stage of the Abbey Theatre in December 1904. Yeats made major revisions of the play for performance in 1906, after which he declared:

> It is now as right as I can make it with my present experience, but it must always be a little over-complicated when played by itself. It is one of a cycle of plays dealing with Cuchulain, with his friends and enemies. One of these plays will have Aoife as its central character, and the principal motive of another will be the power of the witches over Cuchulain's life. The present play is a kind of cross-road where too many interests meet and jostle for the hearer to take them in at a first hearing unless he listen carefully, or know something of the story of the other plays of the cycle.[1]

Yeats' next Cuchulain play was a prose play, *The Golden Helmet,* which was produced in 1908. Yeats completed a revised version, this time in verse and bearing the title *The Green Helmet,* in 1910. He said in a note: 'The play is founded upon an old Irish story, *The Feast of Bricriu,* given in *Cuchulain of Muirthemne,* and is meant as an introduction to *On Baile's Strand.*[2]

In 1917 and 1919, Yeats completed two additional plays, *At the Hawk's Well* and *The Only Jealousy of Emer,* basing them on the model of Japanese *Noh* drama. He said of them: ' "At the Hawk's Well" and "The Only Jealousy of Emer" are the first and last plays of a series of four dealing with Cuchulain's life. The others are my "Green Helmet" and "Baile's Strand".'[3] Although he spoke of the cycle as being complete and gathered the plays into their proper sequence as a play cycle in the 1934 edition of *Collected Plays*, Yeats realised that the series was not yet finished. He wrote in 1934: 'I would have attempted the Battle of the Ford and the Death of Cuchulain, had not the mood of Ireland changed.'[4]

Late in the year 1938, his own death near, Yeats undertook to complete his Cuchulain cycle. On 1 January, 1939, he wrote to Edith Shackleton Heald: 'I think my play is strange and the most moving I have written for some years. I am making a prose sketch for a poem — a kind of sequel — strange too, something new.'[5] The play Yeats referred to was *The Death of Cuchulain*, the poem, 'Cuchulain Comforted'. Yeats died four weeks later.

It is clear from his comments that Yeats intended his Cuchulain plays to make up a coherent and unified play cycle. Yeats' clearly expressed intent in this regard has most often been ignored both by producers and critics. Having staged the plays in a single-evening production in 1969, I am convinced that the major patterns of meaning in the plays become apparent only when they are considered together. It was this conviction which prompted the approach taken in the present study.

Because the Cuchulain plays were central to so much of Yeats' life and work, they do indeed provide a 'kind of cross-road' where Yeats' main interests 'meet and jostle'. In the first half of this book, I consider the Cuchulain plays in the context of five of Yeats' main areas of interest. Chapter 1 traces the relationship between the Cuchulain· plays and Yeats' desire to regenerate Ireland by means of an Irish Mystical Order. Chapter 2 considers the Cuchulain plays as an outgrowth of the Celtic revival and of the nationalist movements which grew out of that revival. Chapter 3 relates the plays to that system of wheels and moon phases which Yeats wrote about in *A Vision*. Chapter 4 examines the biographical elements in the plays. Chapter 5 treats Yeats' theatrical theories and the impact of these theories on the form of the Cuchulain plays. The last five chapters are devoted to an examination of the text of each of the five plays in turn. Particular attention is given to those patterns of meaning which emerge only when the plays are considered together.

In the course of this study, I have felt at no time any inclination to take a patronising attitude towards Yeats' work in the theatre. All evidence seems to point to the fact that as a practical theatre worker he was innovative, pragmatic and highly skilled. I suspect that the period of greatest respect for Yeats' theatrical ideas and for his accomplishments as a playwright is yet to come. In the past ten years the discovery of Artaud, the influential work of such directors as Grotowski and Brook, the renewed interest in Gordon Craig have served to make the public aware that there are exciting alternatives to naturalism in the theatre. We may be on the threshold of a period when Yeats' subjective, lyrical drama will no longer be out of phase. If Yeats were to begin to get the careful and competent professional productions he has generally been denied in our time, it would become increasingly difficult to ignore the fact that he was in actuality a highly successful playwright working in a difficult and not always popular form.

It was T. S. Eliot who most clearly described the nature and importance of Yeats' accomplishment as a playwright.

> Yeats had nothing, and we have had Yeats. He started writing plays at a time when the prose-play of contemporary life seemed triumphant, with an indefinite future stretching before it; when the comedy of light farce dealt only with certain privileged strata of metropolitan life; and when the serious play tended to be an ephemeral tract on some transient social problem. . . . Just as, from the beginning, he made and thought his poetry in terms of speech and not in terms of print, so in the drama he always meant to write plays to be played and not merely to be read. . . . It is impossible to disentangle what he did for the Irish theatre from what the Irish theatre did for him. From this point of vantage, the idea of the poetic drama was kept alive when everywhere else it had been driven underground. I do not know where our debt to him as a dramatist ends — and in time, it will not end until that drama itself ends.[6]

It was Eliot also who pointed out that Yeats was the first contemporary writer to use myth as a criticism of modern life by 'manipulating a continuous parallel between contemporaneity and antiquity'. 'Instead of narrative method, we may now use the mythical method. It is, I seriously believe, a step toward making the modern world possible for art . . .'[7] Nowhere can this method be seen to be operating more effectively than in the Cuchulain plays.

Acknowledgements

The author and publishers wish to thank the following for permission to reproduce copyright material: Columbia University Press for the extracts from *The Tragic Drama of William Butler Yeats* by Leonard E. Nathan and from the first volume of *W. B. Yeats: Uncollected Prose* edited by John P. Frayne; Faber & Faber Ltd and E. P. Dutton & Co. Inc. for the extracts from *Yeats: The Man and the Masks* by Richard Ellmann; the Hamlyn Publishing Group Ltd for the extracts from *The New Larousse Encyclopedia of Mythology;* William Heinemann Ltd for the extract from *On the Art of the Theatre* by Edward Gordon Craig; John Murray (Publishers) Ltd for the extract from *Cuchulain of Muirthemne* by Lady Gregory; the *Bulletin of the New York Public Library* for the extracts from 'The Reception of Synge's *Playboy* in Ireland and America, 1907-1912' by Daniel J. Murphy; Thames & Hudson Ltd and Praeger Publishers Inc. for the extracts from *The Celts* by T. G. E. Powell; M. B. Yeats, Miss Anne Yeats and Hart-Davis MacGibbon Ltd for the extract from *Letters of W. B. Yeats* edited by Allan Wade; M. B. Yeats, Miss Anne Yeats, the Macmillan Co. of Canada and Macmillan Publishing Co. Inc., New York, for 'Easter 1916' from *Collected Poems of W. B. Yeats.*

Acknowledgements

The author and publishers wish to thank the following for permission to reproduce copyright material: Columbia University Press for the extracts from *The Tragic Drama of William Butler Yeats* by Leonard E. Nathan and from the first volume of *W. B. Yeats: Uncollected Prose* edited by John P. Frayne; Faber & Faber Ltd and E. P. Dutton & Co. Inc. for the extracts from *Yeats: The Man and the Masks* by Richard Ellmann; the Hamlyn Publishing Group Ltd for the extracts from *The New Larousse Encyclopedia of Mythology;* William Heinemann Ltd for the extract from *On the Art of the Theatre* by Edward Gordon Craig; John Murray (Publishers) Ltd for the extract from *Cuchulain of Muirthemne* by Lady Gregory; the *Bulletin of the New York Public Library* for the extracts from 'The Reception of Synge's *Playboy* in Ireland and America, 1907-1912' by Daniel J. Murphy; Thames & Hudson Ltd and Praeger Publishers Inc. for the extracts from *The Celts* by T. G. E. Powell; M. B. Yeats, Miss Anne Yeats and Hart-Davis MacGibbon Ltd for the extract from *Letters of W. B. Yeats* edited by Allan Wade; M. B. Yeats, Miss Anne Yeats, the Macmillan Co. of Canada and Macmillan Publishing Co. Inc., New York, for 'Easter 1916' from *Collected Poems of W. B. Yeats.*

1 The Ritual of a Lost Faith

The Cuchulain plays are Yeats' major treatment of the Celtic saga materials he thought to be central to a sound Irish nationalism and a sense of the unity of Irish culture. In imagery and ritual form, the play cycle owes a great deal to Yeats' vain attempts in the nineties to create the ceremonies of an Irish Mystical Order. Something of the nature and purpose of the Cuchulain plays is revealed in a comment made by Yeats in 1929 about a prose adaptation of *The Only Jealousy of Emer,* then being prepared for the Abbey stage. In a letter to Sturge Moore Yeats said: 'I always feel my work is not drama but the ritual of a lost faith.'[1] The remark connects the plays with a project Yeats tells of in the *Autobiographies.*

> I planned a mystical Order which would buy or hire the castle, and keep it as a place where its members could retire for a while for contemplation, and where we might establish mysteries like those of Eleusis and Samothrace; and for ten years to come my most impassioned thought was a vain attempt to find philosophy and create ritual for that Order. I had an unshakable conviction, arising how or whence I cannot tell, that invisible gates would open as they opened for Blake, as they opened for Swedenborg, as they opened for Boehme, and that this philosophy would find its manuals of devotion in all imaginative literature, and set before Irishmen for special manual an Irish literature which, though made by many minds, would seem the work of a single mind, and turn our places of beauty or legendary association into holy symbols.[2]

Yeats did not succeed in creating ritual for an Irish Mystical Order, but in his search for materials from which the ritual could be built he 'plunged without a clue into a labyrinth of images'.[3] This experience had a profound effect on all of his work, particularly upon the form and imagery of the Cuchulain plays.

II

Yeats' desire to found an Irish Mystical Order was at least in part an extension of his youthful dream of becoming 'a sage, a magician or a poet'.[4] Wisdom, magic and poetry were connected disciplines for Yeats, for his view of the poet's role in society was essentially shamanistic. He admired the druidical bards of ancient Ireland and wanted to emulate them. The bard, he tells us, 'had to understand not only innumerable kinds of poetry, but how to keep himself for nine days in a trance' and 'believed in the historical reality of even [his] wildest imaginations'.[5] Yeats plunged into occultism and ceremonial magic to prepare himself for such a role, and into nationalist politics to bring into being a social context in which the role could be played with greater effectiveness.

For Yeats, the spiritual regeneration of Ireland seemed to depend on the restoration of the holy places. As a boy he had always been strongly attracted to those features of the Irish landscape which were beautiful in themselves and were connected in the popular imagination with incidents in legend, folk tale or myth. The Lake Isle of Innisfree, for instance, was associated in folk-tradition with the story of a forbidden tree, a monster and the love of a young man for a beautiful maiden. Yeats' desire to retire to the island and live 'as Thoreau lived, seeking wisdom' was a boyhood dream that he did not abandon until he was twenty-two or twenty-three.[6] He tells us that he cannot remember 'whether I chose the island because of its beauty or for the story's sake'.[7]

This association of landscape and legend was for Yeats the very heart of his sense of Irishness. When he began to discover as a young man how much of the mythological heritage of Ireland was lost to the modern Irishman, he became convinced that the restoration of that heritage was the most important contribution he could make to the cause of Irish nationalism. He saw his own youthful development as having been impoverished by his ignorance of the stories of Cuchulain, Conchubar and Maeve.

> When I was a child I had only to climb the hill behind the house to see long, blue, ragged hills flowing along the southern horizon. What beauty was lost to me, what depth of emotion is still perhaps lacking in me, because nobody told me, not even the merchant captains who knew everything, that Cruachan of the Enchantments lay behind those long, blue, ragged hills:[8]

In the first draft of the *Autobiographies* Yeats is explicit about the part that was to be played by the Mystical Order in countering the spiritual impoverishment which had resulted from Ireland's loss of her ancient mythological heritage.

> An obsession more constant than anything but my love itself was the need of mystical rites — a ritual system of evocation and meditation — to reunite the perception of the spirit, of the divine, with natural beauty. I believed that instead of thinking of Judea as holy we should [think] our own land holy, and most holy where most beautiful. Commerce and manufacture had made the world ugly; the death or pagan nature-worship had robbed visible beauty of its inviolable sanctity. I was convinced that all lonely and lovely places were crowded with invisible beings and that it would be possible to communicate with them. I meant to initiate young men and women in this worship, which would unite the radical truths of Christianity to those of a more ancient world, and to use the Castle Rock for their occasional retirement from the world.[9]

The mystic sense of the union of spiritual and natural beauty that Yeats hoped to create through his rituals is akin to that expressed by Cuchulain in *On Baile's Strand.*

> And we will hunt the deer and the wild bulls;
> And, when we have grown weary, light our fires
> Between the wood and water, or on some mountain
> Where the Shape-Changers of the morning come . . .
> The head grows prouder in the light of the dawn
> And friendship thickens in the murmuring dark
> Where the spare hazels meet the wool-white foam.[10]

III

Though Yeats was convinced that he found in the ancient Irish sagas support for his assumptions about the spirituality of the pagan Celts, the sagas gave no more than ambiguous hints about the philosophical system which underlay that spirituality or the rituals in which it found expression. In his attempt to reconstruct the culture and beliefs of ancient Ireland, Yeats augmented the material gained from Celtic sources with ritual and philosophy whose source might at first seem somewhat remote from the ancient Irish Celts.

A principal source of doctrine for Yeats was that body of Hindu, Buddhist and occultist beliefs that made up the teachings of Madame Helena Blavatsky. Philologists had pointed out that Sanskrit, Greek and Gaelic were sister tongues of the great Aryan language group and comparative mythologists had pointed out remarkable parallels in the cultural patterns of the ancient Aryan cultures. Yeats had little doubt that the beliefs prevalent in Hindu tradition, and among the Greeks of Homer's time, were essentially those held by the ancient Druids. Although Yeats was a member of the Theosophical Society for only a short time (from 1887 to 1890) certain of Madame Blavatsky's ideas became central to his thought. Madam Blavatsky taught the doctrine of reincarnation, the idea that all existence is arranged cyclically, and the belief that in a trance state the soul can leave the body and make contact with other souls and disembodied spirits.

As a theosophist, Yeats also became acquainted with the doctrine of correspondences, a teaching which explained the efficacy of ceremonial magic and accounted for the mysterious power of symbols in art and in nature. Virginia Moore quotes a letter of Yeats' which states the doctrine concisely: 'Every organ of the body has its correspondences in the heavens; and the seven principles which made the human soul and body correspond to the seven colours and the seven planets and the notes on the musical scale.'[11] The persistence of such correspondences on every level of existence has its root in the world of the spirit, for the material world is built on a pattern which itself 'corresponds' to the nature of spiritual reality. Things below resemble things above. Nature is filled with the 'signatures' of spiritual forces. Such a view of reality provided a framework hospitable to Yeats' belief 'that all lonely and lovely places were crowded with invisible beings and that it would be possible to communicate with them'.[12] Indeed, Yeats' most comprehensive study of the categories of Irish fairies was printed in Madame Blavatsky's magazine, *Lucifer,* in 1889.[13]

Of even more direct influence on Yeats' experiments in Celtic mysticism, was his association with MacGregor Mathers and the Order of the Golden Dawn. Mathers, like Blavatsky, was a student of the esoteric tradition with a deep but undisciplined erudition in the field of comparative religion and mythology. Mathers, however, was more interested in ceremonial magic than in the philosophical aspects of the occult. Because of the emphasis on ritual and ceremonial magic in the Order of the Golden Dawn, Yeats noted immediately that work in the Order affected him quite differently from the work he had done in the Esoteric Section of the Theosophical Society.

After I had been moved by ritual, I formed plans for deeds of all kinds I wished to return to Ireland to find there some public work; whereas when I had returned from meetings of the Esoteric Section I had no desire but for more thought, more discussion.[14]

The ritual which Mathers had created for the Golden Dawn, partly from his own reading and partly from his wife's seership, constituted an elaborate ritual application of that doctrine of correspondences which Yeats had first learned from Madame Blavatsky. In the Order rituals and in the 'knowledge lectures' by which Order members prepared themselves for ritual involvement, Mathers managed to integrate a number of the major symbolic systems by which, in various cultures, the pattern of spiritual reality has been represented. Thus kabbalistic, alchemical, Rosicrucian and astrological systems of symbolism were correlated and used interchangeably in the Order together with symbols drawn from the Tarot, numerology, the Greek and Egyptian mystery religions and other seasonal rituals.

When, in 1890, Yeats joined the Golden Dawn he

discovered what he conceived to be a coherent programme for spiritual progress consistent with his long-held ambition to become sage, magician and poet. At the heart of the system was the kabbalistic teaching that the source of all things in the universe is *Ain Soph Aour,* Infinite or Limitless Light. Israel Regardie says that

> this is to be understood as an infinite ocean of brilliance wherein all things are held as within a matrix, from which all things are evolved, and it is that divine goal to which all life and all things eventually must return.[15]

This divine source of all being manifests itself in the ten branches of the Tree of Life. The ten branches or *Sephiroth* represent all aspects of creation. For the individual the branches of the Sephirothic tree represent levels of spirituality. The system of degrees instituted by Mathers in the Order of the Golden Dawn corresponded to the ten Sephiroth. The initiate worked his way, degree by degree, to a more exalted spiritual condition, approaching ever nearer the source of all being. The Supernals, the three highest branches of the Tree of Life, are to be thought of, according to Regardie, 'as an exalted condition of consciousness rather than of substance'.[16] Regardie himself associates the Supernals with what Jung calls the Collective Unconscious.[17]

The kabbalists held that Creation and the Fall of Man were one and the same event. Incarnation and the birth of consciousness marked a shattering of the pristine unity of the human soul and the spiritual source from which it came. The Golden Dawn provided a programme for the soul's slow progress in undoing the curse of creation, and rejoining the primal source of all life. If Regardie is right in identifying the Supernals as equivalent to the Collective Unconscious (what Yeats was to call *Anima Mundi*) then we have in the teachings of the Golden Dawn a dramatic metaphor of the need for psychic reintegration, and in the Order rituals a programme for the working out of that integration of the conscious mind with the deepest levels of the unconscious that Jung calls 'individuation'.[18]

It was under the influence of the Golden Dawn that Yeats' vague ambitions for the spiritual regeneration of Ireland crystallised into a plan for the establishment of an Irish Mystical Order which would use specifically Celtic symbolism. It was within the organisational framework of the Golden Dawn that Yeats carried out some of his most important experiments towards the creation of the Celtic rituals. Mathers himself was an enthusiastic Celticist as well as a student of magical lore and he undertook to work with Yeats on the creation of the rituals. A number of other Golden Dawn members joined with Yeats in a series of practical experiments which would develop materials for the rituals through joint vision. The visions would be induced by means of a technique taught by Mathers within the Golden Dawn. By this technique visions could be evoked and controlled through the use of symbols. Yeats describes his first introduction to the practice, known in the Order literature as 'skrying'.

> He [Mathers] gave me a cardboard symbol and I closed my eyes. Sight came slowly, there was not that sudden miracle as if the darkness had been cut with a knife, for that miracle is mostly a woman's privilege, but there rose before me mental images that I could not control: a desert and a black Titan raising himself up by his two hands from the middle of a heap of ruins. . . .
> I had soon mastered Mathers' symbolic system, and discovered that for a certain minority . . . the visible world would completely vanish, and that the world summoned by the symbol would take its place.[19]

Yeats had, of course, hoped from the beginning that his chief collaborator in evolving the rituals would be Maud Gonne. At every opportunity he worked at the symbolism with her, hoping to win her love through joint collaboration on a project that combined her two main interests, nationalism and the occult.

> Maud Gonne entirely shared these ideas, and I did not doubt that in carrying them out I should win her for myself. . . . At every moment of leisure we obtained in vision long lists of symbols. Various trees corresponded to cardinal points, and the old gods and heroes took their

places gradually in a symbolic fabric that had for its centre the four talismans of the Tuatha de Danaan, the sword, the stone, the spear and the cauldron, which related themselves in my mind with the suits of the Tarot.[20]

IV

According to the evidence of Yeats' letters, the winter of 1897-98 was a period of particularly intense visionary activity among the little group of Celtic adepts Yeats had chosen from the membership of the Golden Dawn to work with him 'on the gods'. In preparation for a series of experiments in group-vision, they had plunged into a study of Irish saga material and of the commentaries on that material by mythologists and Celtic scholars.

John Rhys' 1886 Hibbert lectures on *Celtic Heathendom* made a particularly vivid impression. Commenting on the story of Finn and the Salmon of Knowledge, Rhys mentions a magic well known as the Well of Connla. He quotes an account of the well by Prof. O'Curry.

In those very early times there was a certain mystical fountain which was called Connla's Well (situated, so far as we can gather, in Lower Ormond). As to who this Connla was, from whom the well had its name, we are not told; but the well itself appears to have been regarded as another Helicon by the ancient Irish poets. Over this well there grew, according to the legend, nine beautiful mystical hazel-trees, which annually sent forth blossoms and fruits simultaneously. The nuts were of the richest crimson colour, and teemed with the knowledge of all that was refined in literature, poetry, and art. No sooner, however, were the beautiful nuts produced on the trees, than they always dropped into the well, raising by their fall a succession of shining red bubbles.[21]

However obscure the identity of Connla may have been to Celtic scholars, to Yeats and his friends he was known as Connla the Druid. So often did they invoke Connla in the winter of 1897-98 that he began to appear of his own accord to Mrs MacGregor Mathers in Paris, even though she knew nothing of his part in the London experiments.[22]

Out of the preoccupation with the Well of Connla grew a series of visions of considerable significance to our study of the Cuchulain plays. On 1 January, 1898, Yeats wrote a letter to Dorothea Hunter, a seer reputed to have 'a faculty of clearly discerning in symbolic picture the essence of a myth or legend'.[23] Yeats speaks in the letter of a series of visionary experiences centring around a magic well situated at the foot of a mountain ash. Mrs Hunter has identified this as being a reference to the Well of Connla. According to Mrs Hunter, 'Those who gaze therein may, if they can find a guide, be led to the Fount of Perpetual Youth. The ash berries fall into the waters and turn them to fire. Connla, the Druid, is the Guardian of the Well.[24]

In his letter Yeats asks Mrs Hunter to come early to a meeting of the Celtic adepts.

> I want to talk to you and your husband about a certain part of our Celtic project in which you can be a great help. I am following out a plan laid down long ago, and after consultation with our chiefs. It is going to be a great movement in the end. I do not want you to mention this among the other members for the present as I want us all to do a little irresponsible experimentation for a while. I have had a number of visions on the way home, greatly extending the symbolism we got tonight. The souls of ordinary people remain after death in the waters and these waters become an organized world if you gather up the flames that come from the waters of the well when the berries fall upon it, and make them into a flaming heart, and explore the waters with this as a lamp. They are the waters of emotion and passion, in which all but purified souls are entangled, and have the same relation to our plane of fixed material forms as the Divine World of fluid fire has to the heroic world of fixed intellectual form.[25]

Richard Ellman quotes extracts from a record of several meetings of the experimenters in which the whole group in joint-vision visits a well guarded by a venerable figure Yeats apparently addresses as 'Cuala'. Birgit Bjersby identifies this as a misreading by Ellman of the name 'Conla'.[26]

D.E.D.I. [Yeats] performed a Celtic ceremony of invocation. This transported us to a mountainous district where in the midst of the hills we found ourselves before an ancient well. Leaning over the well on our left grew a mountain-ash tree laden with red berries that kept dropping, dropping into the water, so ripe that they seemed like drops of blood reddening the pool as they sank. Then appeared a venerable figure, luminous but human, the figure of a man with a white beard. He knelt beside the well and looked into the water. D.E.D.I. addressed him as 'Cuala' and asked if he could tell us how he came to be here and connected with this well. Then looking with him into the water we saw that it was full of many reflections, as of horses and chariots and battles in constant procession and we understood that once he had been involved in much stir and strife in the world and had renounced it all in pursuit of his ideal. . . .

When we left the Guardian at his station we saluted with the X sign and again when we passed Manaanan for it seemed befitting; and when at last we mounted through the dark Lethe-like waters we brought with us still the light from the throne. Two of our number had not brought enough of this light with them and when we reached the well, they noted the leafless ash-trees and the chill and cheerless aspect of the scene which was not so to the rest. So we all waited together till the ash-tree budded again and the scene assumed warmth and life. Then D.E.D.I. vanished as before.[27]

Yeats' experiments in joint-vision did not yield him the ritual for an Irish Mystical Order. However, the direct relationship between this vision and the ritual play, *At the Hawk's Well,* which Yeats wrote almost two decades later, is unmistakable.

Yeats' uncle George Pollexfen, whose consuming interest was astrology, also shared in the project. Yeats tells us that the old man's 'slow and difficult clairvoyance added certain symbols'.[28] George Russell (AE) carried on his own series of visionary excursions among the Celtic gods, reporting the results to Yeats. Of particular interest was the appearance of a white fool. In a letter written to AE in August 1899, Yeats discusses this vision and ponders the meaning of certain symbolic details of his own recent dreams.

My dear Russell: When you write to me about the symbol please tell me the figures you saw as well as the conclusions you come to. I saw the white door today and the white fool; he was followed out of the door by a marriage procession who had flowers and green boughs. Last night I had a dream of two lovers, who were being watched over by a blackbird, or raven, who warned them against the malice and slander of the world. Was this bird a transformation of Aengus or one of his birds?

You are perhaps right about the symbol, it may be merely a symbol of ideal human marriage. The slight separation of the sun and the moon permits the polarity which we call sex, while it allows of the creation of an emotional unity. . . . I may be getting the whole story of the relation of man and woman in symbol — all that makes the subject of *The Shadowy Waters*. If you can call up the white fool and have the time I wish you could make a sketch of him, for Dalua seems to becoming important among us. Aengus is the most curious of all the gods. He seems both Hermes and Dionysus. He has some part in all enthusiasm. I think his white fool is going to give me a couple of lines in *The Shadowy Waters*.[29]

The lines alluded to are the opening lines of the 1900 version of *The Shadowy Waters*.

> 'His face has never gladdened since he came
> Out of that island where the fool of the wood
> Played on his harp.'[30]

As these documents show, an important synthesis of diverse but parallel symbolic systems was taking place in the minds of Yeats and his associates. Under the catalytic influence of ceremonial magic, druidical lore from the old sagas, ritual patterns from the mythologies of the world, Hindu doctrine from Madame Blavatsky, magical symbols from alchemy, the Kabbalah, and the Tarot, and mystic insights from AE were beginning to come together into a more or less coherent vision of the world of the spirit. Yeats'

letters contain references to cycles and elemental forces, to
figures such as the fool and the guardian of the well, and to
shape-changing birds of ambiguous omen. The symbolic
features of the visionary world which Yeats explored in the
nineties was obviously a prime source of the inconography of
the Cuchulain cycle.

The actual composition of the rituals of the Irish Mystical
Order continued to present Yeats with apparently insur-
mountable difficulties. The rituals which have been preserved
in Yeats' notes seem incoherent and incomplete. Richard
Ellman comments that 'a great deal is said in them about the
secret quest but little information is given about what that
quest is after or how it can be carried out'.[31] Work on the
Celtic rituals suffered a severe setback in 1900 when a quarrel
split the Golden Dawn into three factions and brought
permanent estrangement between Yeats and Mathers. In
1903, when Maud Gonne married John MacBride, Yeats
abandoned the project altogether.

V

By the turn of the century, Yeats was deeply involved in the
Irish theatre movement, a movement closely connected, in
his mind at any rate, with the spiritual aims which had
motivated work on the Irish Mystical Order. In an essay
written in 1899 he spoke of the need in the present age for a
theatre which would serve as 'the preparation of a priesthood'.

> Blake has said that all art is a labour to bring again the
> Golden Age, and all culture is certainly a labour to bring
> again the simplicity of the first ages, with knowledge of
> good and evil added to it. The drama has need of cities
> that it may find men in sufficient numbers, and cities
> destroy the emotions to which it appeals, and therefore
> the days of the drama are brief and come but seldom. It
> has one day when the emotions of cities still remember the
> emotions of sailors and husbandmen and shepherds and
> users of spear and bow; as the houses and furniture and
> earthen vessels of cities, before the coming of machinery,
> remember the rocks and the woods and the hillside; and it

has another day, now beginning, when thought and scholarship discover their desire. In the first day, it is the art of the people; and in the second day, like dramas acted of old times in the hidden places of the temple, it is the preparation of a priesthood. It may be, though the world is not old enough to show us any example, that this priesthood will spread their religion everywhere, and make their Art and the Art of the people.[32]

The dream of establishing in Ireland a ritual theatre like that of Aeschylus and Sophocles, which came to dominate Yeats' imagination, had its roots in the somewhat older dream of establishing on Irish soil rites like those of Eleusis and Samothrace.

The ancient Celtic saga materials were as important to Yeats' theatre work as they were to his work on the Irish Mystical Order. When Alfred Nutt offered to supply Yeats with translations of the old Gaelic epics if he would undertake to pick the best versions and put his English upon them, he declined. Lady Gregory took up the project, making or finding the translations herself.[33] The result was her *Cuchulain of Muirthemne,* the book which Yeats used as the basis for his Cuchulain plays. In the Cuchulain plays, which Yeats wrote between the years 1902 and 1939, we can trace the growth of Yeats' power to adapt certain of the ideas which had their origin in the work on the Celtic rituals to the requirements of theatrical presentation.

In *On Baile's Strand,* the first written of the Cuchulain plays, Yeats took Shakespeare as his model. The early version of the play owes something to the technique of *King Lear* but the resemblance is superficial. After much revision of the play, Yeats, who regularly attended and wrote about the Shakespeare productions at Stratford-on-Avon, seems to have penetrated to the heart of Shakespeare's techniques. In the final version of *On Baile's Strand,* Yeats uses the fool in a way which closely parallels Shakespeare's treatment of the fool in *Lear,* that most symbolic of Shakespeare's plays. In *The Green Helmet,* Yeats experimented boldly in an effort to capture the peculiar tone of the Irish sagas themselves. He adapts imagery, stagecraft and theme to a *genre* he calls 'heroic farce'.

A decade of theatre management convinced Yeats that a drama whose aim was spiritual regeneration could not be readily accommodated by a national theatre, which must be popular to survive. He searched for a form of drama which would not require elaborate and expensive staging and which would allow him to return to the concept of theatre as sacred ritual. He found this form in the Japanese *Noh* play.

The stories used by the writers of Japanese *Noh* reminded Yeats of old Irish legends and beliefs. Those beliefs he now thought of as differing little from those of the Japanese Shinto worshipper.[34] The *Noh* plays themselves were the rituals of the Japanese warrior caste. The Zen Buddhist doctrines which underlay them did not differ significantly from the doctrines propounded by Madame Blavatsky and the knowledge lectures of the Golden Dawn. The adventure which provided the subject-matter of the *Noh* drama was often parallel to the subject-matter of the folk tales and superstitions which Yeats and Lady Gregory had collected from the Galway peasants in the nineties. The central incident of the *Noh* play, Yeats tells us, 'is often the meeting with ghost, god, or goddess at some holy place or much-legended tomb; and god, goddess, or ghost reminds me at times of our own Irish legends and beliefs . . .'[35]

In 1916 and 1919, Yeats produced two *Noh* plays based on incidents in the life of the Irish hero Cuchulain. The first, *At the Hawk's Well,* enacts the initiation of the Celtic warrior; the second, *The Only Jealousy of Emer,* is a resurrection ritual. It was a version of this play that prompted Yeats' comment that his work was 'not drama but the ritual of a lost faith'.[36]

VI

As Morton Seiden has pointed out, much of the material derived from Yeats' work on the Irish Mystical Order was to find its way into *A Vision,* the curious private mythology Yeats evolved with the aid of his wife's mediumship.[37] It is not surprising therefore to find Yeats making explicit reference to the system of *A Vision* in *The Only Jealousy of Emer.* As I will demonstrate in some detail in Chapter 3

Yeats used this system to structure the ritual framework of the entire Cuchulain cycle.

If we approach the five Cuchulain plays as a connected cycle beginning with *At the Hawk's Well* and ending with *The Death of Cuchulain,* we find that each play can be assigned to an important phase on the great wheel of symbolic moon phases which is at the heart of the system of *A Vision.* We also find that each play may be seen as a crisis point in the life of a single man. Moreover, the plays form a sequence of seasonal rituals similar to those by which the ancient Celts were thought to mark the changes of the seasons. The plays abound in imagery suggestive of that material Yeats originally prepared for the initiation rituals to be used in his Irish Mystical Order.

The Death of Cuchulain, the play which completes the play cycle, was written just before Yeats' death. He had returned to many of his old preoccupations, including thoughts about the abandoned Castle of the Heroes.[38] The completed play cycle is intensely personal, yet somehow embraces the story of Ireland. It has much to say about the love of the masculine sun for the 'cold, sliding, slippery-footed moon' which is the feminine nature and about that 'sexual love founded upon spiritual hate' which Yeats knew so intensely. But it is also a schooling in heroism, as Yeats intended the rituals of the Irish Mystical Order to be a schooling in heroism. It brings vividly before the eyes of modern Ireland the figure of 'that famous man Cuchulain' and the ancient heroic ideal for which he stands.

2 That Famous Man Cuchulain

I

Cuchulain, the hero of Yeats' play cycle, was a personage of considerable symbolic importance to the Irish nationalist movement. It was to Standish O'Grady that Yeats gave credit for reintroducing to modern Ireland the Old Gaelic epics in which Cuchulain is the dominant figure. ' "It is that famous man Cuchulain. . . ." In the eighties of the last century Standish O'Grady, his mind full of Homer, retold the story of Cuchulain that he might bring back an heroic ideal.'[1]

The impact of O'Grady's work had been great upon the young poets and artists of Yeats' circle. On first reading O'Grady's *History of Ireland, Heroic Period,* published in 1878, George Russell (AE) had felt like a man 'who suddenly feels ancient memories rushing at him, and knows he was born in a royal house, that he had mixed with the mighty of heaven and earth and had the very noblest for his companions'.[2] Yeats saw the book as 'the starting point of what may yet prove a new influence in the literature of the world'.[3] Reviewing O'Grady's *The Coming of Cuchulain* in 1895, Yeats said:

> It is probable that no Englishman can love these books as they are loved by the many Irishmen who date their first interest in Irish legends and literature from the 'History'. There is perhaps, too, something in their tumultuous vehemence, in their delight in sheer immensity, in their commingling of the spirit of man with the spirit of the elements, which belong to the wild Celtic idealism rather than to the careful, practical ways of the Saxon.[4]

O'Grady himself, in the hyperbolic terms which were to become typical of the claims of the Celtic revival, did not hesitate to proclaim the superiority of the Gaelic epics over their Greek counterparts.

I cannot help regarding this age and the great personages moving therein as incomparably higher in intrinsic worth than the corresponding ages of Greece. In Homer, Hesiod, and the Attic poets, there is polish and artistic form, absent in the existing monuments of Irish heroic thought, but the gold, the ore itself, is here massier and more pure, the sentiment deeper and more tender, the audacity and freedom more exhilarating, the reach of imagination more sublime, the depth and power of the human soul more fully exhibit themselves. . . . Out of the ground start forth the armies of her demigods and champions — an age bright with heroic forms, loud with the the trampling of armies and war-steeds, with the roar of chariot-wheels, and the shouting of warriors.[5]

Yeats was certainly in agreement that here was the unrefined ore necessary for the forging of a great literature. In a letter to O'Grady in 1898 he said:

There is humour and fantasy as well as miraculous poetry in our old legends, and one can find in them all kinds of meanings. They will some day be the themes of poets and painters in many countries, and the substance of a new romantic movement. . . . They are the greatest treasure the Past has handed down to us Irish people, and the most plentiful treasure of legends in Europe.[6]

During the nineties, Yeats devoted a great deal of his effort to an attempt to reclaim for Ireland her long-neglected Celtic heritage and to turn the attention of young Irish writers towards the Celtic subject-matter. 'Do there not lie hid among those spear heads, and golden collars over the way in the New Museum, suggestions of that age before history when the art legends and wild mythology of earliest Ireland rose out of the void?'[7]

Although the need to restore the Celtic element in Irish culture became a central tenet of Irish nationalist doctrine, there was sharp disagreement as to how this restoration should be accomplished. Douglas Hyde founded the Gaelic league to work for the de-Anglicising of Ireland and the restoration of a distinctly Irish nationality. To Hyde this meant the restoration of Gaelic sports, dress, manners, customs and language.[8] Yeats, on the other hand, argued that the restoration of the Gaelic language was not the key to establishing an Irish identity.[9] If Irish writers would turn to Irish subjects, particularly Celtic subjects, they could create in English a literature as distinctly Irish as American literature is distinctively American. Literary revival, not linguistic restoration, was what Ireland needed. 'When we remember the majesty of Cuchullin and the beauty of sorrowing Deirdre we should not forget that it is that majesty and that beauty which is immortal, and not the perishing tongue that first told of them.'[10]

Both Hyde's Gaelic League and Yeats' literary movement had a profound impact on the growth and direction of political nationalism. Historian Thomas O'Neill describes the political force generated by the Gaelic League.

> As year succeeded year the Gaelic League grew and spread throughout Ireland. Branches were formed in which not only the Irish language but Irish history as well were taught. Traditions of the past were revived and the Gaelic League classes were not only places of study but of entertainment. Irish music was played and Irish songs sung. Traditional dances were practised. The doctrine of Irishness was inculcated. All of this was non-political in intent but in practice it could not be divorced from politics. It moulded a new generation whose outlook was fundamentally Irish. It was only a matter of time before that attitude would reflect itself in the political field. . . . There were some like the poet, William Rooney, who railed at the Gaelic League's rule against interfering in politics. For the most part, however, Douglas Hyde and his associates merely pursued their course, unwittingly creating a revolution.[11]

The political impact of the work of Yeats and other members of the Irish literary movement was equally strong.

> Reaching back into Irish mythology for its heroes, such as Cuchulain, the literary movement provided new inspiration for an old dream. National sentiment in Ireland had long

found a romantic refuge, and the literary movement was even more romantic than the language revival. Writers like Yeats revolted against the tradition of earlier national poets whose aim was political. In his writings he would preach no political gospel. . . . Nonetheless the literary revival was political. It inspired the imagination. It created the ancient heroes and it won new admirers for the beautiful woman who in tradition personified Ireland — Cathleen Ni Houlihan.[12]

Padraic H. Pearse was among those who, in his own words, 'sprung from the Gaelic League or have received from the Gaelic League a new baptism and a new life of grace'.[13] A gifted poet and scholar, Pearse's vision of Ireland's destiny and his own had been shaped by the ideals of Gaelic literature. He saw himself in the image of the Celtic hero Cuchulain. Yeats' portrayal of Cuchulain's reckless courage and heroic joy in *The Green Helmet* had commanded his admiration.[14] It was in the name of the ancient heroes that Pearse summoned the youth of Ireland to assert their manhood in defence of a national ideal.

Fearghus, Conchubar, Cuchulain, Fion, Oisin, Oscar — these were more to the Gael than mere names of great champions and warriors of a former time: they represented to him men who had gone before, who had fought the good fight, who had passed from earth to the mystic Tir na n-og, who had become gods, but whose spirits, heroic and immortal, still lived after them. And though well-nigh two thousand years have rolled away since those mighty heroes trod this land of ours, yet is their spirit not dead: it lives on in our poetry, in our music, in our language, and, above all, in the vague longings which we feel for a something, we know not what, — our irresistible, overmastering conviction that we, as a nation, are made for higher things. Oh! that this hero-spirit were stronger than it is! Oh! that men could be brought to realize that they are MEN, not animals, — that they could be brought to realize that, though 'of the earth, earthy,' yet that there is a spark of divinity within them! And men *can* be brought to realize this by the propagation of a literature like that of the Gael,

— a literature to which nature-love and hero-love shall form the key-words, a literature which shall glorify all that is worthy of glory, — beauty, strength, manhood, intellect, and religion.[15]

On Easter Monday 1916, Padraic Pearse and James Connolly at the head of a band of about 700 relatively untrained men seized the Dublin Post Office and proclaimed the establishment of an Irish Republic. The rebels held off the forces of the British Empire for a week. When the rebels surrendered, Pearse, Connolly and thirteen other leaders of the insurrection were tried for treason, found guilty and shot. The heroic sacrifice of the Easter rebels galvanised Ireland into a sense of her nationhood. Independence became inevitable.

The career of Padraic Pearse reminds us that Yeats and others who participated in the Celtic revival did succeed in establishing a kind of school for heroes, though not exactly the kind Yeats had hoped to found with his Irish Mystical Order. In a sense, by their action, Pearse and Connolly had restored that lost age of heroes. The Irish government commemorated the event by a statue of Cuchulain. Was this a recognition that, for the moment at least, the old gods had returned? Yeats was still brooding upon such matters when, just before his death, he wrote the final song of the Cuchulain cycle.

> What stood in the Post Office
> With Pearse and Connolly?
> What comes out of the mountain
> Where men first shed their blood?
> Who thought Cuchulain till it seemed
> He stood where they had stood?[16]

A central aim of Yeats and the other writers of the Celtic movement was to establish on the foundation of the ancient Irish legends a literature and a drama which would substitute a positive nationalism for the negative and divisive passions which have gripped the Irish throughout their modern history. As Phillip L. Marcus has pointed out, the legends 'represented a subject that, while intensely national, was uncoloured by modern politics or sectarian religious controversy and thus might appeal to writers of differing persuasions and to a wider, more heterogeneous audience.'[17] According to Yeats, his original aim was to found a school

> that could have substituted, as only a literature without satirical or realistic prepossessions could, positive desires for the negative passion of a national movement beaten down into party politics, compelled for a century to attack everything.[18]

In the end, Irish bitterness proved too great; the negative passions did not give way before Yeats' 'spiritual propaganda'; even the Abbey Theatre eventually became a home for the satire and the realism which Yeats had set out to circumvent. Yeats' plays about the Irish hero Cuchulain remain as a monument to the noble dream of an Irish nation founded on a 'heart-uplifting pride'[19] rather than on the hatred, envy, bitterness and suspicion of a land where 'neighbour wars on neighbour, and why there is no man knows'.[20] Considering the plays in relation to the Irish nationalist movement, we detect a bitter and ironic ambiguity in the term 'ritual of a lost faith'.

II

Although nationalist considerations were in a large measure responsible for Yeats' interest in the Celtic saga materials, he had little sympathy with those nationalist writers whose idea of reclaiming the Celtic materials was to treat them as historical accounts of Ireland's past, somewhat distorted by centuries of oral transmission. Historical reading of the old sagas tended to obscure their mythological significance and dull their power to stir the imagination. Yeats was, as we saw in Chapter 1, more interested in revitalising Ireland's ancient mythology to provide a living faith for modern Ireland, than in piecing together a pseudo-history of the Irish race. When Douglas Hyde's *The Story of Early Gaelic Literature* was published in 1895, it upheld the view that the sagas were based on the actual history of Ireland. Yeats attacked Hyde's position in the *Bookman*.

Dr. Hyde throws in his lot with those who hold them historical in the main; and this choice seems to an obstinate upholder of the other theory but a part of the one capital defect in his criticism. He is so anxious to convince his little group of enthusiasts of the historical importance of the early Irish writings, of the value to modern learning of the fragments of ancient customs which are mixed up with their romance, that he occasionally seems to forget the noble phantasy and passionate drama which is their crowning glory. . . . This defect is probably caused to some extent by the traditions of Irish learning which are hopelessly dry-as-dust, but if our own profoundly imaginative Irish scholar cannot throw off the ancient chains we are indeed lost.[21]

Neither Yeats' criticism, nor the neatly-turned compliment with which it was coupled, deflected Hyde from his espousal of the historical approach. His *Literary History of Ireland,* published in 1899, carried the historical interpretation of the sagas even further.

Yeats' interpretation of the saga material was greatly influenced by his own activities as a folklorist and by his reading of such students of mythology as Alfred Nutt, John Rhys, and D'Arbois de Jubainville. Yeats saw in the fairy tales and folk beliefs of the Irish peasants the remnants of an ancient faith which, in spite of Christianity, had been kept relatively intact down to the end of the seventeenth century. This ancient faith he saw as 'a great tapestry' which hangs behind all Irish history.[22] Nor did he share the common belief of folklorists that 'this exultant world of fancies is passing away'.[23]

Much, no doubt, will perish — perhaps the whole tribe of folk-tales proper; but the fairy and ghost kingdom is more stubborn than men dream of. It will perhaps, in Ireland at any rate, be always going and never gone. I have talked to men who believe they have seen it.[24]

Yeats consciously interwove fairy lore which he had gathered from the peasantry into his retelling of the Cuchulain stories, giving them texture and linking them to what he considered an ancient but still living faith.

Each of the three mythologists whom Yeats most frequently mentions, Nutt, Rhys and Jubainville, contributed significantly to his understanding of myth and greatly influenced his handling of the Cuchulain materials. In a letter to the editor of the *Daily Express* in 1895, Yeats says of D'Arbois de Jubainville's *Mythologie Irlandaise* that

> it is scarcely possible to understand Irish bardic and folk lore at all without its vivid and precise account of the ancient Pagan mythology of Ireland and of the descent of the mischievous fairies and spirits from the ancient gods of darkness and decay, and of the descent of the beautiful and kindly people of the raths and thorn trees from the gods of light and life.[25]

John Rhys carried the examination of this system of opposites even further, holding that the Irish myths told of the adventures of sungods and culture heroes. Morton Seiden summarises Rhys' views thus:

> Rhys . . . postulates that in Celtic heliolatry a *symbolic* wheel of the sun represents, as a rule, the revolving seasons, the adventures of nature gods or heroes, and the waxing and waning day. In the mythological battles of the Tuatha de Danaan and the Formorians, ancient Irish nature deities, moreover, he said that there are symbolized certain conflicting opposites; these opposites he called man and woman, life and death, light and darkness, day and night, and summer and winter.[26]

According to Professor Myles Dillon,

> Alfred Nutt suggested that the association of the gods with earth-mounds (such as New Grange, which was the dwelling of Oengus) went back to a stage of nature-worship when rivers, trees, wells and mounds were worshipped. He went on to suggest a common origin for certain features of Greek and Irish mythology, especially the doctrine of re-birth, which was part of the cult of Dionysus.[27]

Yeats was of course fully alive to the link between the two ancient Aryan cultures, Irish and Greek. At one point he even put forward a suggestion that the Irish schoolchild learn both Irish and Greek and study both literatures together.

> Let him translate Greek into Irish and learn that our chariot-fighting Red Branch resembled the chariot-fighting Greeks and Trojans; that D'Arbois de Joubainville spent his life in the study of Irish for no other reason; that the sacred grove where Oedipus was carried off by the gods differed in nothing from the groves where, according to Connaught tales, men, women and children are carried off; that Greek literature was founded on a folk belief differing but little from that of Ireland; that Roman, like English literature, was founded upon the written word.[28]

Some time during the 1890s Yeats began to study Sir James Frazer's *The Golden Bough* with its monumental documentation of the thesis that at the centre of all religion is the death and rebirth of a god of fertility. The ideas of these writers fitted well with what he had learned and experienced in the Order of the Golden Dawn and he eagerly adopted their doctrine. Their insights would enable him to restore to the myths their ancient glory.

> To the old folk-lorist fables and fairytales were a haystack of dead follies, wherein the virtuous might find one little needle of historical truth. . . . Rhys and many more have made us see in all these things old beautiful mythologies wherein ancient man said symbolically all he knew about God and man's soul, once famous religions fallen into ruin and turned into old wives' tales, but still luminous from the rosy dawn of human revery.[29]

III

The main source of stories about Cuchulain and the other heroes of ancient Ulster is the *Táin Bó Cúailnge*. This ancient epic was probably composed between the fourth and seventh centuries A.D. It tells of the court of Conchubar Mac Nessa, King of Ulster, at about the time of Christ. In the society described in the *Táin,* totem and tabu, headhunting, and fighting from chariots in single combat are prominent elements. The central episode of the Táin is a war between

Ulster and Connaught over the ownership of the Brown Bull of Coolney. Cuchulain is the central hero of this war and it is on the story of his defence of Ulster that the *Tain* focuses. As in the *Aeneid,* however, certain other tales are included as prefatory material to the main story. Fergus, for instance, describes the boyhood deeds of Cuchulain and fills in the warriors of Connacht as to the background of the Ulster heroes, just as Aeneus uses Dido's curiosity as justification for unfolding the whole story of the Sack of Troy. It has, in fact, been suggested that the present form of the *Táin* may have been influenced by the *Aeneid.*[30] The oldest surviving manuscripts containing the *Táin* date from the twelfth century.

Lady Gregory, in retelling the stories of Cuchulain in her *Cuchulain of Muirthemne,* arranged the stories of the life of the hero in chronological order, toned down the more grotesque passages describing Cuchulain's 'transformations', and tended to make him more heroic by moderating the supernatural aid he received in times of difficulty. In this she followed the practice of Standish O'Grady. It was on Lady Gregory's book that Yeats based his Cuchulain plays.

In his treatment of the Cuchulain stories, Yeats ignored altogether the story of the great Cattle Raid of Coolney. He centred his treatment rather on Cuchulain's slaughter of his own son and his subsequent fight with the sea. This incident provided the subject-matter for *On Baile's Strand.* Around this central play, Yeats placed the four others. Taken together the five plays span the life of the hero from his initiation as a warrior to his eventual death. On the whole, the life of Cuchulain emerges in Yeats' play cycle as tighter, more coherent and more fully human than in the old sagas.

In *At the Hawk's Well,* Cuchulain, young, vigorous and proud, journeys into Scotland to seek the waters of immortality. He comes upon a hollow in the rock where three dried hazels drop their nuts and withered leaves. A girl who has been guarding the well now seems to have sunk into a senseless stupor. An old man tries to warn Cuchulain that a curse will fall on him if he remains in this place.

Suddenly the spirit of a hawk takes possession of the girl.

The old man warns Cuchulain that if he looks into her eyes while she is in that state of possession he will never know love unmixed with hate — that he may indeed unwittingly destroy his own children. Cuchulain, doom-eager and destined to live the life of a hero, gazes fully into the hawk-woman's eyes.

The hawk-woman lures Cuchulain from the well as the waters of immortality begin to rise. She eludes him and Cuchulain returns. Hearing the clash of arms in the distance, he leaves to fight Aoife, the warrior queen who will become the mother of the child he is destined to kill.

There is, in Lady Gregory's *Cuchulain of Muirthemne*, no mention of any such meeting with the hawk-goddess. The story of Cuchulain's battle with Aoife is, however, briefly recounted.

So then Cuchulain and Aoife attacked one another and began a fierce fight, and she broke Cuchulain's spear in pieces, and his sword she broke off at the hilt. Then Cuchulain called out, 'Look, the chariot and the horses and the driver of Aoife are fallen down into the valley and are lost!' At that Aoife looked about her, and Cuchulain took a sudden hold of her, and lifted her on his shoulders, and brought her down to where the army was, and laid her on the ground, and held his sword to her breast, and she begged for her life, and he gave it to her. And after that she made peace with Scathach, and bound herself by sureties not to go out against her again. And she gave her love to Cuchulain; and out of that love great sorrow came afterwards.[31]

Yeats, in choosing not to present the encounter with Aoife directly on stage but to treat it symbolically, has shifted the emphasis in the story from Aoife herself to the spirit which animates her. This spirit Cuchulain first encounters as a great grey hawk which attacks him as he climbs the mountain side, then as the shadow by which the guardian of the well is possessed. It is after the 'unappeasable shadow' has shown itself to Aoife and 'the fierce women of the hills' that they offer sacrifice and arm for battle. Cuchulain's relationship to this spirit is represented on stage by the ritual of the hawk dance in which he participates.

In *The Green Helmet,* Cuchulain undertakes to answer the challenge of a Red Man who has come from the Country-under-Wave and engaged in a game of head-for-head with two other champions of Ulster, Conall and Legaire. When Conall and Legaire found that the red giant could allow himself to be beheaded without suffering harm, they had become frightened and had refused to offer their heads as agreed. Cuchulain himself accepts the challenge in their place. The Red Man, instead of beheading him, declares him champion of the land.

The plot of *The Green Helmet* is a skilful interweaving of two episodes from Lady Gregory's *Cuchulain of Muirthemne:* 'Bricriu's Feast, and the War of Words of the Women of Ulster' and 'The Championship of Ulster'. In Lady Gregory's account, Bricriu, a Red Branch noble with a reputation for sowing discord, declares that he will hold a feast. On receiving the invitation, Fergus says to the men of Ulster, 'We will not go, for if we do, our dead will be more than our living, after Bricriu has set us to quarrel with one another.'[32]
Their reluctance to attend angers Bricriu.

'I will stir up strife', said Bricriu, 'between the kings and leaders, the heroes of valour, and the swordsmen, till everyone makes an end of the other, if they will not come with me to my feast.' 'We will not go for the sake of pleasing you,' said Conchubar. 'I will stir up anger between father and son, so that they will be the death of one another,' said Bricriu; 'if I fail in doing that, I will make a quarrel between mother and daughter; if that fails, I will set the women of Ulster one against the other, so that they will come to deadly blows, and be striking one another on the breast.'[33]

The men of Ulster agree to attend the feast after first placing their host under guard in another place. This precaution has little effect, so great is Bricriu's talent for sowing discord. He first promotes a dispute among the three leading Red Branch heroes, Legaire, Conall and Cuchulain, over who shall receive 'the hero's portion' — a choice cut of meat along with which go many additional honours. No sooner is peace restored — by arranging a series of contests to determine the championship of Ulster — than a dispute breaks out among the wives of the three heroes over who is fairest and most deserving of honour. The question of precedence is solved by breaking holes in the wall so that all three ladies can enter simultaneously. The dispute among the ladies turns into a war of words.

The last of a series of contests arranged to determine the championship of Ulster brings the three heroes face to face with a stranger who claims to be looking for a man capable of keeping his word. When asked what test is to be applied, the stranger replies.

> 'Here is this axe,' he said, 'and the man into whose hands it is put is to cut off my head to-day, I to cut his head off to-morrow. And as you men of Ulster have a name beyond the men of all other countries for strength and skill, for courage, for greatness, for highmindedness, for behaviour, for truth and generosity; for worthiness, let you find one among you that will hold to his word and keep to his bargain.'[34]

Legaire is the first to take up the challenge. When he has severed the stranger's head from his body, the stranger rises, gathers up his head and his axe, and strides from the hall, his neck streaming with blood. When the stranger returns to claim Legaire's head according to the bargain, Legaire loses his nerve and refuses to offer it. The same thing happens when Conall accepts the challenge. Again the stranger survives decapitation. Conall, like Legaire, breaks his word. Then it is Cuchulain's turn.

Cuchulain executes a spectacular decapitation of the stranger, hurling the head to the top of the rafters, so that the whole house shakes. When the stranger returns, Cuchulain's nerve does not fail. He stretches his neck on the chopping block. Instead of taking Cuchulain's head, the stranger strikes the floor with the blunt side of the axe. He reveals himself as Curoi, son of Daire. He is judge of the championship of Ulster.

'Rise up, Cuchulain,' he said. 'Of all the heroes of Ulster, whatever may be their daring, there is not one to compare with you in courage and in bravery and in truth. The Championship of the heroes of Ireland is yours from this out, and the Champion's Portion with it, and to your wife the first place among all the women of Ulster. And whoever tries to put himself before you after this,' he said, 'I swear by the oath my people swear by, his own life will be in danger.'[35]

In adapting this story for dramatic presentation, Yeats compresses it considerably. Bricriu and Curoi are combined in one character, the Red Man. This supernatural character still maintains Bricriu's penchant for mischief-making. Indeed Yeats has in all likelihood restored Bricriu to the status he may once have had in the old mythology, that of god of discord. It is interesting that it is just such a god, Bricriu of the Sidhe, who takes possession of Cuchulain's body in *The Only Jealousy of Emer*.[36] In Yeats' play Cuchulain is in Scotland at the time of the original challenge of the Red Man. He returns to take up the challenge which has been accepted by Legaire and Conall in his absence, but which they are afraid to carry out. This makes Cuchulain's selfless heroism all the more impressive. It also allows us to see *The Green Helmet* as a sequel to *At the Hawk's Well*.

In *On Baile's Strand* Cuchulain agrees to take an oath of obedience to Conchubar, High King of Ulster. No sooner is the oath taken than a young warrior from Aoife's country strides into the room. Cuchulain's heart warms to the boy but Conchubar orders Cuchulain to fight him. Cuchulain finds himself attacking Conchubar in defence of the boy. Somebody shouts that Cuchulain has been bewitched by the young stranger. Stung by this accusation, Cuchulain turns on the youth, accepts his challenge and kills him.

When he finds it is his own son he has killed, Cuchulain goes mad, wades into the sea slashing murderously at the waves. The tide apparently drowns him.

The plot of *On Baile's Strand* is based on 'The Only Son of Aoife', an episode in Lady Gregory's *Cuchulain of Muir-*

themne. In Lady Gregory's version of the story Cuchulain knows that he has left Aoife with child. Aoife's hatred of Cuchulain is based on her jealousy of his wife Emer.

> The time Cuchulain came back from Alban, after he had learned the use of arms under Scathach, he left Aoife, the queen he had overcome in battle, with child. . . .
>
> It was not long after the child was born, word came to Aoife that Cuchulain had taken Emer to be his wife in Ireland. When she heard that, great jealousy came on her, and great anger, and her love for Cuchulain was turned to hatred; and she remembered her three champions that he had killed, and how he had overcome herself, and she determined in her mind that when her son would come to have the strength of a man, she would get her revenge through him. She told Conlaoch her son nothing of this, but brought him up like any king's son; and when he was come to sensible years, she put him under the teachings of Scathach, to be taught the use of arms and the art of war. He turned out as apt a scholar as his father, and it was not long before he had learnt all Scathach had to teach.[37]

Aoife sends Conlaoch into Ireland with three commands upon him: first, never to give way to any living person; second, not to refuse a challenge from the greatest champion alive; third, not to tell his name on any account. He lands at Baile's Strand at a time that Conchubar is holding his court there.

Conlaoch first fights Conall and defeats him. Then Cuchulain challenges the young champion. The two are evenly matched and Cuchulain finds himself pressed very hard. He calls for his spear.

> And he called for the Gae Bulg, and his anger came on him, and the flames of the hero-light began to shine about his head, and by that sign Conlaoch knew him to be Cuchulain, his father. And just at that time he was aiming his spear at him, and when he knew it was Cuchulain, he threw his spear crooked that it might pass by him. But Cuchulain threw his spear, the Gae Bulg, at him with all his might, and it struck the lad in the side and went into his body, so that he fell to the ground.[38]

Conlaoch identifies himself and Cuchulain is overcome by grief as his son dies. As Cuchulain laments the death of his son, Conchubar makes a decision.

'There is trouble on Cuchulain,' said Conchubar; 'he is after killing his own son, and if I and all my men were to go against him, by the end of the day he would destroy every man of us. Go now,' he said to Cathbad, the Druid, 'and bind him to go down to Baile's Strand, and give three days fighting against the waves of the sea, rather than kill us all.'[39]

Cathbad does as he is bidden. After venting his wrath on Aoife by splitting a stone into quarters, Cuchulain fights the waves. Lady Gregory's version concludes: 'Then he fought with the waves three days and three nights, till he fell from hunger and weakness, so that some men said he got his death there. But it was not there he got his death, but on the plain of Muirthemne.'[40]

In adapting this story, Yeats adds a sub-plot involving a blind man and a fool who are in some sense the shadows of Conchubar and Cuchulain. He makes Cuchulain unaware that he has left Aoife with child and eliminates the scene in which Conlaoch reveals his identity. This makes possible the powerful scene in which the blind man reveals the truth to Cuchulain and Cuchulain goes mad with grief. It is this madness, not a druidical spell, which leads him to fight the waves. By removing the motive of jealousy as an explanation of Aoife's actions, Yeats makes her a more impressive character. Her actions are simply a manifestation of the curse which falls upon all those who choose the heroic life. Like Cuchulain, she is fated always to mix hatred in love.[41] The ambiguity in the old legends surrounding the death of Cuchulain Yeats uses as an opportunity to introduce the death and resurrection theme of *The Only Jealousy of Emer* into his play cycle.

In *The Only Jealousy of Emer*, Cuchulain's wife Emer tries to summon the spirit of her husband back after his apparent drowning on Baile's Strand. She has Cuchulain's mistress, Eithne Inguba, kiss the lips of Cuchulain's lifeless body. It is not Cuchulain's spirit that returns but a changeling — the ugly, distorted spirit, Bricriu. Bricriu offers to bring Cuchulain back if Emer will give up any claim to his love. Bricriu grants Emer second-sight and she sees the spirit of her husband with the moon goddess, Fand. He is about to kiss Fand and become immortal like herself. Emer becomes jealous for the first time and, to take Cuchulain from Fand, renounces her love, bringing her husband back to the arms of his mistress.

Lady Gregory's account of Cuchulain's sojourn with the goddess Fand is found in an episode of *Cuchulain of Muirthemne* which is itself entitled 'The Only Jealousy of Emer'.

In Lady Gregory's story, Cuchulain tries to kill an enchanted bird for his mistress, Eithne Inguba, and is put under a spell by two women of the Sidhe. He is unconscious for a year. When he regains consciousness, one of the women appears again and informs Cuchulain that Fand, who has been deserted by Manannan, god of the sea, has fallen in love with him. The messenger's name is Liban and she is the wife of Labraid of the quick sword. Labraid sends a request that Cuchulain give him 'one day's help against Senach of the crooked body, and against Eochaid Juil, and against Eoghan of Inbhir, that is Eogan of the River's Mouth'.[42]

After a number of complications, Cuchulain fights the battle for Labraid, and stays a month with Fand. When he leaves, he agrees to meet her at a yew tree at the head of Baile's Strand.

> But when all this was told to Emer, there was great anger on her, and she had knives made ready to kill the woman with; and she came, and fifty young girls with her, to the place whery they had settled to meet. . . .

> 'No harm shall be done to you by her,' said Cuchulain; ' and she shall not reach to you at all. Come into the sunny seat of the chariot, opposite myself, for I will defend you against all the many women of the four points of Ulster; for though Forgall's daughter may threaten,' he said, 'on the strength of her companions, to do some daring thing, it is surely not against me she will dare it.[43]

Although threats of force are of no avail, Emer is able to win back Cuchulain by her willingness to give him up.

> 'It is certain,' said Emer, 'that I will not refuse this woman if you follow her. But all the same, everything red is beautiful, everything new is fair, everything high is lovely, everything common is bitter, everything we are without is thought much of; everything we know is thought little of, till all knowledge is known. And O Cuchulain,' she said, 'I was at one time in esteem with you, and I would be so again, if it were pleasing to you.'
>
> And grief came upon her, and overcame her. 'By my word, now,' said Cuchulain, 'you are pleasing to me, and will be pleasing as long as I live.'
>
> 'Let me be given up,' said Fand. 'It is better for me to be given up,' said Emer. 'Not so,' said Fand 'it is I that will be given up in the end, and it is I that have been in danger of it all this time.'
>
> And great grief and trouble of mind came on Fand, because she was ashamed to be given up, and to have to go back to her home there and then; and the great love she had given Cuchulain troubled her. . . .[44]

Fand goes back to her husband Manannan. This development outrages Cuchulain.

> It is then there was great anger on Cuchulain, and he went with great leaps southward to Luachair, the place of rushes; and he stopped for a long while without drink, without food, among the mountains, and where he slept every night, was on the road of Midluachan.[45]

Conchubar sends druids to calm Cuchulain. They put an enchantment on him, and then administer a drink of forgetfulness. The druids give a drink of forgetfulness to Emer as well that she may forget her jealousy. Manannan shakes his cloak between Cuchulain and Fand so that they will never meet again.

Yeats uses many of the details of Lady Gregory's narrative, but in a way that their significance is radically altered. In Yeats' play cycle, the Fand episode follows Cuchulain's fighting with the waves. Cuchulain's unconscious state, the result of a spell cast upon him by two women in the original story, is now the result of his apparent drowning at the end of *On Baile's Strand.* The trance state is simultaneous to the meeting with Fand rather than prior to it. In making this change, Yeats alters the meaning of the entire episode. In Yeats' play, the trance state is an instance of the soul leaving the body. This makes possible the possession of the body by the spirit Bricriu. It also makes clear that the meeting with Fand (a naturalistic meeting between two lovers in Lady Gregory's story) is symbolic of a state of Cuchulain's soul and is not merely another amorous adventure.

Yeats also places in an entirely new context Emer's renunciation of Cuchulain's love. In the original story, Emer and Fand seem to be engaged in a contest of self-sacrifice out of love for Cuchulain. Fand withdraws from the field apparently because she is impressed by Emer's queenly qualities and, in the end, Emer wins back the love of Cuchulain. In Yeats' play, however, renunciation is a weapon given to Emer to give her power over Fand. As such it has significance within the symbolic pattern of the play.

Bricriu is also an interpolation original to Yeats. In Lady Gregory's story it is Manannan himself who comes riding out of the sea. Yeats, incidentally, drops all reference to Fand's marriage to Manannan. In fact in the prose version of the play, *Fighting the Waves,* he refers to her as Manannan's daughter.[45]

In *The Death of Cuchulain,* Cuchulain is wounded six times in battle and, knowing that he is about to die, ties himself to a pillar-stone so that he may die on his feet. As he waits for death, Queen Aoife, older now, but a wild, warlike figure yet, appears before him. She seems about to kill him when she hears a step. It is a blind old beggarman come to gather Cuchulain's head to sell for twelve pennies. It is at the hand of this old man that Cuchulain meets his death.

Yeats bases this play on certain incidents from the episodes, 'The Gathering at Muirthemne' and 'Death of Cuchulain', in Lady Gregory's *Cuchulain of Muirthemne.* In Lady Gregory's story, the enemies of Cuchulain gather to destroy him. Cuchulain realises his danger but is ready to plunge into battle regardless.

> And then one of the daughters of Catalin took the appearance of a crow, and came flying over him and saying mocking words, and she bade him go out and save his own house and his lands from the enemies that were destroying them. And though Cuchulain knew well by this time it was witchcraft was being worked against him, he was ready as before to rush out when he heard the sounds and the shouting of battle; and there came trouble and confusion on his mind with the noise of striking and of fighting, and with the sweet sounds of the harps of the Sidhe.[47]

To save Cuchulain from the death which awaits him should he plunge precipitously into battle, Emer and Conchubar engage Niamh, his best-loved mistress, to put him under oath not to go to battle unless she gives him leave. But Badb, one of Catalin's three deformed and one-eyed daughters, takes on the shape of Naimh and urges him to go into battle. Later, when Naimh denies having released him from his bond, he refuses to believe her.

In the battle, Cuchulain is fatally wounded. He asks permission of his enemies to go to the lake and drink.

> There was a pillar-stone west of the lake, and his eye lit on it, and he went to the pillar-stone, and he tied himself to it with his breast-belt, the way he would not meet his death lying down, but would meet it standing up. Then his enemies came round about him, but they were in dread of going close to him, for they were not sure but he might be still alive.[48]

The Grey of Macha, one of Cuchulain's chariot horses, returns from the dead and makes three attacks on Cuchulain's enemies. Lugaid, son of Curoi, then cuts off Cuchulain's head. Conall avenges Cuchulain's death and Emer delivers a long lament to the head of Cuchulain. When Conall returns with the heads of Cuchulain's enemies, Emer sings the Lay of the Heads. She has herself buried with Cuchulain.

Yeats uses many of the details of this story in his final Cuchulain play but rearranges them so that the final play will

cohere with the rest of the cycle. He substitutes Eithne
Inguba for Niamh, brings Aoife onto the scene and has
Cuchulain's head taken by the blind man, a character from
On Baile's Strand. The characteristics of the daughters of
Catalin in their various forms are split between the crow-
headed war goddess, the Morrigu, and Maeve, who is
described as having an eye in the middle of her forehead.[49]
Yeats replaces Emer's Lay of the Heads with a dance because,
in the words of the old man who introduces the play, 'where
there are no words there is less to spoil'.[50]

Yeats' Cuchulain cycle ends with a reference to Pearse and
Connolly and the statue of Cuchulain which stands in the
Dublin Post Office. It is remarkable that Pearse and Yeats,
the two Irishmen who took the most active part in shaping
the fate of modern Ireland, should have been enamoured of
the same mythological hero. While Pearse and Connolly prepared for the Easter Uprising, Yeats was rehearsing *At the
Hawk's Well* for a performance in Lady Cunard's drawing-
room. The activities seem to belong to two different worlds,
yet they were strangely connected.

The questions asked in the end song of *At the Hawk's Well*

> Who but an idiot would praise
> Dry stones in a well?
>   . . .
> Who but an idiot would praise
> A withered tree?[51]

would appear to find their answer in a poem of Pearse's.

> Since the wise men have not spoken, I speak
>   that am only a fool;
> A fool that hath loved his folly,
> Yea, more than the wise men their books or
>   their counting houses, or their quiet
>   homes,
> Or their fame in men's mouths.[52]

Yeats had characterised Cuchulain as 'the fool — wandering
passive, houseless and almost loveless'.[53]

Padraic Pearse would have had little patience with Yeats'

neo-paganism. His nationalistic aspirations didn't look to Irish Mystical Orders or a revival of druidical ceremonies. Pearse dreamed of an Ireland, Gaelic, free and Roman Catholic. Yet, as Yeats wrote in 1937, 'in the imagination of Pearse and his fellow soldiers the Sacrifice of the Mass had found the Red Branch in the tapestry; they went out to die calling upon Cuchulain.'[54]

3 The Burning Wheel of Love

I

By the year 1902, Yeats' theatrical work had begun to draw his attention from the search for rituals for an Irish Mystical Order. It was true, however, that his plans for an Irish theatre remained closely related to his plans for establishing the Order. He wished all his writings, his plays in particular, 'to have a secret symbolic relation to these mysteries [of the Irish mystical order], for in this way I thought there would be a greater richness, a greater claim upon the love of soul, devotion without exhortation or rhetoric. . .'.[1] Dramatic ritual for the Mystical Order and ritual drama for an Irish theatre tended to merge.

When Yeats received word of Maud Gonne's marriage to John MacBride, in February 1903, he abandoned plans for the Mystical Order altogether. Norman Jeffares comments on Yeats' emotional reaction to the marriage.

> Once she was married there was nothing to look forward to, even with diminished hope. The puzzle to him had been that, when they went to see the Lia Fail, Maud had appeared to understand his plans, especially those for the Castle of the Heroes, to be built of Irish stone and decorated with the four jewels of the Tuatha de Danaan, with perhaps a statue of Ireland. . . . It seemed impossible to him that she should not marry him, knowing his love and his plans for Ireland. Her marriage carried conviction that all hope of achieving the loveliness of his dreams was gone. . . .[2]

Maud's marriage brought Yeats face to face with some central problems in his life which he had up to now evaded. The immediate and dramatic effect that this new outlook had on his work may be seen in the changes it prompted in the text of *On Baile's Strand,* the first version of which was near completion when he received word of Maud's marriage in 1903. By 1906, Yeats had completely rewritten the first half of *On Baile's Strand* in a way that not only made it a better play, but also brought it into line with his new outlook on life, and with the future course of his philosophic development and dramatic technique. In the revised version of *On Baile's Strand* he directly adopted 'the burning wheel of love' with its alternate sides of love and hate as a dramatic theme. He also began to come effectively to terms with the contradictions within his own personality.

II

By the end of 1902, Yeats' first version of *On Baile's Strand* was near completion. He struggled to make final changes so that it could be published by Dun Emer Press. On 16 December he wrote to Lady Gregory: 'After that comes *Cuchullain* and this must be amended at once for my sister, and then the wind up of this [book].'[3] On 3 January, 1903, he hoped 'in a couple more days to have got *Cuchullain* finally right and sent to my sisters'.[4] On 15 January, he found 'that *Cuchullain* wants new passages here and there'.[5] His sisters did publish *On Baile's Strand* under the Dun Emer imprint later that year, as part of the volume *In the Seven Woods*. It was produced on 27 December, 1904, the first play to be presented by the National Theatre Society in their new quarters in the Abbey Theatre. The text used was essentially that published in the Dun Emer edition of *In the Seven Woods*.

The 1903 version of *On Baile's Strand* is an interesting but seriously flawed play. It is, as Peter Ure has pointed out, 'essentially a simple transposition of the story of Cuchulain's quarrel with Conchubar, his slaying of his own son and subsequent madness and death, into a play suitable for performance on the Abbey stage'.[6] However, the characterisation of Cuchulain bears the mark of Yeats' uncertainties about his own personality and motivations in the period preceding Maud Gonne's marriage. The plotting bears evidence of Yeats' tendency to evade certain central issues which relate closely to his own life. The unity of the entire play is undermined by Yeats' indecision as to what part magic should play in ritual drama.

In *The Tragic Drama of William Butler Yeats,* Leonard E. Nathan accurately defines some of the confusions.

> The weaknesses of plot result in a confusion of thematic emphasis. A long discussion between Cuchulain and his followers concerning different types of love is meant as dramatic irony looking forward to Cuchulain's failure to recognize his son. But the discussion seems excessively long for this function and has nothing to do with the central opposition of Cuchulain and Conchubar, for Cuchulain's passion for fierce, undomesticated women suggests that Conchubar, as his opposite, must cherish virtues of gentle nature and passive love. But Conchubar hardly represents such virtues in this version of the play; thus Cuchulain's preference for heroic love over domestic love is not clearly brought into effective relationship with the play's main theme, which hinges upon the opposition of Cuchulain and Conchubar. The same may be said of the conflict between father and son; though a matter central to the play, this conflict is not clearly related to the central theme. Had Yeats (as he would do in the later version) set Cuchulain's relationship to his son in contrast to Cuchubar's relationship to his children, the conflict of Cuchulain and the Young Man would have enhanced and clarified the theme.[7]

Nathan points to the deep split in the personality of Cuchulain which tends to rob the play of dramatic unity. It is difficult to reconcile the capriciously wilful Cuchulain who urges his followers to ignore the High King for the sake of prolonging a boyish conversation:

> Come nearer yet;
> Though he is ringing that old silver rod
> We'll have our own talk out. They cannot hear us.[8]

with the Cuchulain who in such stirring and solemn words speaks of the deeds that could be accomplished if he had had a son like the young stranger:

> He would avenge me
> When I have withstood for the last time the men
> Whose fathers, brothers, sons, and friends I have killed
> Upholding Ullad; when the four provinces
> Have gathered with the ravens over them.
> But I'd need no avenger. You and I
> Would scatter them like water from a dish.[9]

Nathan points to two other major difficulties. Although the play abounds with references to the supernatural, Yeats has failed to demonstrate convincingly that the supernatural is really relevant to the main action of the play. In Nathan's words, 'the supernatural . . . [is] neither the symbol for an extraordinary psychological state nor an objective reality in its own right'.[10] Further, the naturalistic fool and blind man of the original version of *On Baile's Strand* are (in the first scene of the play at any rate) stock, low-comedy, Irish peasant figures. Their inclusion appears to be an arbitrary attempt to broaden the application of the significance of the main plot by creating an analogous sub-plot according to principles Yeats had outlined in an essay on 'Emotion of Multitude'.[11] They seem inadequately integrated into the thematic structure of the play, and therefore lose much of their effect.

So great was Yeats' dissatisfaction with the 1903 version of *On Baile's Strand,* that he rewrote the entire first section of the play, right to the entrance of the young stranger whom Cuchulain fails to recognise as his son. In the 1906 version of *On Baile's Strand,* Yeats centres the play's entire thematic structure squarely on the conflict between the values of Cuchulain and the values of Conchubar. As Richard Ellman has suggested, this conflict owes much of its vividness to the soul-searching Yeats underwent after finding he had lost Maud Gonne to John MacBride.

> Yeats blamed his own timid, critical intellect for restraining his impetuous nature so that when he should have embraced he had feared and qualified and idealized. He had lost the capacity for acting on instinct which men like MacBride, lacking the critical mind, possessed.[12]

The conflict between Conchubar and Cuchulain was, to some extent, the dramatisation of a conflict between two parts of Yeats' own nature, a conflict which had been made acute by the traumatic impact of the news of Maud's marriage.

The strong emphasis given the conflict between Cuchulain and Conchubar serves to unify the play. Every scene, every detail in the play, is now carefully shaped so that it serves either to clarify or to mirror the central conflict. In the 1906 version of the play, the meeting between Cuchulain and Conchubar has been arranged specifically to discuss Cuchulain's insubordination and the necessity of an oath of allegiance. Since the incident which has prompted Concubar's concern is the arrival on a unguarded shore of 'a youngster out of Aoife's country', then a discussion of Cuchulain's love for Aoife becomes relevant to the main conflict. In the revised play, Cuchulain is strong and proud from the beginning, displaying none of those Richard II qualities which so confused us in the 1903 version.

The oath of allegiance required of Cuchulain is administered in the 1906 version in a 'fire and sword' ritual. During the ceremony, three 'singing women' chant a choral ode. The introduction of the ceremony and the ode which accompanies it completely refocuses many of the elements in *On Baile's Strand;* it is also a development of great importance in Yeats' growth as a ritual dramatist.

In a letter to Florence Farr written on 16 February, 1906, at a time when he was working on the revision of *On Baile's Strand,* Yeats spoke of 'a strange little play' into which he obviously intended to pour many of his feelings about Maud Gonne and her 'indomitable kind of woman'. He had written a choral ode for it.

> I have a sketch of a strange little play about the capture of a blind Unicorn, and I have written a choral ode about witches which contain these lines — suggested in some vague way by your letter, only suggested I mean, in phantasmal exaggeration of some sentence.

> Or, they hurl a spell at him
> That he follow with desire
> Bodies that can never tire

Or grow kind, for they anoint
All their bodies joint by joint
With a miracle working juice,
That is made out of the grease
Of the ungoverned unicorn;
But the man is thrice forlorn
Emptied, ruined, wracked and lost
That *they* follow, for at most
They will give him kiss for kiss
While they murmur 'After this
Hatred may be sweet in the taste.'
Those wild hands that have embraced
All his body can but shove
At the burning wheel of love
Till the side of hate comes up.

The hero had been praising an indomitable kind of woman
and the chorus sing of her evil shadow. The unicorn in the
little play is a type of masterful and beautiful life, but I
shall not trouble to make the meaning clear — a clear vivid
story of a strange sort is enough. The meaning may be
different with everyone.[13]

Yeats abandoned the play about the blind unicorn almost
immediately but used the choral ode he had written for it as
an accompaniment to the 'sword and fire' ritual of *On Baile's
Strand*. In its new context, the ode retained for him almost
all the associations it had had in the abandoned play. With
the ceremony and the ode providing a ritual centre for the
play, Yeats was now able to treat directly many of the issues
which had been treated only obliquely in the 1903 version of
On Baile's Strand.

On closer examination we find that the conflict between
the values of Cuchulain and the values of Conchubar is
merely one aspect of a deeper theme treated by the play. *On
Baile's Strand*, in the 1906 version, is about 'an indomitable
kind of woman', Aoife, and the evil shadow which she casts
over those who dare to love her. Love is a 'burning wheel'
and when it is propelled by desires strong enough, it is
inevitable that the 'side of hate' should come up. The wheel
of love becomes a symbol of the fate of Cuchulain. Its

operation is what the Fool senses but cannot 'puzzle out' in the first scene. It is the turning of the wheel that makes Cuchulain's destruction of his son inevitable, that animates the conflict between Cuchulain and Conchubar, that makes us sense that the argument about witchcraft is no arbitrary device but an organic part of the play. In introducing the wheel of love and of fate, Yeats has come upon the image that he will use to provide a framework for the entire Cuchulain cycle. As we shall see, it will also become a central symbol in all his thought.

Cuchulain uses sun and moon imagery to extend the metaphor of the wheel of love and hate. His speech is an elaboration of an idea Yeats found in Blake's writings that 'sexual love is founded upon spiritual hate'.[14]

> I never have known love but as a kiss
> In the mid-battle, and a difficult truce
> Of oil and water, candles and dark night,
> Hillside and hollow, the hot-footed sun
> And the cold, sliding, slippery-footed moon —
> A brief forgiveness between opposites
> That have been hatreds for three times the age
> Of this long-'stablished ground.[15]

There is much mention of this war of opposites in the 1906 version of *On Baile's Strand*. Typically it is described as a struggle between elemental spirits. (Fire and water vie for dominance in the blood. Fire is used to drive spirits of the air from the great hall.) Such imagery is closely related to the magical tradition as Yeats knew it from Blake, the alchemists and the Golden Dawn. The discussion of Cuchulain's obstinate and heroic folly in continuing to love the woman whose every move is calculated to harm him is brought to the centre of the debate with Conchubar and thus to the thematic centre of the play. We are led to conclude that Yeats' final abandonment of all hope that Maud will reciprocate his love has somehow freed him to treat, without evasion, the evil shadow cast over others by a beautiful, indomitable woman. It seems also that abandonment of all hope of setting up an Irish Mystical Order has brought about a much freer use of magical imagery in Yeats' dramatic poetry.

In the 1906 revision of *On Baile's Strand,* magic becomes central. It is no longer an arbitrary decoration. Sun and moon imagery, wheels of love and hate, symbols of masculinity and femininity, predominate. Cuchulain's imagery is a tapestry of allusions to battles between elemental spirits. He alludes to some hermetic or kabbalistic vision of the origin of the world, in which he has seen 'the heavens like a burning cloud/Brooding upon the world,'[16] and laments that now the 'old fiery fountains' from which life originally sprang 'are far off/And every day there is less heat o' the blood'.[17] Fire imagery illuminations line after line of Cuchulain's dialogue and at the centre of the play Yeats places the fire ritual with its accompanying choral ode which ties the magical and psychological elements of the play together into a dramatic unity. In a very real sense, Irish ritual theatre was born with the 1906 revision of *On Baile's Strand.*

Yeats' growing mastery of dramatic structure is evident in his skilful adaptation of the fool and the blind man to a dramatic function consistent with the new pattern of the play. In the version of 1903, the blind man and fool were represented as naturalistic, low-comedy, almost burlesque types. 'Barach, a tall thin man with long ragged hair, dressed in skins, comes in at the side door. He is leading Fintain, a fat blind man, who is somewhat older.'[18] They were ordinary peasants, their nuisance value generally notorious around the court. Cuchulain and the young kings knew them by reputation.

> They always flock together; the blind man
> Has need of the fool's eyesight and strong body,
> While the poor fool has need of the other's wit,
> And night and day is up to his ears in mischief
> That the blind man imagines.[19]

In the 1906 version of the play, these two characters are no longer given names, but are referred to simply as Blind Man and Fool. A detailed story about the blinding of Fintain in the 1903 version of the play is reduced to a mysterious reference. 'That was before you were blinded for putting a curse on the wind.'[20] Yeats, now under the influence of Gordon Craig,[21] sees them as masked figures. The play is carefully restructured so that they appear only before Cuchulain and the audience.

In making these changes, Yeats has considerably enhanced the symbolic significance of the Fool and Blind Man. In the earlier version of the play, they were low-comedy extensions (or shadows) of Cuchulain and Conchubar. Now they are far more than this. In some sense they represent the forces which govern the lives of all men.

> Life drifts between a fool and a blind man
> To the end and nobody can know his end.[22]

In a note written in 1934 Yeats linked them to the wheel imagery which we have noted at the centre of this play, referring to them as 'those combatants who turn the wheel of life'.[23] When, some thirteen years after the composition of the final version of *On Baile's Strand,* Yeats was to work his wheel symbolism into that complex metaphysical system outlined in *A Vision,* he would make much of two symbolic figures, Hunchback and Fool. The Blind Man and Fool of *On Baile's Strand* seem to represent an early formulation of this symbolism. The Fool seems also to be related to the Fool of Faery, that familiar visitor through vision to Yeats' friend George Russell (AE). This mysterious figure, connected in Yeats' mind with the god Aengus, had a special place of prominence in all visionary experience. Certainly in the 1906 version of *On Baile's Strand* Yeats had moved Blind Man and Fool far beyond their original position of low-comedy characters generalising a theme or providing 'comic relief' in an otherwise tragic plot.

Magic, in the final version of *On Baile's Strand,* has become a central theme of the play. It is the Fool's allegiance to the witches that first draws the Blind Man's scorn, while it is Cuchulain's dancing that is the central issue of Conchubar's attack on him. It is worth considering for a moment what manner of dance is implied by Conchubar's remark

> He came to land
> While you were somewhere out of sight and hearing,
> Hunting or dancing with your wild companions.[24]

The dance danced by Cuchulain and his wild companions

could scarce be other than the great, circular dance, used by dervishes, initiates to the ancient mysteries, devotees of gnostic religions and the members of modern magical societies, for the production of trance states conducive to the evocation of spirits. This is the dance that Yeats would attribute to the Judwalis in the first edition of *A Vision.* In a short story published in the nineties, entitled *Rosa Alchemica,* Yeats described the dance as practised by the members of an Irish Mystical Order established by Michael Robartes.

The dance wound in and out, tracing upon the floor the shapes of petals that copied the petals of the rose overhead, and to the sound of hidden instruments which were perhaps of an antique pattern, for I have never heard the like; and every moment the dance was more passionate, until all the winds of the world seemed to have awakened under our feet. After a little I had grown weary, and stood under a pillar watching the coming and going of those flame-like figures; until gradually I sank into a half-dream, from which I was awakened by seeing the petals of the great rose, which had no longer the look of mosaic, falling slowly through the incense-heavy air, and, as they fell, shaping into the likeness of living beings of an extraordinary beauty. Still faint and cloud-like, they began to dance, and as they danced took a more and more definite shape, so that I was able to distinguish beautiful Grecian and august Egyptian faces, and now and again to name a divinity by the staff in his hand or a bird fluttering overhead; and soon every mortal foot danced by the white foot of an immortal; and in the troubled eyes that looked into untroubled shadowy eyes, I saw the brightness of uttermost desire as though they had found at length, after unreckonable wanderings, the lost love of youth.[25]

What ancient ceremonies Cuchulain carries out in those magical places 'where the spare hazels meet the wool-white foam',[26] we are not told, but his intimacy with the 'pale windy people'[27] is undeniable and it is of course a major source of Conchubar's hostility towards him.

There is no reason to doubt Yeats' contention that the major source of *A Vision* was his wife's automatic script. Yeats undoubtedly used his wife's gifts as a medium in much the same way that MacGregor Mathers had used those of his wife in composing the rituals of the Golden Dawn and that Yeats himself had intended to use those of Maud Gonne in composing the rituals of the Irish Mystical Order. The main features of the system that the spirits dictated to him through his wife, however, were already available to him from his study of Blake, the Kabbalah, Blavatsky and Rosicrucianism. In fact, the most important features of that system were inherent in his way of looking at experience by the time he revised *On Baile's Strand* in 1906. In the course of that revision there seems to have emerged the beginnings of a plan for a cycle of Cuchulain plays, linked together by continuous narrative, but each representing one of a series of connected rituals, replacing the abandoned rituals of the Irish Mystical Order. How conscious was the process by which Yeats first began to give effect to the plan I do not presume to say. When, however, Yeats published almost simultaneously, in 1919, the poem 'The Phases of the Moon' and the play *The Only Jealousy of Emer,* then, in 1921, added a note linking the two works, all was intelligible.

III

In a note included in *Four Plays for Dancers,* a 1921 volume containing *At the Hawk's Well, The Only Jealousy of Emer,* and two other plays based on Japanese *Noh* drama, W. B. Yeats made the following comment:

> While writing these plays, intended for some fifty people in a drawing-room or a studio, I have so rejoiced in my freedom from the stupidity of an ordinary audience that I have filled 'The Only Jealousy of Emer' with those little known convictions about the nature and history of a woman's beauty, which Robartes found in the *Speculum* of Gyraldus and in Arabia Deserta among the Judwalis. The soul through each cycle of its development is held to incarnate through twenty-eight typical incarnations, corresponding to the phases of the moon, the light part of

the moon's disc symbolizing the subjective and the dark part of the objective nature, the wholly dark moon (called Phase 1) and the wholly light (called Phase 15) symbolizing complete objectivity and complete subjectivity respectively. In a poem called, 'The Phases of the Moon' in *The Wild Swans at Coole* I have described certain aspects of this symbolism which, however, may take 100 pages or more of my edition of the Robartes papers, for, as expounded by him, it purports to be a complete classification and analysis of every possible type of human intellect, Phase 1 and Phase 15 symbolizing, however, two incarnations not visible to human eyes nor having human characteristics. The invisible fifteenth incarnation is that of the greatest possible bodily beauty and the fourteenth and sixteenth those of the greatest beauty visible to human eyes. Much that Robartes has written might be a commentary on Castiglione's saying that the physical beauty of a woman is the spoil or monument of the victory of the soul, for physical beauty, only possible to subjective natures, is described as the result of emotional toil in past lives. Objective natures are declared to be always ugly, hence the disagreeable appearance of politicians, reformers, philanthropists, and men of science. A saint or sage before his final deliverance has one incarnation as a woman of supreme beauty.

In writing these little plays I knew that I was creating something which could only fully succeed in a civilization very unlike ours. I think they should be written for some country where all classes share in a half-mythological, half-philosophical folk-belief which the writer and his small audience lift into a new subtlety. All my life I have longed for such a country, and always found it impossible to write without having as much belief in its real existence as a child has in that of the wooden birds, beasts, and persons of his toy Noah's Ark. I have now found all the mythology and philosophy I need in the papers of my old friend and rival, Robartes.[28]

It is to these papers, which Yeats is to publish as *A Vision,* that we must look for the mythological and philosophical framework not just of *The Only Jealousy of Emer* but of Yeats entire Cuchulain cycle. The poem Yeats mentions, 'The Phases of the Moon', provides a key to the symbolism of *The Only Jealousy of Emer;* on close examination it also yields up the scenario for the spiritual adventures of Cuchulain through all five of the Cuchulain plays, including *The Death of Cuchulain,* the play that Yeats completed just before his death in 1939.

Both 'The Phases of the Moon' and the five-play Cuchulain cycle tell the story of the progress of the human soul as it moves from absorption in the objective world to subjective realisation and back again to absorption in the objective world. This process may be illustrated by Yeats' great wheel of moon phases. It is worth looking at this system in some detail and considering its application to the Cuchulain cycle.

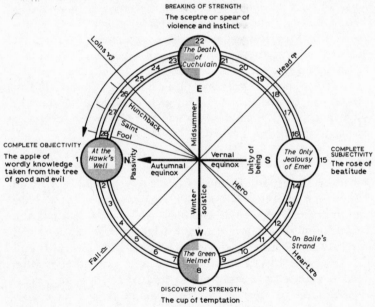

IV

To W. B. Yeats, all human experience was cyclical. His principal symbol for illustrating this was a great wheel around the circumference of which were arranged the twenty-eight phases of a symbolic moon. Alternatively, he saw life as moving between objectivity and subjectivity on a pair of interpenetrating gyres. This view of life was in harmony with everything he had learned in his years of study of occult doctrine. It was a view he also associated with doctrines he believed made up the beliefs of pre-Christian Ireland and some beliefs held by Irish peasants to the present day. As he says in a late poem,

> Many times man lives and dies
> Between his two eternities,
> That of race and that of soul,
> And ancient Ireland knew it all.[29]

Yeats explains his wheel symbolism thus in a passage from *A Vision:*

This wheel is every completed movement of thought or life, twenty-eight incarnations, a single incarnation, a single judgment or act of thought. Man seeks his opposite or the opposite of his condition, attains his object so far as it is attainable, at Phase 15 and returns to Phase 1 again.[30]

It is clear from Yeats' note on *The Only Jealousy of Emer,* and from certain speeches within the play, that this play is meant to be a dramatisation of Phase 15 on the great wheel of moon phases. But it is also clear that the Woman of the Sidhe is herself meant to be taken as a moon goddess at the stage of the full moon. The Ghost of Cuchulain asks:

> Who is it stands before me there
> Shedding such light from limb and hair
> As when the moon, complete at last
> With every labouring crescent past,
> And lonely with extreme delight,
> Flings out upon the fifteenth night?[31]

Given Cuchulain's identity as a Celtic solar hero, what we have here is obviously a crisis point in the romance of the Sun and the Moon.

But the Ghost of Cuchulain identifies the Woman of the Sidhe as the same supernatural personage he met at the hawk's well.

> I know you now, for long ago.
> I met you on a cloudy hill
> Beside old thorn-trees and a well.
> A woman danced and a hawk flew,
> I held out arms and hands;[32]

There she exhibited tendencies opposite to those that characterise her in her present phase.

> but you,
> That now seem friendly, fled away,
> Half woman and half bird or prey.[33]

The Woman of the Sidhe herself makes the contrast between her two appearances explicit.

> Hold out your arms and hands
>   again;
> You were not so dumbfounded when
> I was that bird of prey, and yet
> I am all woman now.[34]

Here, as the goddess Fand, she is all light, all beauty. In *At the Hawk's Well* she was referred to as 'the unappeasable shadow' and was associated with images of darkness. In that play too, Cuchulain was referred to in terms which suggested his solar identity. It appears to be an inescapable conclusion that if *The Only Jealousy of Emer* represents the solar hero and the moon goddess at Phase 15 on the great wheel (the phase of the full moon), then *At the Hawk's Well* represents their situation at Phase 1 (the phase of the new moon). If *At the Hawk's Well* is a dramatisation of Phase 1 on the great wheel and *The Only Jealousy of Emer* a dramatisation of Phase 15, then it should not surprise us that the other plays of the cycle also find their appropriate positions on the wheel of symbolic moon phases. I would place *The Green Helmet* at Phase 8 on the great wheel and *The Death of Cuchulain* at Phase 22. *On Baile's Strand* falls at Phase 12, which Yeats terms 'the phase of the hero' — an appropriate phase for the central play of the Cuchulain cycle.

V

The hypothesis that all five of the Cuchulain plays can be located in sequence on the great wheel of lunar phases receives striking confirmation if we consider the symbols with which Yeats decorates the drawing of the great wheel on page 66 of *A Vision,* and relate them to the imagery of the Cuchulain plays.

Opposite Phase 1 on the drawing is the Apple of Worldly Knowledge taken from the Tree of Good and Evil. We are reminded of the tree symbolism in *At the Hawk's Well* and particularly of the hazels which drop nuts into the well, nuts which bear such a close resemblance to those nuts of wisdom which drop into the Well of Connla. We recall the words of the musicians. 'Wisdom must live a bitter life.'[35] Now the Gaelic name Aoife is an equivalent of the English Eva. It is clear that *At the Hawk's Well* recounts a Celtic variation of the Garden of Eden story. It is also clear that the story of the Garden and of the Dawn of Consciousness are associated in Yeats' mind with Phase 1 and the phases immediately following it on the great wheel.

Opposite Phase 8 in the drawing is the Cup of Temptation, a symbol which seems particularly appropriate to the imagery and theme of *The Green Helmet.* Opposite Phase 15 is the Rose of Beatitude, an alternate symbol for the absolute beauty represented in the play by the full moon. At Phase 22 is the Sceptre or Spear of Violence and Instinct, a symbol appropriate to the fate that the hero meets in *The Death of Cuchulain.*

As I have pointed out, the cycle of Cuchulain plays may be seen as the story of the romance between the Sun and the Moon. Read this way, the emphasis is thrown on the moon goddess herself in her changing aspects as we follow her through the course of a full lunar month. The most prominent plays in this pattern are *At the Hawk's Well* and *The Only Jealousy of Emer,* representing as they do the dark and the full of the moon respectively. But when we read with the emphasis on Cuchulain, the sun hero himself, the plays assume the pattern of a solar year and we may trace the career of the sun as he moves through the changing seasons of his yearly cycle.

VI

In *A Vision* Yeats instructs us in the technique to be used in relating the solar year to the great wheel of lunar phases.

> I am told to give Phases 1, 8, 15, 22 a month a piece the other phases the third of a month, and begin the year like the early Roman year in the lunar month corresponding to March, when days begin to grow longer than nights:
>
> | | | |
> |---|---|---|
> | March . | . | . Phase 15 |
> | April . | . | . Phases 16, 17, 18 |
> | May . | . | . Phases 19, 20, 21 |
> | June . | . | . Phase 22 |
>
> and so on.[36]

If we apply this table of correspondences to the positions we have assigned the Cuchulain plays on the great wheel, we begin to see the plays in one of their most important aspects, as seasonal rituals marking certain crisis points in the solar year. Thus *At the Hawk's Well* (placed by this reasoning in September) may be seen as a ritual marking the autumnal equinox. *The Green Helmet* marks the winter solstice, *The Only Jealousy of Emer* the vernal equinox, and *The Death of Cuchulain* the summer solstice. *On Baile's Strand* would be placed by this reasoning in early February, at the time of the old Celtic festival of *Imbolc*.

Such a system of rituals keyed to the solar year closely parallels the religious rituals of primitive peoples and the rituals of such magical societies as the Golden Dawn. A study of the Golden Dawn papers published by Israel Regardie reveals the importance of ceremonies marking equinox and solstice in the lives of order members.[37] Behind the Cuchulain cycle is a complex system of ritual. It is when we study the Cuchulain cycle as a whole, that we realise how little Yeats changed his basic aim when he shifted his attention from the Castle of the Heroes to Irish Ritual Theatre.

Although Yeats, as a believer in the multilevel symbol, disapproved of John Rhys' too exclusive interpretation of the Cuchulain myth in terms of solar imagery, there can be little doubt that the festivals of some form of primitive heliolatry

provide the structural basis for the Cuchulain cycle. Throughout the five plays, Cuchulain is constantly referred to in
terms of solar imagery. When he first appears in *At the
Hawk's Well,* he is dressed like a young sun god. The Old Man
says:

> If I may judge by the gold
> On head and feet and glittering in your coat,
> You are not of those who hate the living world.[38]

In *The Green Helmet,* Emer speaks of 'His mind that is
fire,/His body that is sun', and declares that she is 'moon to
that sun', and 'steel to that fire'.[39] In *On Baile's Strand* it is
said of Cuchulain:

> He burns the earth as if he were a fire,
> And time can never touch him.[40]

He refers to himself explicitly as an offspring of the Sun God.

> My father gave me this.
> He came to try me, rising up at dawn
> Out of the cold dark of the rich sea.[41]

Cuchulain's speeches are filled with fire imagery and with
references to his own fiery origin and Conchubar comments
somewhat ironically that Cuchulain's father 'came out of the
sun'.[42]

Cuchulain refers to his love for Aoife as a 'difficult truce'
of 'the hot-footed sun/And the cold, sliding, slippery-footed
moon'.[43] Cuchulain's fate at the end of *On Baile's Strand* is
described by the Fool in terms which suggest an image of the
sun setting beyond the western sea. 'There, he is down! He is
up again. He is going out in the deep water. There is a big
wave. It has gone over him. I cannot see him now. He has
killed kings and giants, but the waves have mastered him.'[44]

It is Emer, in *The Only Jealousy of Emer,* who places the
apparent death of Cuchulain in the waves in its cyclical
context. Just as the setting sun does not die, Cuchulain is not
dead. The death of Cuchulain would have cosmic significance
— like the death of the sun.

> The very heavens when that day's at hand,
> So that his death may not lack ceremony,

Will throw out fires, and the earth grow red with blood.
There shall not be a scullion but foreknows it
Like the world's end.[45]

In *The Death of Cuchulain,* Cuchulain contrasts his unchanging solar nature with the nature of all that are governed by the changing moon.

You thought that if you changed I'd kill you for it,
When everything sublunary must change,
And if I have not changed that goes to prove
That I am monstrous.[46]

It is the final death of the hero that suggests most clearly his identity as a sun god. As Cuchulain stands tied motionless to a pillar, a Blind Man begins to feel from his ankles to his neck. As the Blind Man's hands reach Cuchulain's neck and he moves to cut off Cuchulain's head, the stage is plunged into darkness. When the lights come on, Cuchulain's head is represented by a black parallelogram. The ritual pattern here seems derived from events associated with solar eclipse — surely one of the most frightening and mysterious events in the life of the sun as seen by primitive man.

VII

W. B. Yeats's remark in a letter to Sturge Moore that he looked upon his work not as drama 'but the ritual of a lost faith' was no idle comment. If we study closely the imagery and the thematic structure of the individual Cuchulain plays, we discover how carefully Yeats has keyed them to their function as seasonal ritual.

The imagery of *At the Hawk's Well* suggests the autumn of the year. The withered leaves of the hazel which the guardian of the well has been raking, the salt sea wind which seems so ominous, the dropping of the hazel nuts — all these are signs of the approach of winter and they evoke in us those emotions of fear and foreboding that primitive man must have felt with the coming of fall. This pattern of imagery is supported by the related image of the setting sun and by the attitudes of an old man who is in the autumn of life.

At the autumnal equinox, daylight and darkness, the time

of waking and sleeping, are evenly balanced. The world stands poised between light and darkness, between the vital processes of summer and the long sleep of winter. The songs of the musicians reflect this situation.

> The heart would be always awake,
> The heart would turn to its rest.[47]

And again:

> 'Why should I sleep?' the heart cries,
> For the wind, the salt wind, the sea wind,
> Is beating a cloud through the skies;
> I would always wander like the wind.'[48]

But later:

> 'O wind, O salt wind, O sea wind!
> Cries the heart, 'it is time to sleep;
> Why wander and nothing to find?
> Better grow old and sleep.'[49]

The Old Man's lighting of a fire at the beginning of *At the Hawk's Well* is an act symbolic of man's resistance to the winter he knows will come. The hearth imagery in the final songs of the musicians looks ahead to that desolate season.

If, as I have suggested, *The Green Helmet* is a ritual for the winter solstice, this gives it a setting of mid-December, exactly at the time at which the story of *Sir Gawayne and the Green Knight,* the Arthurian variant on the same myth, is said to have taken place. It is not difficult to see why both Yeats and the fourteenth-century Gawayne author saw the myth of the mysterious challenger with his game of head-for-head as particularly applicable to the situation of the winter solstice.

It is difficult for the modern mind to recapture fully the feelings of primitive man when faced with seasonal change. Environmental change of any kind awakens terror if we do not understand the processes which cause the change. One is continually fearful that change will go too far, that the environment will cease to support life. Myth reassures man of the cyclical nature of change; ritual enables him to participate in the rhythms of nature, and holds a promise that he may even control those rhythms through imitative magic. The myth which is the source of both *Sir Gawayne and the Green Knight* seems to have its roots in such a seasonal ritual, a ritual particularly appropriate to the winter solstice.

Through October, November and early December the days become ever shorter, while the sun appears to lose its life-giving power even during those hours which darkness does not dominate. The sun is losing a battle with the forces of darkness; man's greatest fear is that the sun will finally be extinguished altogether. It is only when the sun has been brought face to face with the possibility of total extinction on the shortest day of the year, when the forces of darkness appear to be within reach of total victory, that a reprieve is granted the sun. The crisis past, the days begin to lengthen, the sun gains strength and the darkness is pushed back. If we recognise that Cuchulain is a solar hero, it is not difficult to trace the connection between the situation at the winter solstice and the plot pattern of *The Green Helmet.*

In *The Green Helmet,* Cuchulain, the sun hero, is ranged against the forces of darkness which appear to be in the service of Bricriu, a god of discord. It is only after Cuchulain has submitted cheerfully to the supreme test, offering himself for total extinction at the hands of the forces of darkness, that he is chosen champion and faces the future with a full confidence of growing power. The sense of exultation at the end of *The Green Helmet* comes from our having participated in a ritual of affirmation. It is parallel to the wild joy of primitive celebrants when they assert their faith in the cyclical pattern of the seasons through ritual celebrations held at the extreme low point of the sun god's powers — the winter solstice.

If *On Baile's Strand* is located at Phase 12 on the lunar wheel, its setting on the solar wheel would be the first part of February. Now there was an ancient Celtic festival held at precisely that time of year. It was known as *Imbolc* and was associated with the goddess Brigit, a potent fertility figure. Whatever rites were practised by the Celts at this time, they no doubt centred around the power of the nature goddess both in her benevolent and malevolent aspects. The fire ceremony at the centre of *On Baile's Strand,* the song of the women about the destructive aspects of the feminine principle, the sacrifice of Cuchulain's son, and Cuchulain's own contest with the waves, all suggest some forgotten pattern of ritual centring around the worship of a nature goddess and the sacrificial death of her sun-god consort.

The resurrection of the solar-hero takes place in *The Only Jealousy of Emer,* a play which, in our scheme, is a ritual for the vernal equinox. Spring has, of course, been the occasion for rituals of rebirth in all the religions of the world.

The Death of Cuchulain begins as a midsummer ritual at Phase 22 on the great wheel. Just as the winter solstice was a time of Discovery of Strength for the sun and the beginning of its recovery, so the summer solstice is a time of the Breaking of Strength,[50] after which the sun begins to lose its battle with the forces of darkness. In the course of the play, we are taken through the last six phases of the great wheel (perhaps this is what Cuchulain's six antagonists and six mortal wounds symbolise) until, with the death of Cuchulain, the solar year has run its course.

When the Blind Man harvests Cuchulain's head for twelve pennies we are ready to begin Phase 1 again. The year will begin once more. That Yeats meant to present the story of Cuchulain by means of a series of seasonal rituals can hardly be doubted. Not only does his presentation of Cuchulain's death take on many of the aspects of a solar eclipse, but the Blind Man who brings darkness to the solar hero is paid twelve pennies for his head, one for each month of the solar year.

VIII

A religious calendar based on solstice and equinox was very much in keeping with the traditions of such magical societies as the Golden Dawn. It was also in keeping with the practices of those mediterranean cultures which were the source of much of the occult tradition. As far as northern Europe and the British Isles are concerned, such a solar orientation of the calendar is pre-Celtic. The Celts themselves appeared to care little about solstice and equinox. In relating the rituals of the Cuchulain cycle to the crisis points in the solar year, Yeats

was returning to a view of the year which had been held by
the builders of Stonehenge and other such structures, a
thousand years before the arrival of the Celts.

Close study of the movements of the sun and the
calculation of solstice and equinox is a feature of a settled,
agricultural society. Many such societies came under the
domination of the Celts when they swept westward in a series
of invasions about 500 B.C. The Celts themselves had an
heroic, pastoral culture. Their calendar ignored solstice and
equinox. The *Larousse Encyclopedia of Mythology* puts the
matter concisely.

> Although the sun appears to have been invoked at *Beltine*
> the Celtic year had no solar orientation. There is nothing
> of the solstice or equinox and one is reminded of Caesar's
> comment that the Celts measured time by nights instead of
> days.[51]

The important holidays on the Celtic calendar fell in
November, February, May and August, not, as in agricultural
societies, in September, December, March and June. The
scheme on which Yeats bases the Cuchulain cycle is a
synthesis of the two systems. Although the Cuchulain plays
are associated with solstice and equinox, as befits ritual
dramas dealing with events in the life of a sun hero, they are
also closely associated with the rituals of the ancient Celtic
holidays which themselves had no solar orientation. Yeats
takes the ancient Celtic calendar and applies it to the great
wheel, shifting it as he does so to a solar axis. Thus *At the
Hawk's Well,* which is, as we have seen, a ritual for the
autumnal equinox, becomes associated with the Celtic New
Year, *Samain,* a holiday which fell on November first on the
Celtic calendar. The other major Celtic holidays are likewise
shifted, so that the rituals of each are in some sense
represented by one of the Cuchulain plays. When we examine
the rituals and legends of the main Celtic festivals we become
aware of yet other ritual patterns which Yeats has established
in the Cuchulain plays.

The myths and rituals associated with the ancient Celtic
festival of *Samain* are certainly suggestive of the atmosphere
of *At the Hawk's Well.* The *Larousse Encyclopedia of*

Mythology describes the emotions aroused by *Samain*.

> The beginning of the Celtic New Year was a particularly important event and the Mythological Cycle contains in its many references to *Samain* evidence of ritual acts which took place at this time. On the eve of the feast, time appeared to belong neither to the old year nor to the new. There was a feeling that this lack of distinction in time was matched by a similar indistinct boundary between the world of man and that of his gods. Although man had taken possession of the land after their defeat the *Tuatha De Danaan* were still powerful and could affect man's welfare. Whereas the mythical heroes of the Celts could venture bravely into the *side* to meet their gods either as allies or enemies, the ordinary people felt less sanguine about the possibility that on the eve of *Samain* the people of the *side* left their domain and wandered in the world of man. Furthermore the beginning of the year was a solemn event coming as it did at the beginning of winter, to a people whose agricultural economy was still liable to failure.[52]

The dispute between the Old Man and the Young Man in *At the Hawk's Well* obviously relates to the inability to distinguish between the rights of the old and the new year on the eve of *Samain*. The possession of the guardian of the well by an 'unappeasable shadow' and the momentary filling of the magic spring are manifestations of the interpenetration of spiritual and material worlds at *Samain*. That Yeats saw such supernatural events as recurring annually is evident in a line from an early prose draft of the play.

> *Old Man.* I know you will drink it. Will you swear to let me drink first? But believe me, it is better for you to go away. You are young, you can come again some other year.

In the finished play, the musicians express the fears associated with *Samain*.

> *Second Musician.* I am afraid of this place.[54]

And later

First Musician [singing or half-singing].
>   O God, protect me
>   From a horrible deathless body
>   Sliding through the veins of a sudden.[55]

Another set of interrelated *Samain* myths throws light on the mysterious relationship between Cuchulain and the goddess who has such a disastrous effect on his life.

> There is less fear in those myths of *Samain* centred on the union of male deities with a mother-goddess figure. Such is the myth of the Dagda's union with the Morrigan by the River Unius and with Boann, the goddess of the River Boyne. Possibly at this feast, too, there were rites performed to ensure the fertility of the land during the coming year.[56]

That Yeats saw the mating with a goddess as a central motif of the Cuchulain cycle from the very outset is borne out by the Fool's speech in *On Baile's Strand*: 'There are some that follow me. Boann herself out of the river and Fand out of the deep sea. Witches they are, and they come by in the wind, and they cry, 'Give a kiss, Fool, give a kiss', that's what they cry.'[57] In the same play, Conchubar challenges Cuchulain to undertake such a union.

>   Being swift of foot,
>   And making light of every common chance,
>   You should have overtaken on the hills
>   Some daughter of the air, or on the shore
>   A daughter of the Country-under-Wave.[58]

Cuchulain curtly replies, 'I am not blasphemous'. He knows that to undertake such a union is to assume the role of a god oneself. He is unwilling to pretend to such a role before Conchubar. Yet *At the Hawk's Well* and *The Only Jealousy of Emer* tell of two such unions with the goddess.

T. G. E. Powell, in his description of the Celtic gods, says of the Dagda:

> The name Dagda, used normally with the definite article, means the Good God, but not good in the ethical sense, but good-at-everything, or all-competent. He is the father

of the tribe, its protector and benefactor, and it may be said at once that this is the basic type of all the Celtic male dieties whether in Ireland or beyond.[59]

Of the marriage of the Dagda he says:

> The Dagda's mate at *Samain* was, as has been indicated, a nature goddess. In the name Morrigan, Queen of Demons, she occurs frequently in Irish texts, but the name is interchangeable with other horrific ones such as *Nemain,* Panic, and *Babd Catha,* Raven of Battle, while other conjunctions include a whole range of horse — more strictly, mare — attributes and symbolism. The Celtic goddesses in fact also conform to a general type, but not tribal, or social, for they are of the land or territory to be placated, taken over, or even enslaved, with the occupancy of the ground. They display both fertility and destructive aspects, and may be symbolized in the sun and moon no less than in zoomorphism, and topography.[60]

The twin aspects of fertility and destructiveness exhibited by the Celtic goddess was to become a major theme of the Cuchulain cycle. The territorial associations of the Celtic goddess leads directly to a consideration of Celtic kingship ritual. In the Celtic rituals of kingship, the king contracted a marriage with a female diety who represented his kingdom. The ceremony recalled the Dagda's marriage to Morrigan. Such a system of ritual would appear to be the source of many of the details of Yeats' treatment of the story of Cuchulain. T. G. E. Powell comments:

> The subject of kingship ritual is too elaborate to be discussed at length here, but some principal aspects may be mentioned. In the first place the Irish king was thought of as being the mortal mate of the territorial nature goddess. At Tara it was Etain, or Medb, who accepted the kings as husbands. The goddess handed them the goblet, the symbolic act of marriage in Celtic society, and in other mythological stories, the young king meets her at a well or spring where she awaits him in the guise of a beautiful maiden. The king must needs posses a mortal wife, although her ritual function is not so clear as is that of the

queen in Aryan India. The Tara kingship stories are much concerned with instancing 'perfect reigns' in which there are plentiful harvests and other ideal conditions, but the king must grow old and with his ageing came the risk of the decline in the prosperity of the people of the land. At this stage the goddess takes on the aspect of a repulsive hag, withering with the king's declining powers, and emphasized the need for a new mate who will ensure the continuation of prosperity. There can be little doubt that the Celtic king, in fully pagan times at least, met a violent but ritual end, and there are a number of somewhat veiled allusions to deaths by weapon wounds, drowning and burning, in the midst of high magic, in the presence of the hag and the tribal god.[61]

Yeats, who advised that Rhys' solar reading of Celtic myth be qualified by the ideas contained in Frazer's *Golden Bough*, was fully aware of this aspect of Celtic ritual. In Yeats' treatment Cuchulain combines attributes of sun god and divine king, as well as being the prototype of such national heroes as Charles Stuart Parnell and Padraic Pearse.

In *At the Hawk's Well* Cuchulain, the young king, meets the goddess at a well or spring where she waits him in the guise of a maiden. The contrast between the bitterness of the Old Man and Cuchulain's faith in his luck can be seen as the contrast between the attitude of the old and the new king as the goddess prepares to take a new mate. *The Death of Cuchulain* may be seen as just such a ritual murder as that described by Powell. Cuchulain's six wounds, his affixing himself to the sacred pillar, the ceremonious winding of Aoife's veil about him, his trance-like state as his head is taken from him, all have about them an atmosphere of 'high magic'. The dance of the severed heads is, as Yeats has pointed out,[62] derived from a very old ritual involving the nature goddess and her slain victim. If Aoife herself represents an aspect of the territorial goddess, her presence is accounted for, as is the change she has undergone.

> *Cuchulain.* Your hair is white.
> *Aoife.* That time was long ago,
> And now it is my time. I have come to kill you.[63]

In Yeats' hands, the transformation of the goddess from beautiful maiden to hag becomes a complex symbol. Instead of limiting his treatment to those changes which denote age alone, Yeats makes full use of the tradition that the nature goddesses have remarkable shape-changing powers. The Badb, for example, may appear in her bird form, the raven or crow, 'to gloat over bloodshed, inducing panic and weakness among the contending warriors'.[64] In Yeats' Cuchulain cycle this 'shape-changing' power is not used capriciously by the goddess but is linked to the cyclical changes she undergoes as moon goddess. Thus the form of the goddess changes as she moves through the phases of the great wheel. Since the fate of the hero is worked out in terms of his relationship to the goddess, and since the changing form of the goddess is symbolic of the changing aspect of the feminine principle with which he must come to terms, the wheel of the hero's fate becomes one with 'the burning wheel of love'.

In *At the Hawk's Well* — Phase 1 on the great wheel — the main aspect of the goddess is her hawk-like form. In *The Only Jealousy of Emer* — Phase 15 — her nature is symbolised by the image of a 'white sea-bird alone'.[65] In *The Death of Cuchulain* — approaching Phase 1 again — she takes the form of the Morrigu, crow-headed goddess of war. The changing phases of the moon and the altering bird form are two symbols for the same cyclical movement in life. Moon imagery and bird imager are linked together in the speeches of the Woman of the Sidhe and the Ghost of Cuchulain in *The Only Jealousy of Emer,* and both are related to the great wheel.

> *Ghost of Cuchulain.*   I know you now, for long ago
>   I met you on a cloudy hill
>   Beside old thorn-trees and a well.
>   A woman danced and a hawk flew,
>   I held out arms and hands; but you,
>   That now seem friendly, fled away,
>   Half woman and half bird of prey.
> *Woman of the Sidhe.*   Hold out your arms and hands again;
>   You were not so dumbfounded when
>   I was that bird of prey, and yet
>   I am all woman now.

Ghost of Cuchulain.   I am not
> The young and passionate man I was,
> And though that brilliant light surpass
> All crescent form, my memories
> Weigh down my hands, abash my eyes.[66]

Yeats' treatment of the changing aspect of the nature goddess is typical of his handling of mythological elements in art. Taking a simple pattern from Celtic mythology such as the transformation of the goddess from beautiful maiden to hag, Yeats alters it so that it fits into his system of cycles and antinomies.

Yeats' treatment serves to bring into sharp relief the ironies of the heroic personality, for Cuchulain desires the goddess when she is at her most destructive and rejects her when she is at her most loving. Those women none can kiss and thrive have shoved at the burning wheel of love until the side of hate has come up. They have murmured to Cuchulain and hatred is sweet to his taste.[67]

XI

Joseph Campbell has commented that in pagan religious disciplines the 'Meeting of Sun and Moon' is everywhere symbolic of the instant when the mind turns inward and realises an identity between the individual and the universe, and when all opposites (eternity and time, male and female, Hermes and Aphrodite) are brought together in one order of act.[68] The story of the romance of the sun and moon, plotted in the system of *A Vision* and dramatised in Yeats' Cuchulain cycle is capable of just such a reading. It symbolises both a cosmological and a psychological process. It is a function of the Doctrine of Correspondences that cosmological and psychological processes are parallel.

The Cuchulain cycle tells of the moon's changes in a single lunar month, of the sun's adventures in the course of a single solar year, of the events in the life of a Celtic warrior from his initiation to his death. But it also tells of the progress of the human soul through a series of incarnations and of the adventures of a soul in the course of a single incarnation. Although I do not intend to undertake a detailed description of the complex esoteric system which Yeats offers in *A Vision,* a discussion of certain of the incarnations mentioned in *A Vision* may be helpful in understanding patterns of imagery, theme and plot in the Cuchulain plays.

Yeats' most concise statement of the cycle of incarnations is contained in the dialogue poem 'The Phases of the Moon' with which he introduces Book I of *A Vision.* In the poem, Michael Robartes expounds the theory of the moon phases and the incarnations they represent:

> Twenty-and-eight the phases of the moon,
> The full and the moon's dark and all the crescents,
> Twenty-and-eight, and yet but six-and-twenty
> The cradles that a man must needs be rocked in;
> For there's no human life at the full or the dark.
> From the first crescent to the half, the dream
> But summons to adventure, and the man
> Is always happy like a bird or a beast;
> But while the moon is rounding towards the full
> He follows whatever whim's most difficult
> Among whims not impossible, and though scarred,
> As with the cat-o'-nine-tails of the mind,
> His body moulded from within his body
> Grows comelier. Eleven pass, and then
> Athena takes Achilles by the hair,
> Hector is in the dust, Nietzsche is born,
> Because the hero's crescent is the twelfth.
> And yet, twice born, twice buried, grow he must,
> Before the full moon, helpless as a worm.
> The thirteenth moon but sets the soul at war
> In its own being, and when that war's begun
> There is no muscle in the arm; and after,
> Under the frenzy of the fourteenth moon,
> The soul begins to tremble into stillness.
> To die within the labyrinth of itself![69]

This section of the poem seems to give a complete summary of the adventures of Cuchulain as Yeats presents them in the Cuchulain cycle from *At the Hawk's Well* to *The Only Jealousy of Emer.* Particularly significant is the statement that there is no human life at the full or the dark of the moon. This accounts not only for the fact that Cuchulain is captured by Fand in *The Only Jealousy of Emer,* leaving his inert body to be possessed by the spirit Bricriu, but also for the fact that when the waters of immortality rise in *At the Hawk's Well* Cuchulain is not present and a mysterious sleep comes upon the Old Man. Phases 1 and 15 are supernatural incarnations, marking the only occasions when spirit world and natural world interpenetrate. The Japanese *Noh* play provided Yeats with a dramatic form for the representation of such an interpenetration of worlds. The dance provided him with a symbol of supernatural incarnation. He uses dance in *At the Hawk's Well* (Phase 1) and in *The Only Jealousy of Emer* (Phase 15). Emer's dance at the end of *The Death of Cuchulain* marks a return to Phase 1.

Robartes' words about the 'always happy' hero turning at Phase 8 to follow 'whatever whim's most difficulty/Among whims not impossible' would seem to characterise the attitude of the hero in *The Green Helmet.* The plot of *On Baile's Strand* finds its echo in the words of Robartes. The words 'twice born, twice buried' describe the fate of the soul at Phase 12, the hero's crescent. The words are highly suggestive in the light of the double tragedy which befalls Cuchulain in *On Baile's Strand.* He first kills the copy of himself he meets in the person of his son, then is himself overcome by the waves. Then he is re-born as a result of Emer's sacrifice in *The Only Jealousy of Emer.* In Robartes' description of Phases 13 and 14 we can trace the fate of Cuchulain at the end of *On Baile's Strand.* Internal conflict, loss of strength, frenzy and the final dying of the soul 'into the labyrinth of itself' are all identifiable as stages in Cuchulain's psychological state after the death of his son.

In connection with our discussion of the hero's crescent, one other observation about the system of incarnations should be made. Yeats, seeing life as a war of opposites, held that each man's destiny was worked out in the interplay between Will and Mask, Creative Mind and Body of Fate. A man's Mask corresponds to the Will of the incarnation which is opposite him on the great wheel. Thus the hero (at Phase 12) has for his Mask the Hunchback (Phase 26). This counterposing of Hero and Hunchback has great significance for the symbolism of the Cuchulain cycle. Yeats speaks of the Hunchback as a phase for which it is difficult to find examples from personal experience. If we study Yeats' description of this symbolic type, however, we can see aspects of the Hunchback in at least three of the persons who are set against the hero in the Cuchulain plays.

The most obvious characteristic of the Hunchback, physical deformity, we see in the Bricriu of *The Only Jealousy of Emer*. The Figure of Cuchulain, when possessed by Bricriu, wears a distorted mask and has an arm withered in the socket. This play quite explicitly dramatises the relationship between man and his Mask. The Ghost of Cuchulain represents the Will of the Hero, the Figure of Cuchulain represents his Mask, derived from the phase of the Hunchback. The two other personages set up against Cuchulain who bear some of the characteristics of the Hunchback are Conchubar in *On Baile's Strand* and his 'shadow'. the Blind Man. Yeats' comments on the Hunchback in *A Vision* could well apply to Conchubar's mechanical over-emphasis of social values at the expense of spiritual and emotional ones.

> The moral abstract being no longer possible, the *Will* may seek this substitute through the knowledge of the lives of men and beasts, plucked up, as it were, by the roots, lacking in all mutual relations; there may be hatred of solitude, perpetual forced bonhomie, yet that which it seeks is without social morality, something radical and incredible.[70]

Yeats, earlier in the discussion, has stressed the Hunchback's tendency to betray.

> . . . and he is full of malice because, finding no impulse but in his own ambition, he is made jealous by the impulse of others. He is all emphasis, and the greater that emphasis the more does he display his sterility. If he live amid a theologically minded people, his greatest temptation may be to defy God, to become a Judas, who betrays, not for thirty pieces of silver, but that he may call himself a creator.[71]

This statement throws a great deal of light on Conchubar's

motivation in *On Baile's Strand* and on his relations with the more vital Cuchulain; it also accounts for the Blind Man's malicious behaviour towards the Fool. The reference to Judas is interesting in light of the Blind Man's betrayal of Cuchulain in *The Death of Cuchulain* for twelve pennies.

Robartes describes Phase 15, the phase of *The Only Jealousy of Emer*, thus:

> All thought becomes an image and the soul
> Becomes a body: that body and that soul
> Too perfect at the full to lie in a cradle,
> Too lonely for the traffic of the world:
> Body and soul cast out and cast away
> Beyond the visible world.[72]

Owen Aherne replies:

> All the dreams of the soul
> End in a beautiful man's or woman's body.[73]

Even the part played by Bricriu seems to be indicated by Robartes' words.

> . . . there is no deformity
> But saves us from a dream.[74]

The key to the symbolism of the ending of *The Death of Cuchulain* seems to me to be contained in Robartes' description of Phases 26, 27, and 28.

> Hunchback and Saint and Fool are the last crescents.
> The burning bow that once could shoot an arrow
> Out of the up and down, the wagon-wheel
> Of beauty's cruelty and wisdom's chatter —
> Out of that raving tide — is drawn betwixt
> Deformity of body and of mind.[75]

In the scene with Eithne Inguba, Cuchulain enters the first of the last three phases, the phase of the Hunchback. Suspecting that she has betrayed him because she wants a younger, friendlier man, he lashes out at her with savage cynicism and then thwarts her attempt to salvage her honour by means of an heroic gesture. Cuchulain displays in this scene a cynicism worthy of Conchubar or the Blind Man. He leaves orders that, should he die, Eithne should be given to Conall Caernach, 'because the women/Have called him a good lover'.[76] As Aoife enters, Cuchulain moves into the phase of the Saint. In a scene of incredible tenderness, he passively accepts her intent to kill him. At the entrance of the Blind Man, Cuchulain moves into the phase of the Fool. As the Blind Man prepares to take his head, Cuchulain murmurs about a soft, feathery shape he sees in a vision. As Cuchulain passes from Phase 28, his head is represented by a black parallelogram. He has passed into Phase 1 where, in Robartes' words:

> Because all dark, like those that are all light,
> They are cast beyond the verge, and in a cloud,
> Crying to one another like the bats:
> But having no desire they cannot tell
> What's good or bad, or what it is to triumph
> At the perfection of one's own obedience;
> And yet they speak what's blown into the mind;
> Deformed beyond deformity, unformed,
> Insipid as the dough before it is baked,
> They change their bodies at a word.[77]

The unsubstantial nature of souls at Phase 1 of the new cycle reminds us of the harlot's song at the end of *The Death of Cuchulain*. The harlot speaks of Conall, Cuchulain and Usna's boys, but complains:

> I adore those clever eyes,
> Those muscular bodies, but can get
> No grip upon their thighs.[78]

The form that the unbaked dough of Cuchulain's spirit will take when that 'first thin crescent is wheeled around' has important implications for modern Ireland. Cuchulain's next incarnation will be in the Dublin Post Office among those rebels of Easter Week 1916, 'who thought Cuchulain till it seemed/He stood where they had stood'.[79]

4 The Rag-and-Bone Shop of the Heart

And when the Fool and Blind Man stole the bread
Cuchulain fought the ungovernable sea;
Heart-mysteries there, and yet when all is said
It was the dream itself enchanted me:
Character isolated by a deed
To engross the present and dominate memory.
Players and painted stage took all my love,
And not those things that they were emblems of.

.   .   .

Those masterful images because complete
Grew in pure mind, but out of what began?
A mound of refuse or the sweepings of a street,
Old kettles, old bottles, and a broken can,
Old iron, old bones, old rags, that raving slut
Who keeps the till. Now that my ladder's gone,
I must lie down where all the ladders start,
In the foul rag-and-bone shop of the heart.

from 'The Circus Animals' Desertion'[1]

I

There is in all the works of W. B. Yeats a constant interplay of personal and impersonal elements. Yeats would say 'subjective and objective elements'. The tension between the subjective and objective in Yeats' art has roots in a quarrel between Yeats and his father over the legitimacy of personal utterance in poetry. As a young man, Yeats had been deeply moved by a rather badly-written poem containing 'the actual thoughts of a man at a passionate moment of life'. He was certain that he had discovered in personal emotion the true source of poetic power. He went to his father with the discovery.

> We should write out our own thoughts in as nearly as possible the language we thought them in, as though in a letter to an intimate friend. We should not disguise them in any way; for our lives give them force as the lives of people in plays give force to their words. Personal utterance, which had almost ceased in English literature, could be as fine an escape from rhetoric and abstraction as drama itself. But my father would hear of nothing but drama; personal utterance was only egotism. I knew it was not, but as yet did not know how to explain the difference. I tried from that on to write out of my emotions exactly as they came to me in life, not changing them to make them more beautiful. ... It is so many years before one can believe enough in what one feels even to know what the feeling is.[2]

As in so many other matters, W. B. Yeats became deeply influenced by J. B. Yeats' opinion without entirely abandoning his own position. He never ceased to write out of his own emotions exactly as they came to him in life, choosing themes which mirrored his own preoccupations and plots which ran parallel to his private life. At the same time he guarded himself against the charge of mere egotism by adopting where possible the dramatic form, attributing his own emotions to characters of his own invention and to characters he drew from the mythological materials with which he worked. He even went so far as to give something of a dramatic framework to books of his lyric poetry. In the 1899 edition of *The Wind Among the Reeds* he attributes lyric poems which are obviously intensely personal statements of his own emotions in various moods to three separate speakers, Aedh, Hanrahan and Michael Robartes, using them 'more as principles of mind than as actual personages'.[3] Throughout his creative life Yeats would tend to work his lyrical verse into the form of dramatic monologue or even dialogue to evade the problem set him by his father at the outset of his career. On the other hand, the dialogue of his verse dramas tends always towards the lyric, and the plays abound in autobiographical material and emotions which derive directly from his personal experience. In a late poem, 'The Circus Animals' Desertion', Yeats accurately states the relationship between his plays and his life. The 'masterful images' which move so impressively through Yeats' ritual drama are complete in themselves. Having grown 'in pure mind' they have a life of their own and require no reference to Yeats' biography to explain their meaning within the works themselves. But each and every one of them finds its origin in the 'rag-and-bone shop' of the poet's heart. This is particularly true of the images which dominate the plays of the Cuchulain cycle.

Yeats, like Padraic Pearse, saw himself in the image of Cuchulain. His letters reveal the extent to which the story of Cuchulain absorbed his time and energy during some of the most creative periods of his life. At times of crisis he turned ever to the figure of Cuchulain — the hero who symbolised for him 'creative joy separated from fear'.[4] In the Cuchulain plays Yeats created a kind of psychological autobiography. At each of the major crisis points in his own life he wrote another Cuchulain play. The last two works he completed before his death in 1939 were a play and a poem about the death of Cuchulain.

II

In Yeats' Cuchulain plays, the hero Cuchulain seeks the love of a goddess whose nature shifts like the phases of a symbolic moon. She is the feminine principle — that woman's beauty which may be a white frail bird at one phase, and a hawk, or a crow-headed war-goddess at another. Yeats dramatises the tragic effect of that dark shadow which falls upon the man who dares to love a goddess. Cuchulain first meets the goddess in the shape of a woman possessed by the spirit of a hawk. He has come to the Hawk's Well seeking the waters of immortality. At the well he meets an Old Man who cries out against his own hopeless fifty-year-old vigil at the Hawk's Well and against the dancers who have cheated him of his youth.

Yeats was fifty years old when, in the spring of 1916, he wrote *At the Hawk's Well.* From the age of twenty-three he had been devoted to Maud Gonne. In a poem introducing the volume *Responsibilities,* published in 1914, Yeats had asked forgiveness of his ancestors

> that for a barren passion's sake,
> Although I have come close on forty-nine,
> I have no child, I have nothing but a book,
> Nothing but that to prove your blood and mine.[5]

The Old Man's complaints against the dancers have auto-biographical roots.

The attitude of the young Cuchulain in *At the Hawk's Well,* on the other hand, recaptures the mood of Yeats on that day in 1889 when he met Maud Gonne for the first time. There was no denying the danger of the heroic values she represented, nor the strength of the lure they offered to him.

> She vexed my father by praise of war, war for its own sake, not as the creator of certain virtues but as if there were some virtue in excitement itself. I supported her against my father, which vexed him the more, though he might have understood that . . . a man young as I could not have differed from a woman so beautiful and so young.[6]

Yeats paid no more heed to his father's concern over Maud's influence on him than did Cuchulain to the Old Man's warning not to gaze into the hawk-woman's unmoistened eyes. In another poem from *Responsibilities* Yeats refers to the great passion that robbed him of his youth, and he links Maud Gonne to the image of a predatory bird.

> And what of her that took
> All till my youth was gone
> With scarce a pitying look?
> How could I praise that one?
> When day begins to break
> I count my good and bad,
> Being wakeful for her sake,
> Remembering what she had,

> What eagle look still shows,
> While up from my heart's root
> So great a sweetness flows
> I shake from Head to foot.[7]

The sweetness remained at the centre of Yeats' love, linked as it was to the continuing power that 'eagle look' held over him. But there was bitterness too, and a strong sense of the barrenness of the passion to which he had devoted so much of his life. The Old Man in *At the Hawk's Well* who has been waiting at the well for fifty years expresses this bitterness. His awareness of having been cheated is an awareness similar to that of Yeats who, at fifty, realised that he had given to Maud that which he could not replace — his youth — and had received little or nothing in return. As the Old Man says,

> You have deluded me my whole life through,
> Accursed dancers, you have stolen my life.
> That there should be such evil in a shadow.[8]

The conflict between the heroic values with which Maud's image was associated in Yeats' mind and the domestic comforts for which he longed was particularly acute around 1916. The conflict is underlined by the musicians' song.

> 'The man that I praise',
> Cries out the leafless tree,
> 'Has married and stays
> By an old hearth, and he
> On naught has set store
> But children and dogs on the floor.
> Who but an idiot would praise
> A withered tree?'[9]

In *At the Hawk's Well* sexual desire and commitment to the heroic life seem inextricably mixed. So it was for Yeats. In his nationalist activities in the 1890s there was, he confessed, 'much patriotism, and more desire for a fair woman'.[10] Richard Ellman comments:

Like other young men, he wanted to prove his courage and strength to his beloved and to himself. But we should not allow his own confession of a multiplicity of motives to blind us to the larger idealism which animated all that he did for his country.[11]

Be that as it may, for Yeats patriotism and sexual desire remained for ever curiously linked. Even as he thinks of the heroes of Ireland's past in the poem 'September 1913', the image of the sexual lure recurs.

> Yet could we turn the years again,
> And call those exiles as they were
> In all their loneliness and pain,
> You'd cry, 'Some woman's yellow hair
> Has maddened every mother's son':
> They weighed so lightly what they gave.[12]

On one level of meaning, the ritual of *At the Hawk's Well* is related to the pattern of Yeats' relationship with Maud Gonne. By 1916 Yeats fully realised how closely linked had been his hopeless passion for Maud and his commitment to heroic activities, but he also had begun to look upon her as one who had passed through his life 'to allure and to destroy'. The emotional tone of the play reflects his attitude towards the relationship in all its complexity. From this personal element comes much of the play's emotional power.

III

The Green Helmet was written in the period immediately following the riots over Synge's *Playboy of the Western World*. Into this play Yeats poured his contempt for the mobs that tried to deny the *Playboy* its hearing and his own sense of exultation at having faced them down. On that occasion, his was

> . . . the laughing lip
> That shall not turn from laughing, whatever rise or fall;
> The heart that grows no bitterer although betrayed by all;
> The hand that loves to scatter; the life like a gambler's throw.[13]

On the Abbey stage that night Yeats experienced the moment when a man is most truly himself, the moment of the heroic act. This experience provided a theme for the Cuchulain play, *The Green Helmet.*

The trouble which erupted in 1907 had been long brewing. The Irish Literary Theatre combined in 1902 with a company of actors under the direction of Willie and Frank Fay. The new organisation called itself the Irish National Theatre Society. Yeats was president, Maud Gonne, Douglas Hyde and George Russell, vice-presidents. In 1904, a wealthy English friend of Yeats, Miss Horniman, provided them with a theatre building of their own. The Abbey Theatre. In 1906, the Irish National Theatre Society was reorganised and Yeats, Lady Gregory and John Synge were established as directors with wide powers for setting the policy of the organisation.

From the outset, Yeats' Irish theatre movement had been embroiled in controversy. Although the Irish public, and particularly the Irish newspapers, were incredibly sensitive to attacks on the stereotypes which dominated Irish thinking on politics, religion and art, Yeats and his colleagues set out to rid Irish drama of such deadening cliches. Even the first two seasons of the Irish Literary Theatre had provoked outcries from quite divergent quarters. Most serious was the objection of some Roman Catholics to the questionable orthodoxy of Yeats' *Countess Cathleen,* for the suspicion that Yeats was attempting to use the theatre to promote a heterodox, even pagan, point of view was an important part of the prejudice against his theatrical ventures. Yeats commented in 1901:

> We do not think there is anything in either play [of the 1901 season] to offend anybody, but we make no promises. We thought our plays inoffensive last year and the year before, but we were accused the one year of sedition, and the other of heresy.[14]

When the Irish National Theatre Society was formed in 1902 there was deep resentment among what Yeats called the Harp and Pepperpot nationalists that an organisation which included in its membership Unionists and suspected Anglophiles should have appropriated the name 'Irish National Theatre'. When Miss Horniman, a wealthy Englishwoman, presented the players with a theatre of their own, on the condition that it be run according to Mr Yeats' ideals and not become the home of political propaganda, suspicions of the movement became acute among the little societies which dominated the Irish nationalist movement. Yeats, for his part, refused to compromise. Although his own *Cathleen ni Houlihan* had roused the enthusiasm of the ultra nationalists, he stoutly insisted that it had not been intended as a propagandist play. The directors of the Abbey Theatre laboured to make it an institution of artistic integrity, choosing plays for their literary and dramatic merit and not for their political viewpoint. The Irish extremists saw the Abbey as an institution held captive by Unionists and Anglophiles and devoted to the pursuit of strange gods.

Aside from Yeats himself, the chief target of the Harps and Pepperpots was John Synge. His portraits of the Irish peasantry were held to be libels on the Irish character and his plots were held to be defamatory to the purity of Irish womanhood. When in 1907 the Abbey produced his play, *The Playbody of the Western World,* he was accused of having invented a 'barbarous jargon' for his characters, which they punctuated with 'elaborate and incessant cursing'.[15]

But the enemies of the Abbey did not limit themselves to strong verbal criticism of the theatre's policy and of Synge's work. On the opening night of *The Playboy of the Western World,* organised rioting interrupted the performance. It was the beginning of a full week of such disturbances at the Abbey. Like Cuchulain, in *The Green Helmet,* Yeats was in Scotland when the trouble began. Lady Gregory wired him news of the rioting. Daniel Murphy gives this account:

> Yeats returned from Scotland in time for the Tuesday performance. Lady Gregory had in the meantime given seats to some Trinity students in order to have a favourable claque. Holloway said they were drinking and, before long, fighting with the rest of the audience; one of them had to be ejected by Synge. Before the performance began, Yeats made a speech in which he invited all to a public discussion of the play Monday next at the Abbey. As soon as the play started, the disturbances began. Yeats tried three times to talk to the audience, and three separate attempts were made to continue the play.[16]

Wednesday brought more rioting. The *Freeman's Journal* reported:

> Cat calls, strident bugle notes, and the fierce demonstrations added to the general din. . . . For fully five minutes not a word spoken on the stage could be heard . . . but from then to the end of the act the dialogue was not completely smothered. . . . The second act, however, was all uproar, and concluded among a hurricane of uproar. The interval between the acts was occupied by a fist fight in the vestibule, and the singing of 'The Peeler and the Goat'. The third act was unintelligible, played amid bugle calls, hisses, applause and boos. After the performance, the house had to be cleared by the police, and demonstrators marched, under police surveillance, through Abbey Street and O'Connell Street.[17]

The brawlers who disrupted performances at the Abbey that week certainly provided a model for the quarrelling pack of charioteers and stable-boys in *The Green Helmet*. Conall describes the mob in that play:

> There, do you hear them now? Such hatred has each for
>   each
> They have taken the hunting-horns to drown one another's
>   speech
> For fear the truth may prevail.[18]

A number of the speeches in *The Green Helmet* reflect Yeats' sense of alienation from Irish attitudes which was the immediate result of the *Playboy* riots. Conall refers to Ireland as 'this unlucky country that was made when the Devil spat'.[19] And he makes reference to a well-known Irish tendency.

> Here neighbour wars on neighbour, and why there
>   is no man knows,
> And if a man is lucky all wish his luck away,
> And take his good name from him between a day
>   and a day.[20]

The real test of Yeats' courage came the Monday following

the riots when the promised debate took place, Greene and Stephens, Synge's biographers, describe the scene.

When the debate took place, as Yeats had promised, on Monday night, Synge was not present, but apparently everyone else in the Dublin literary world was. Mary Colum, who was then a student, wrote an eyewitness account of it and the Dublin newspapers gave it full coverage. Yeats made what was certainly one of the most courageous utterances of his life to an audience almost totally hostile and threatening. The riots and the bitter controversies that had erupted out of them were to have a lasting effect on him — even more than upon Synge, 'so absorbed in his own vision of the world that he cares for nothing else.' But Yeats never weakened in his commitment to the ideals he had so belligerently expounded. As he stepped out on the stage that night his audience knew that he was unruffled by their hostility as were the immaculate evening clothes he had put on as a further note of defiance. Mary Colum wrote that when they refused to listen to him he reminded them that he was the author of *Cathleen Ni Houlihan.* 'The audience, remembering that passionately patriotic play, forgot its antagonism for a few moments and Yeats got his cheers. . . . I never witnessed a human being fight as Yeats fought that night, nor knew another with so many weapons in his armory.'[21]

It was on the stage of the Abbey that night that Yeats realised in his own life the heroic ideal he had always embraced — the ideal of the laughing lip, the steady heart, and hand that scatters life like a gambler's throw. And it was his courageous stand that night that secured for the Abbey the right to the title of Irish National Theatre, while maintaining its strong stand against merely propagandist plays. The *Green Helmet* was truly his.

IV

As we saw in Chapter 3, the final version of *On Baile's Strand* owes much to the effect upon Yeats of receiving the shocking news that Maud Gonne had married John MacBride. Yeats had been about to deliver a lecture on that day in 1903 when he received the news that Maud had married MacBride, a soldier-adventurer-revolutionary — an unequivocal man of action. He could never remember a word of what he said in that lecture. He only knew that he got through it somehow.[22] Richard Ellman describes Yeats' initial reaction to the news.

> Yeats blamed his own timid, critical intellect for restraining his impetuous nature so that when he should have embraced he had feared and qualified and idealized. He had lost the capacity for acting on instinct which men like MacBride, lacking the critical mind, possessed. Maud Gonne's marriage was therefore an indictment; instead of condemning her, he condemned himself, 'took all the blame, out of all sense and reason.'[23]

It was in the Cuchulain play, *On Baile's Strand,* that he dramatised this internal conflict. Ellman comments:

> The real struggle is between the warrior Cuchulain, instinctively loving and hating, and the crafty king Conchubar who forces Cuchulain to slay unwittingly his own son. Cuchulain's tragic fate, like Yeats' own, is caused by his listening to the voice of apparent reason; instead of following his impulse to make friends with the unknown warrior, he allows Conchubar to persuade him that the cry of his heart is witchcraft, and discovers too late the identity of his opponent.[24]

By the time he completed his revision of *On Baile's Strand,* Yeats no longer took 'all the blame, out of all sense and reason', but introduced, as a major theme of his play, the 'evil shadow' invariably cast by a certain 'indomitable kind of woman'.

When Maud's marriage to John MacBride ended in separation, Yeats re-established something of the old relationship with her. However, he had begun to long deeply for domestic roots, and Maud, now converted to Roman Catholicism, would not consider divorce. By the spring of 1916, Yeats had already spoken of marriage to Miss Georgie Hyde-Lees, stepdaughter of Olivia Shakespear's brother.

Then the Easter insurrection suddenly changed everything. John MacBride was one of those who, with Pearse, Connolly and the others, had engineered the seizure of the Dublin Post Office and the declaration of an Irish Republic. When the uprising was put down, he was one of the men the English shot. Yeats was later to celebrate his bravery along with that of the others.

> This other man I had dreamed
> A drunken, vainglorious lout.
> He had done most bitter wrong
> To some who are near my heart,
> Yet I number him in the song;
> He, too, has resigned his part
> In the casual comedy;
> He, too, has been changed in his turn,
> Transformed utterly:
> A terrible beauty is born.[25]

At the time, however, Yeats was less preoccupied by John MacBride's transformation through martyrdom than by the realisation that Maud Gonne was now free to marry him. He rushed to her side. Joseph Hone tells the story.

> Yeats' first impulse was to ask Maud Gonne to marry him now that she was free, and yet before going to France he all but made a compact with Lady Gregory, for the sake of the Abbey Theatre (which at this time largely depended for its existence on the donations of rich Irish Unionists), and as a 'refuge from some weakness in myself', not to marry unless Maud Gonne renounced all politics, including amnesty for political prisoners.[26]

As might have been expected, Maud was a good deal more interested in bringing about the release of the political prisoners and in making the greatest possible revolutionary capital out of the executions than she was in marriage to Yeats at this time.

In the summer of 1917, Yeats proposed marriage to Maud's daughter, Iseult, whom she introduced to the public as her 'adopted niece'.[27] When Iseult refused him, Yeats returned to his original plans and renewed his proposal to Miss Hyde-Lees. She accepted him and they were married on 20 October, 1917.

The events of 1916 and 1917 had a profound effect on Yeats. He did not spare himself examination of conscience over his behaviour. Fearing he had given pain to Miss Hyde-Lees by his pursuit of Maud and pain to Maud by his proposal to Iseult, he allowed his soul 'to die into the labyrinth of itself', there to explore those 'intricacies of blind remorse' which Cuchulain speaks of in *The Only Jealousy of Emer* and to come to terms with the principle of femininity which had manifested itself so strongly in the persons of the three beautiful women with whom his life had become entangled.

The Only Jealousy of Emer is the result of that struggle within 'the labyrinth of the mind' which resulted from Yeats' marriage crisis. In the moon goddess Fand, the young mistress Eithne and the selfless and loving Emer, Yeats has given us moving portraits of the three women he proposed to in that remarkable year, Maud, Iseult and Georgie. As Cuchulain's soul reaches its point of extreme subjectivity, then begins to move again towards the objective, we become aware of a change of direction in Yeats' own spiritual biography. From the point of his marriage on, Yeats will move towards a greater and greater objectivity in his poetry and a greater and greater objective involvement in life.

Yeats completed *The Death of Cuchulain* a few weeks before his own death in 1939. It is a courageous and moving play. Yeats does not sentimentalise the dying Cuchulain but treats the hero's death with a full measure of the wry irony and courage with which he faced the approaching end of his own life. An Old Man from Mythology opens the play, pouring out all of Yeats' splenetic fury at a theatre and a society which have rejected the ideals which make life an heroic adventure. In a scene which recaptures the strange tension and tenderness of a visit Maud Gonne paid the poet in the summer of 1938,[28] Yeats shows the dying Cuchulain visited by Aoife, the warrior queen with whom he has sustained a love-hate relationship throughout his adult life. When Cuchulain dies, it is simply the anonymous force of darkness, symbolised by a blind old beggerman, which overcomes him. His soul takes on its own first shape again, a soft feathery shape,

And is not that a strange shape for the soul
Of a great fighting-man?[29]

The wheel of life, for Cuchulain as for Yeats, has come full circle. In his seventy-four years of life W. B. Yeats learned a great deal about the mysteries of the human heart. Much of what he learned is chronicled in the Cuchulain plays.

5 Players and Painted Stage

I

Any study of the Cuchulain plays must take into account Yeats' ideas about how they should be acted and staged. Yeats subjected himself to a long, self-directed apprenticeship in the technical aspects of play production and for extended periods it became literally true that

> Players and painted stage took all my love,
> And not those things that they were emblems of.[1]

This apprenticeship had as great an influence on the form of the Cuchulain plays as his involvement in magic and in the nationalist movement had on their content. If we are to understand the Cuchulain plays in their theatrical, as well as their philosophical and literary context, it will be necessary to examine certain of Yeats' ideas about the staging of ritual drama. I propose to trace the course of the evolution of Yeats ideas about play production, and then to consider their impact on the Cuchulain plays.

II

One of the most difficult problems to be faced by the producer of the Cuchulain plays is the difficulty of deciding how to approach the singing of the songs and the speaking of the verse. Yeats himself had very definite ideas on the matter. He found himself equally annoyed by the modern musician who, 'through the over-development of an art that seems exterior to the poet, writes so many notes for every word that the natural energy of the speech is dissolved and broken and the words made inaudible', and the modern actress who puts into her voice 'so many different notes, so run[s] up and down the scale under an impulse of anger and scorn that one had hardly been more affronted by a musical setting'.[2]

Musical settings must be such as to disturb neither the rhythms of the poetic line nor the naturalness and audibility of the words. And actors should adopt the practice of orators who 'speak difficult passages, where there is some delicacy of sound or of thought, upon one or two notes'.[3] 'Where one requires the full attention of the mind, one must not weary it with any but the most needful changes of pitch and note, or by irrelevant gesture.'[4] All art is, Yeats believed, 'a monotony on external things for the sake of an interior variety, a sacrifice of gross effects to subtle effects, an asceticism of the imagination.'[5] Ritual tragedy required a most careful control of vocal elements.

During the nineties, Yeats and the actress Florence Farr had carried on a series of experiments in an attempt to find a more satisfactory way of setting lyric poetry and choral odes to music. When the Irish Literary Theatre was founded they turned their attention to the problem of speaking dramatic verse to musical notes. They evolved a system of controlled declamation which Yeats imagined to be connected to a lost art which was older than singing.[6] Miss Farr's greatest success was with the choral work in Greek tragedy, where she 'used often definite melodies of a very simple kind, but always when the thought became intricate and the measure grave and slow, fell back upon declamation regulated by notes.'[7]

The effect of this 'declamation regulated by notes' was similar to a technique Yeats had heard practised by Irish peasants. 'I have heard Irish country-women, whose singing is called 'traditional Irish singing', speak their little songs precisely as Miss Farr does some of hers, only with rather less drama.'[8]

A system of notation gave them some trouble. Since the speaking voice seems to make use of smaller intervals than that used in modern music they tried a system of notation which involved quarter-tones. Composer Arnold Dometsch was consulted.

Mr. Dometsch put us back to our first thought. He made us a beautiful instrument, half psaltery, half lyre, which contains, I understood, all the chromatic intervals within the range of the speaking voice; and he taught us to regulate our speech by the ordinary musical notes.[9]

Florence Farr, who had a naturally beautiful speaking voice, achieved some striking effects, but the same effects could not always be produced by another speaker following her system of notation. As a matter of fact the consistency of her own performances was less than reliable. At any rate, speaking to the psaltery did tend to restore emphasis to the rhythms of the poetic line and for this Yeats was grateful.

> Modern acting and recitation have taught us to fix our attention on the gross effects till we have come to think gesture, and the intonation that copies the accidental surface of life more important than the rhythm; and yet we understand theoretically that it is precisely the rhythm that separates good writing from bad, that is the glimmer, the fragrance, the spirit of intense literature.[10]

Yeats was certain that 'if people would listen for a while to lyrical verse spoken to notes, they would soon find it impossible to listen without indignation to verse as it is spoken in our leading theatres.'[11]

Not all of Yeats' acquaintances and fellow workers were instant converts to his ideas about the speaking of verse. While George Moore was in the process of recasting *The Countess Cathleen* and *The Heather Field* Yeats attempted to explain the technique to the new leading lady Moore had chosen for his play. Moore tells the story.

> The experienced actress went on the stage, and while she recited my mind turned over all the possible Carden Tyrrells in the Green Room Club; but Yeats had been listening, and as soon as I had congratulated her began to talk to her about his method. My anger was checked by the thought that the quickest way, and perhaps the only way, to rid ourselves of Yeats would be to ask him to go on the stage and read his verses to us. There was no choice for him but to comply, and when he left the stage I took him by the arm, saying: 'One can hear that kind of thing, my dear fellow, on Sunday, in any Methodist chapel.'[12]

Bernard Shaw, in a letter to Florence Farr, pointed out that she and Yeats had merely adopted the old practice of intoning. 'There is no new art in the business at all,' he said.

'Yeats only thinks so because he does not go to church.'[13]
Shaw, of course, favoured 'an athletic articulation'.

> With that you can give effect to the real thing, which is,
> your sense of the meaning of the words, your emotional
> and intellectual conviction. That is the only thing that
> makes speech tolerable. Without it cantilating can do
> nothing except intensify ordinary twaddling into a nerve
> destroying crooning like the maunderings of an idiot-
> banshee. Remember that even in singing, it is the Irish
> defect to lose grip and interest by neglecting the words and
> thinking only of the music. Cats do the same thing when
> they are serenading one another but the genuineness of
> their emotion gives them poignancy.[14]

Annie Horniman thought that Yeats, being tone deaf, was
being led into a ridiculous position by more musically
sophisticated colleagues.

> Personally I consider that he is being treated as a blind
> man would be if he were insulted by ugly faces being
> pulled at him by people who spoke politely to him all the
> while. Quarter tones are such extremely delicate things
> that no amateur is to be trusted with them except in very
> rare cases. If you do anything with notes, do them
> 'purely'; or else leave them alone altogether and trust to
> the ordinary speaking voice and its various degrees of
> tones.[15]

Florence Farr herself observed that all the claims that
Yeats made for the new technique had been made for the
ritual singing of the High Mass and for the singing of
recitative in opera by the inventors of those art forms. Yet no
trace of ecstasy remains in the delivery of either. In the end,
all depends on the quality of imagination in the speaker.

> When beginners attempt to speak to musical notes they fall
> naturally into the intoning as heard throughout our lands
> in various religious rituals. It is not until they have been
> forced to use their imaginations and express the inmost
> meaning of the words, not until their thought imposes
> itself upon all listeners, and each word invokes a special

mode of beauty, that the method rises once more from the dead and becomes a living art.[16]

One particular effect impressed Florence Farr as being strikingly beautiful. 'There is no more beautiful sound than the alternation of carolling or keening and a voice speaking in regulated declamation. The very act of alternation has a particular charm.'[17] This is an effect that Yeats no doubt remembered when he composed the lines for the musicians in *At the Hawk's Well* for they adapt themselves well to this technique. Nor can it be an accident that the instrument held by the musician in the Dulac costume design so resembles the psaltery Dolmetsch made for Florence Farr. But, by the time Yeats wrote *At the Hawk's Well*, Florence Farr had already left England for Ceylon.

When I had enough knowledge to discover some dramatic form to give her the opportunity she lacked Florence Farr had accepted a post in a Cingalese girls' school that she might hide her ageing beauty. I have the psaltery Arnold Dolmetsch designed for her, certain strings are broken, probably nobody will play on it again, but that I may not injure it by exposure to the air I do not hang it upon the wall to revive old memories.[18]

Although Florence Farr's experiments in speaking to the psaltery had the salutary effect of re-emphasising rhythmic effects in spoken poetry, her method did not constitute an adequate technique for handling verse dialogue. It was the Fay brothers, particularly Frank Fay, who gave Yeats that delivery of dramatic verse, at once beautiful and natural, that he longed to re-establish in the theatre.

The first time Yeats heard William Fay's small company of amateur Irish actors perform an historical play, he had gone home with his 'head on fire'. 'I wanted to hear my own unfinished *On Baile's Strand*, to hear Greek tragedy, spoken with a Dublin accent.'[19]

Yeats decided to give Fay's company his *Cathleen ni Houlihan*. It was produced along with George Russell's *Deirdre* at St Teresa's Hall in April 1902. After the St Teresa's Hall experiment Yeats and Lady Gregory joined forces with the Fays and the Irish Literary Theatre gave way to the Irish National Dramatic Society.

In William Fay's brother Frank, Yeats found a competent actor and gifted speaker of verse who knew enough stage history not to brush aside Yeats' ideas as impractical just because they differed from present usage on the commercial stage. 'He knew everything, even that Racine at rehearsal made his leading lady speak on musical notes and that Ireland had preserved longer than England the rhythmical utterance of the Shakespearean stage.'[20] Gerard Fay comments on the relationship between poet and actor.

> This passionate interest in the spoken word was the strongest link between Frank Fay and Yeats. It persisted through the quarrels of the later years. It was their first link and almost their last, for it was not long before Frank Fay died that Yeats asked him to create a character in a private performance of one of his later Noh plays produced in the drawingroom of 82 Merrion Square, Dublin.
>
> Their discussion on verse-speaking led to Yeats's abandoning some extravagant ideas he had picked up on the subject. They led to Yeats's having Frank Fay's voice in mind when he wrote some of his plays. . . .[21]

To Yeats, Fay's was the ideal reading — masculine and varied, rhythmical and musical, but never dropping into a monotonous chant. Later Yeats was to complain that Fay's acting had too little of the element of passion, but for now Fay seemed an ideal illustration of Yeats' ideas.

> An actor must so understand how to discriminate cadence from cadence and so cherish the musical lineaments of verse or prose, that he delights the ear with continually varied music. This one has to say over and over again, but one does not mean that his speaking should be a monotonous chant: Those who have heard Mr Frank Fay speaking verse will understand me. That speech of his, so masculine and so musical, could only sound monotonous to an ear that was deaf to poetic rhythm, and no man should, as do London managers, stage a poetical drama

according to the desire of those who are deaf to poetical rhythm.[22]

The speeches of Cuchulain in *On Baile's Strand* were written specifically for Frank Fay's speaking voice and vocal technique. Yeats rewrote lines until Frank Fay found them suitable. 'I think I shall get it simple enough for Fay in the end,' he says in a letter written in 1902.[23] The aim of all this careful rewriting was, in the words of Frank's brother William, to make the lines 'as easy to speak as any play of Shakespeare's'.[24] The result, according to William Fay, who produced the play and played the part of the Fool, was

> the most brilliant achievement in theatrical blank verse of our time. As Cuchullain Frank got the best part he had ever had up till then. An epic hero, it is true, should properly be played by a big man, and Frank was far from that; but on the stage he had the power of making you forget his lack of inches, even as Henry Irving could make you forget his excess of them. His delivery of the verse gave a quality to his impersonation that made up for his physical deficiencies.[25]

When, a little later, Sarah Allgood joined the company, the Irish dramatic movement acquired an actress who could bring a similar beauty to the speaking of female roles. Yeats thought of Miss Allgood's work as being a kind of continuation of the early experimentation of Florence Farr. She too could give him exactly what he wanted in the performance of a dramatic lyric, though her technique was her own. 'Her method was "folk-singing" or allied to it, beautifully humble and simple, whereas Florence Farr's was Greek and arrogant.'[26]

No other technical problem so preoccupied Yeats as the problem of getting the songs in his plays properly performed. The second version of *On Baile's Strand* contains two songs, the song of the Fool and the song sung by the three women throughout the Sword and Fire ritual. Yeats intended both of these songs to be spoken to musical notes according to the technique he and Florence Farr had developed.

These songs, like all other songs in our plays, are sung so as to preserve as far as possible the intonation and speed of ordinary passionate speech, for nothing can justify the degradation of an element of life even in the service of an art.[27]

But the words of the ritual song of the women are not to be clearly heard. As important as they are to the deeper meaning of the play they will remain a kind of secret element obscured by the louder voices of Cuchulain and Conchubar.

> Very little of the words of the song of the three women can be heard, for they must be for the most part a mere murmur under the voices of the men. It seemed right to take some trouble over them, just as it is right to finish off the statue where it is turned to the wall, and besides there is always the reader and one's own pleasure.[28]

As we shall see in a later chapter, this effect fits well with the underlying symbolism of the play. But Yeats' instructions in the matter caused great consternation among the actors at rehearsal. Lady Gregory wrote to him describing the difficulties.

> The three women repeat it together. Their voices don't go together. One gets nervous listening for their separate ones. No one knows how you wish it done. Every one thinks the words ought to be heard. I got Miss Allgood to speak it alone, and we thought if it didn't delay the action too long, she might speak it, and at the end she and the others might sing or hum lines of it to a definite tune. If you can quite decide what should be done, you can send directions, but if you are doubtful, I almost think you must come over.[29]

Yeats got Florence Farr to compose a setting for the song, which relieved matters somewhat. He remained convinced, however, that the song should work subliminally with the words not drawing too great a conscious attention to themselves.

Probably the most intense struggle Yeats ever had with performers to get the musical effects he wanted in a play came during the rehearsals for the first production of *At the*

Hawk's Well in 1916. In this play, his first adaptation of the Noh play form to Irish legendary material, Yeats had introduced a chorus of three musicians. The lines of the musicians had been written to be performed with an alternation between keening or carolling and controlled declamation similar to that which had been developed by Florence Farr. Edmund Dulac wrote very simple music to be played on a zither (according to his illustrations really a psaltery), a flute (really a bamboo pipe) and a drum. The whole play was to be performed to the accompaniment of the music but the lines of the actors were on no account to be spoken 'through music' in the fashionable way, and the players must all move to the accompaniment of drum taps.[30]

Because of the importance of the music to this new play form, Dulac himself assumed the role of First Musician. A Mrs Mann and a Mr Foulds, both professional musicians, were engaged for the other two musician roles. Rehearsals got under way in the beginning of March 1916. Trouble began almost immediately. Mrs Mann in particular had many suggestions for improving the form of the play. She particularly objected to the subordinate role the musicians were asked to play. 'In the big London theatres', she said ' the action is stopped from time to time to give the musician his turn.'[31] By 28 March, Yeats had decided that the musicians would 'have to be eliminated when we are through our first performances', for with their set ideas about the theatrical use of music they were giving more and more trouble.[32]

In a letter to John Quinn, Yeats describes an argument between Dulac and Mr Foulds. The letter is dated 2 April, the day of the opening performance, and the continual dissension has begun to get on his nerves.

My dress rehearsal, or really first performance, is given at Lady Cunard's to-day at 3-40, and I am to be there at 3. I shall go to lunch and then lie down for a little and after that I may be able to face the musicians. One of them insists on a guitar, and the scene of the play is laid in Ireland in the heroic age! His instrument is to appear to-day disguised by Dulac in cardboard, but the musician will struggle for the familiar shape.[33]

After a charity performance the following week, Yeats decided not to do the play again until June. One of the main aims of this stratagem was to get rid of the two recalcitrant musicians. In a letter to Lady Gregory Yeats said:

> The music Beecham says is good but one cannot discuss anything with a feud between Dulac and a stupid musician at every rehearsal. It seems better to get very simple music that can be kept under control. I may even repeat the lyrics myself and have no singing and no music but gong and drum played by Dulac and perhaps a dulcimer or flute.[34]

Yeats' deep indignation over such conflicts as these found its way into a comment made by Daniel O'Leary, a character in one of the stories which introduced the final version of Yeats' *A Vision*. 'The realists turn our words into gravel, but the musician and the singers turn them into honey and oil. I have always the idea that some day a musician would do me an injury.'[35]

The rehearsals for *At the Hawk's Well* marked Yeats' last attempt to have his theories about speech and music applied in their purest form.

> I gave up the fight, began writing little dance plays, founded upon a Japanese model, that needed no scenery, no properties, and can be performed in studio and drawingroom, thinking that some group of students might make a little money playing them and gradually elaborate a technique that would respect literature and music alike. Whenever I produced one of these plays I asked my singers for no new method, did not even talk to them upon the subject.[36]

When, in the twenties, the Abbey Theatre produced his translations of *King Oedipus* and *Oedipus at Colonus*, he did not even insist that Florence Farr's techniques for handling choral work be used. As a matter of fact he instructed the producer Lennox Robinson to disregard his essay *Speaking to the Psaltery*. This was

> partly because liturgical singers were there at his hand, but mainly because if a chorus stands stock still in half shadow

music and singing should, perhaps, possess a variety of rhythm and pitch incompatible with intelligible words. The main purpose of the chorus is to preserve the mood while it rests the mind by change of attention. A producer who has a space below the level of the stage, where a chorus can move about an altar, may do well to experiment with that old thought of mine and keep his singers as much in the range of the speaking voice as if they sang 'The west's awake,' or sang round a binnacle. However, he has his own singers to think of and must be content with what comes to hand.[37]

The musical score for both Oedipus plays was by the young American composer George Antheil, and the music was anything but unobtrusive. During the fight scene in *Oedipus at Colonus* there were twelve pianos played at once.[38] Antheil made considerable use of jazz rhythms in his work and Yeats found in it 'something heroic and barbaric and strange'.[39] When he decided to rewrite *The Only Jealousy of Emer* as a prose play and under the title *Fighting the Waves* produce it on the Abbey stage, he engaged Antheil to compose the music for the production. The orchestra demanded by Antheil was so large that it 'roused a distinguished Irish lyric poet to begin a dance play which', he assured Yeats, 'requires but a tin whistle and a large expensive concertina'.[40]

It was not just the size and importance of the orchestra in *Fighting the Waves* which seemed to be in violation of the principles Yeats had been advocating all his life. Antheil's jazz rhythms all but destroyed the intelligibility of the songs which began and ended the play. But Yeats had become skilled at being 'content with what comes to hand'. In a somewhat shocking note on the play he even called the words 'irrelevant'. 'I have left the words of the opening and closing lyrics unchanged, for sung to modern music in the modern way they suggest strange patterns to the ear without intruding upon it their difficult, irrelevant words.'[41]

Yeats realised that the collaboration with Antheil was a betrayal of a number of the principles he had sought to establish earlier in his career. 'The orchestra brings more elaborate music and I have gone over to the enemy. I say to the musician "Lose my words in pattern of sound as the name of God is lost in Arabian arabesques".⁴² One could always argue, of course, that this treatment of the songs in *Fighting the Waves* merely extended the principle established in *On Baile's Strand*, that certain songs in ritual plays are purposely obscure, containing as they do the esoteric meaning of the play. Thus they are not meant to be immediately understood at first hearing. It is a somewhat strained argument, Yeats' lyrics being difficult enough without further obscuring them by word distortions and musical distractions. None the less Yeats used this argument to justify the fact that his words became submerged in Antheil's music in *Fighting the Waves*.

> [The words of the songs] are a secret between the singers, myself, yourself. The plain fable, the plain prose of the dialogue, Ninnette de Valois' dance are there for the audience. They can find my words in the book if they are curious, but we will not thrust our secret upon them. I can be as subtle as I like without endangering the clarity necessary for dramatic effect.⁴³

This treatment is entirely in keeping with that 'ritual of a lost faith' that the play represents for him. 'The Elizabethan singer, according to Edmund Spenser, and his music was simpler than yours, read out his song before he sang it. We will adopt no such arbitrary practice; our secret is our religion.'⁴⁴

But it is to the simple ballad measure that he returns in his last play, *The Death of Cuchulain*. The final song of that play is meant to be totally understood for it is Yeats' final statement of what Cuchulain has meant in his own life and in the life of modern Ireland. It requires in its performance a technique 'beautifully humble and simple', like that of Sarah Allgood.

In the speech of the Old Man at the beginning of *The Death of Cuchulain*, Yeats indicates that he has returned to his old ideas, to his love for that 'old forgotten music'. 'Before the night ends you will meet the music. There is a singer, a piper, and a drummer. I have picked them up here and there about the streets, and I will teach them, if I live, the music of the beggar-man, Homer's music.'[45]

II

By 1902, Yeats had a very clear idea of the practices he objected to in modern acting, but he had only the vaguest idea of the techniques with which they could be replaced.

> When I saw a London play, I saw actors crossing the stage not because the play compelled them, but because a producer said they must do so to keep the attention of the audience. . . . I hated the existing conventions of the theatre, not because conventions are wrong but because soliloquies and players who must always face the audience and stand apart when they speak — 'dressing the stage' it was called — had been mixed up with too many bad plays to be endurable.[46]

Yeats rejected naturalism as an alternative to the arbitrary stage movement and hackneyed conventions of the contemporary stage. The naturalists, by bringing the spirit of science into the theatre, were setting up an environment hostile to poetry. Yeats' ideas about acting style and stage management were based on the principle that in all fine art one must sacrifice gross effect to subtle effect. This would involve a stilling of stage movement so that the subtler movement of the poetry could have its effect.

> We must get rid of everything that is restless, everything that draws attention away from the sound of the voice, or from the few moments of intense expression, whether that expression is through the voice or through the hands; we must from time to time substitute for the movement that the eye sees the nobler movements that the heart sees, the rhythmic movements that seem to flow up into the imagination from some deeper life than that of the individual soul.[47]

Yeats realised that merely getting rid of unnecessary movement on the stage would not of itself create a vivid, poetic acting style. But he did not know enough about the art of acting to go further in his advice to actors. George Moore, on the other hand, being an advocate of the naturalistic school had very precise ideas on the subject. Yeats thought of going on the stage in small parts so that he might master the stage for the purpose of poetic drama. 'I believe that I construct all right — but I have very little sense of acting. I don't see my people as actors though I see them very clearly as men. Moore sees them always as actors.'[48]

When William Fay's little company of Irish amateurs produced his *Cathleen ni Houlihan* together with George Russell's *Deirdre* in 1902, Yeats saw in the 'wonderful simplicity and naivety' of their performance the beginning of a new acting style for poetic drama. 'Their method', he said, 'is better than their performance, but their method is the first right one I have seen.'[49]

There was a stillness and freedom from conventional business in Maud Gonne's performance as *Cathleen ni Houlihan* which conveyed a sense of nobility and tragic power. George Moore thought the role should be played more naturalistically and had suggestions for making the play more conventionally dramatic.

> Moore wanted Cathleen to walk up and down all the time in front of the footlights. When I explained that this would not be true to the play, that she was as it were wandering in a dream, made restless as it were by the coming rebellion, but with no more fixed intention than a dreamer has, he wanted me to re-write the play. Such emotions were impossible in drama; she must be Ireland calling up her friends, marshalling them to battle.[50]

The acting in Russell's *Deirdre,* which Moore thought was 'the silliest he ever saw',[51] was to Yeats a vindication of his own ideas of what acting should be in poetic drama.

> In *Deirdre,* a dim dreamlike play, they acted without 'business' of any kind. They simply stood still in decorative attitudes and spoke . . .[52] They showed plenty of inexperience, especially in the minor characters, but it was the first performance I had seen since I understood these things in which the actors kept still long enough to give poetic writing its full effect upon the stage.[53]

Fay's actors achieved this admirable stillness largely because 'they did not know what else to do'. But a little later Yeats saw Sarah Bernhardt in a production of Racine's *Phèdre* and brought back word to the Irish actors that the style they had stumbled upon could be developed into a very high art indeed. There was a remarkable stillness on the stage throughout the performance of Racine's tragedy.

> I noticed too that the gestures had a rhythmic progression. Sarah Bernhardt would keep her hands clasped over, let us say, her right breast for some time, and then move them to the other side, perhaps, lowering her chin till it touched her hands, and then, after another long stillness, she would unclasp them and hold them out, and so on, not lowering them till she had exhausted all the gestures of uplifted hands. . . . Beyond them stood a crowd of white-robed men who never moved at all, and the whole scene had the nobility of Greek sculpture, and an extraordinary reality and intensity.[54]

After the performances of *Deirdre* and *Cathleen ni Houlihan* Yeats decided to join forces with the Fay brothers. He and Frank Fay began a correspondence on acting and the principles of playing poetic drama which was soon to give Yeats that 'sense of acting' which he had heretofore lacked. Frank Fay's influence and the availability of a group of actors to experiment with greatly accelerated Yeats' mastery of the technical details of the actor's art. He soon ceased to have difficulty thinking of his characters in a theatrical as well as a literary context.

The acting style developed by William Fay in his company was simple and natural without being naturalistic. Frank Fay had a fine sense of the heroic gesture and recognised, with Yeats, that 'Art is art because it is not nature'. 'He was openly, dogmatically, of the school of Talma which permits an actor, as Gordon Craig has said, to throw up an arm calling down the thunderbolts of Heaven, instead of seeming to pick up pins from the floor . . .'[55] There were some much-loved conventions from which he could be weaned with only the greatest difficulty. 'He knew the history of all conventions and sometimes loved them. I would put into his hands a spear instead of a sword because I knew he would flourish a sword in imitation of an actor in an eighteenth century engraving.'[56]

In his contacts with Frank Fay, Yeats was dealing with an actor of a very high order of intelligence. His advice to Fay on matters of role preparation show Yeats' realisation that an actor's first need is an understanding of the nature of the part, and not a flood of advice on external details. When Frank Fay undertook the role of Cuchulain in *On Baile's Strand* he seemed to have a curious inability to understand the part. Yeats explained:

About Cuchullain. You have Lady Gregory's work I know. Remember however that epic and folk literature can ignore time as drama cannot — Helen never ages, Cuchullain never ages. I have to recognise that he does, for he has a son who is old enough to fight him. I have also to make the refusal of the son's affection tragic by suggesting in Cuchullain's character a shadow of something a little proud, barren and restless, as if out of sheer strength of heart or from accident he had put affection away. He lives among young men but has himself outlived the illusions of youth. He is probably about 40, not less than 35 or 36 and not more than 45 or 46, certainly not an old man, and one understands from his talk about women that he does not love like a young man. Probably his very strength of character made him put off illusions and dreams (that make young men a woman's servant) and made him become quite early in life a deliberate lover, a man of pleasure who can never really surrender himself. He is a little hard, and leaves the people about him a little repelled — perhaps this young man's affection is what he had most need of. Without this thought the play had not any deep tragedy. I write of him with difficulty, for when one creates a character one does it out of instinct and may be wrong when one analyses the instinct afterwards. It is as though the character embodied itself. The less one reasons the more living the character. I felt for instance that his boasting was necessary, and yet I did not reason it out. The touch of something hard, repellent yet alluring, self assertive yet self immolating, is not all but it must be there. He is the fool — wandering passive, houseless and almost loveless. Concobhar is reason that is blind because it can only reason because it is cold. Are they not the cold moon and the hot sun?[57]

In the end it is through metaphor that poet can best communicate with actor, bringing about an understanding of the poet's meaning by stirring the imagination of the actor.

As the Abbey Theatre began to earn a wider reputation and a distinctive 'Abbey style' of acting began to develop, Yeats remained dissatisfied with one aspect of the company's technique. From the beginning of the movement no performer, with the possible exception of Maud Gonne in *Cathleen ni Houlihan,* had ever been able to make the fire of passion burn with the pure clear flame Yeats thought was necessary for poetic tragedy. Although the stage management and external acting style of the Abbey company was not objectionably naturalistic, the actors persistently based their performances on observation and not on their own subjective awareness of the forces which lie at the centre of life. Yeats concluded that theirs was essentially a comic art, based on character and not on passion.

After a performance of Synge's *Deirdre of the Sorrows* in 1909 he wrote:

> Then as I watched the acting I saw that O'Donovan and Molly (Maire O'Neill) were as passionless as the rest. Molly had personal charm, pathos, distinction even, fancy, beauty, but never passion — never intensity; nothing out of the brooding mind. All was but observation, curiosity, desire to please. Her foot never touched the unchanging rock, the secret place beyond life; her talent showed like that of the others, social, modern, a faculty of comedy. Pathos she has, the nearest to tragedy the comedian can come, for that is conscious of our presence and would have our pity. Passion she has not, for that looks beyond mankind and asks no pity, not even of God. It realizes, substantiates, attains, scorns, governs, and is most mighty when it passes from our sight.[58]

Molly's performance improved but the flame of passion still did not burn clear.

Last night Molly had so much improved that I thought she may have tragic power. The lack of power and of clarity which I still find amid great charm and distinction, come from lack of construction, through lack of reflection and experience, than from mere lack of emotion. There are passages where she attempts nothing, or where she allows herself little external comedy impulses, more, I think, because they are habitual than because she could not bring emotion out of herself. The chief failure is towards the end. She does not show immediately after the death of Naoise enough sense of what has happened, enough normal despair to permit of a gradual development into the wild unearthly feeling of the last speeches, though these last speeches are exquisitely spoken.[59]

Yeats despaired of ever seeing an Irish actress achieve such tragic effects as Mrs Patrick Campbell, for instance, achieved in his own *Deirdre*. They seemed incapable of the passionate and solitary mood such playing required.

Looking back on the movement in 1919, Yeats realised that the art of the Irish players had been an objective art from the beginning. The vividness of the early playing came from the vividness of the Irish country life that they had imitated.

Our players, too, have been vivid and exciting because they have copied a life personally known to them, and of recent years, since our manager has had to select from the ordinary stage-struck young men and women who have seen many players and perhaps no life but that of the professional class, it has been much harder, though players have matured more rapidly, to get the old, excited, vivid playing.[60]

Even where that early playing had appeared to be purely subjective, a product of the artist's imagination, there had been hidden models.

One of the early players was exceedingly fine in the old woman in *Riders to the Sea*. 'She has never been to Aran, she knows nothing but Dublin, surely in that part she is not objective, surely ˏshe creates from imagination', I thought; but when I asked her she said, 'I copied from my old grandmother'. Certainly it is ´this objectivity, this making of all from sympathy, from observation, never from passion, from lonely dreaming, that has made our players, at their best, great comedians, for comedy is passionless.[61]

To find a fully developed tradition of subjective acting of the kind he wanted for his verse tragedies Yeats had to go to the tradition of the Noh theatre of Ancient Japan. 'If he would become famous as a Noh player . . . he must not observe life, not put on an old face and stint the music of the voice. He must know how to suggest an old woman and yet find it all in the heart.'[62]

The most striking effect of Yeats' constant exposure to actors and acting problems in the early years of the Abbey Theatre was the growth of his interest in the physical aspects of acting. Initially he had been of the opinion that the voice was of such supreme importance in poetic drama that all other aspects of the actor's person must be subordinated to it. He thought of bodily movements as competition for the voice. His rule was simple: the less movement the better. He tells us that he

> once asked a dramatic company to let me rehearse them in barrels that they might forget gesture and have their minds free to think of speech for a while. The barrels, I thought, might be on castors, so that I could shove them about with a pole when the action required it.[63]

As Yeats worked more and more closely with actors in rehearsal at the Abbey, and began to watch their performances with a producer's as well as a playwright's eye, he altered his views considerably. His dislike of arbitrary movement, mechanical gesturing and mere busyness on the stage remained. But he became more and more aware of the aesthetic pleasure that comes from the truly organic use of the body on stage, of the degree to which carefully controlled movement can strengthen the effect of poetic speech, and of the way in which movements of the whole body can communicate directly to the audience the forces at work in the unconscious mind. He began to observe, both in

life situations and in rehearsals, how people used their bodies
as well as their voices, and to apply what he learned in his
work as a stage director. A series of journal entries made in
1909 illustrate the keen interest he took in these matters.

> I noticed in the train, as I came to Queenstown, a silent,
> fairly well-dressed man, who struck me as vulgar. It was
> not his face, which was quite normal, but his movements.
> He moved from his head only. His arm and hand, let us
> say, moved in direct obedience to the head, had not the
> instinctive motion that comes from a feeling of weight, of
> the shape of an object to be touched or grasped. There
> were too many straight lines in gesture and in pose. The
> result was an impression of vulgar smartness, a defiance of
> what is profound and old and simple.[64]

Yeats recognised that the ability to move in an organic
fashion, as though prompted by instinct rather than by
conscious decision, was the source of true stage presence in
an actor. Inexperienced actors always appear to be giving
orders to their bodies, another example of 'the will trying to
do the work of the imagination'.

> I have noticed that beginners sometimes move this way on
> the stage. They, if told to pick up something, show by the
> movement of their body that their idea of doing it is more
> vivid than the doing of it. One gets the impression of
> thinness in the nature.[65]

The stage director must determine whether the problem
stems from self-consciousness at being on stage for the first
time or from a chronic separation of the actor from his
instincts.

> I am watching Miss V———— to find out if her inanimate
> movements when on the stage come from lack of
> experience of if she has them in life. I watched her sinking
> into a chair the other day to see if her body felt the size
> and shape of the chair before she reached it. If her body
> does not so feel she will never be able to act, just as she
> will never have grace of movement in ordinary life.[66]

Yeats well understood the importance of motivation in
creating full and expressive stage movement.

As I write I see through the cabin door a woman feeding a child with a spoon. She thinks of nothing but the child, and every movement is full of expression. It would be beautiful acting. Upon the other hand her talk — she is talking to someone next her — in which she is not interested, is monotonous and thin in cadence. It is a mere purpose in the brain, made necessary by politeness.[67]

In seven years of production work Yeats had developed to a marked degree that 'sense of acting' he felt he lacked in 1902.

Yeats' increasing tendency to consider the actor's physical presence and his bodily movement an important element in the visual design of a production owes a great deal to the ideas of Edward Gordon Craig, the brilliant and revolutionary stage designer whose influence on Yeats we will consider in some detail in a later section of this chapter. Craig felt that acting would never become a truly creative art until actors overcame their 'egoism' and learned to use their bodies and voices as materials in the creation of performances of visual and auditory beauty and symbolic significance. He advocated the reintroduction of the mask to the theatre. The mask serves to depersonalize the actor, makes him cease to rely on facial expression and forces him to pay attention to the movements of his whole body, to rely on physical means of expression, to re-create life itself instead of reproducing everyday situations naturalistically. In the first issue of his theatre magazine, *The Mask,* published March 1908, Craig had said

. . . human facial expression is for the most part valueless.
. . . Masks carry conviction when he who creates them is an artist, for the artist limits the statements which he places upon these masks. The face of the actor carries no such conviction; it is over-full of fleeting expression, frail, restless; disturbed and disturbing. . . .[68]

Working closely with Craig, Yeats sought to introduce masks to the Abbey stage, particularly for such symbolic figures as the Fool in the *Hour-Glass* and the Fool and the Blind Man in *On Baile's Strand.* Eight years after Craig's article on the mask, Yeats echoed its ideas in his introduction to *Certain*

Noble Plays of Japan. 'A mask never seems but a dirty face, and no matter how close you go is yet a work of art; nor shall we lose by stilling the movement of the features, for deep feeling is expressed by a movement of the whole body.'[69]

In the April 1908 edition of *The Mask* Craig further developed his ideas about an ideal art of acting. He advocated that the actor become a kind of superior marionette, using his body as though it were a material apart from himself in the practice of a truly creative, anti-realistic art. Denis Bablet summarises Craig's views on this new kind of actor, whom Craig calls the *über-marionette.*

> The *über-marionette* is the actor who has acquired some of the virtues of the marionette and thus released himself from servitude.

> > The *über-marionette* will not compete with life — rather will it go beyond it. Its ideal will not be the flesh and blood but rather the body in trance — it will aim to clothe itself with a death-like beauty while exhaling a living spirit. Several times in the course of this essay has a word or two about Death found its way on to the paper — called there by the incessant clamouring of 'Life! Life! Life!' which the realists keep up.

> And as some people had mistaken the real meaning of his essay, Craig explained in his preface to the 1925 edition of *On the Art of the Theatre* that 'The *Über-marionette* is the actor plus fire, minus egoism; the fire of the gods and demons, without the smoke and steam of mortality'. His condemnation of realism as contrary to art carries with it the complete abolition of the realistic actor. In the revived art of the theatre, the actor must abstain from servile imitation of nature and from all attempt at impersonation.[70]

Yeats' familiarity with the ideas of Gordon Craig certainly prepared him for the enthusiastic acceptance of Japanese acting technique when he came to study the Noh tradition several years later.

> Therefore it is natural that I go to Asia for a stage convention, for more formal faces, for a chorus that has no

part in the action, and perhaps for those movements of the body copied from the marionette shows of the fourteenth century. . . .

The players wear masks and found their movements upon those of puppets. A swift or a slow movement and a long or a short stillness, then another movement.

At the climax, instead of the disordered passion of nature there is a dance, a series of positions and movements which may represent a battle, or a marriage, or the pain of a ghost in the Buddhist Purgatory.[71]

But it was Mr Ito, the Japanese dancer who danced the part of the Hawk-woman in his first production of *At the Hawk's Well,* who showed Yeats the powerful effect the human body could have when used in this way.

There, where no studied lighting, no stage-picture made an artificial world, he was able, as he rose from the floor, where he had been sitting cross-legged, or as he threw out an arm, to recede from us into some more powerful life. Because the separation ˙ was achieved by human means alone, he receded but to inhabit as it were the deeps of the mind.[72]

As he watched the Japanese dancer, Yeats made an observation that perhaps explained some of the strange power he had felt in the 'rhythmic progression' of Bernhardt's gestures many years before.

I have lately studied certain of these dances, with Japanese players, and I notice that their ideal of beauty, unlike that of Greece and like that of pictures from Japan and China, makes them pause at moments of muscular tension. The interest is not in the human form but in the rhythm to which it moves, and the triumph of their art is to express the rhythm in its intensity.[73]

Yeats had at last discovered a theatrical style to replace the outworn Western tradition where 'for nearly three centuries invention has been making the human voice and the movements of the body seem always less expressive'.[74] And he had come to the point of realising that a truly ritualistic theatre must be based on patterns of physical as well as verbal movement.

If Mr Ito in *At the Hawk's Well* gave Yeats exactly what he wanted, Henry Ainley, the experienced actor who played Cuchulain, was not so fortunate. Ainley seemed incapable of the strong, ritualised, full movements Yeats demanded for the play. He annoyed Yeats by waving his arms 'like a drowning kitten' at rehearsals,[75] and he finally had to undergo the indignity of having Yeats work out all the gestures for the part and present them to him in the form of drawings by Dulac.[76] After the first performances Yeats decided to get rid of Ainley along with the musicians.[77]

After *At the Hawk's Well,* the dance assumed an ever greater importance for Yeats both as a symbol in his poetry and as an art form in the theatre. Ninette de Valois' dance as Fand in *Fighting the Waves* made a lasting impression on him. 'I am deeply grateful for a mask with the silver glitter of a fish, for a dance with an eddy like that of the water, for music that suggested, not the vagueness, but the rhythms of the sea.'[78] Ninette de Valois was the tragi-comedian dancer the Old Man speaks of in *The Death of Cuchulain.* 'I could have had such a dancer once, but she has gone; the tragicomedian dancer, upon the same neck love and loathing, life and death.'[79] But in spite of the difficulty of getting the ritual dance performed properly, there is no doubt of its primacy in the play, no doubt that Yeats has long since abandoned any idea that the physical aspects of ritual should be subordinated to the verbal aspects. Of one thing the Old Man is certain. 'I promise a dance. I wanted a dance because where there are no words there is less to spoil.'[80]

IV

From 1901 to about 1914 all Yeats' thinking about theatre design was dominated by the revolutionary ideas of Edward Gordon Craig. Craig, the son of actress Ellen Terry, had begun his theatre career as an actor. When Yeats first met him in 1901 he was engaged in the production of a series of romantic operas for the Purcell Society in London. Craig was both producer and designer of the operas and every detail of production was made 'to conform to Craig's own controversial but stongly-held theatrical conviction. Yeats immediately undertook a careful study of Craig's design principles and production methods. With Craig's instruction, Yeats rapidly gained confidence in the field.

In 1902 Yeats commented to Frank Fay that he was much more secure in his knowledge of theatrical scenery than in his knowledge of acting. He attributed knowledge of scenery to Craig. 'Two years ago I was in the same state about scenery that I am now in about acting. I knew the right principles but I did not know the right practice because I had never seen it. I have now however learnt a great deal from Gordon Craig.'[81]

Before his meeting with Gordon Craig, Yeats' ideas about stage scenery and costumes were, indeed, somewhat vague and general. As usual, though, he knew what he did not want. He did not want the 'elaborate and rich' mounting which such critics as William Archer insisted was the only suitable setting for poetic drama. Nor did he want the setless production in rehearsal costuming which George Moore was currently advocating. In a letter to the *Daily Chronicle* in 1899 he outlined his views.

> I see in my imagination a stage where there shall be both scenery and costumes, but scenery and costumes which will draw little attention to themselves and cost little money. I have noticed at a rehearsal how the modern coats and the litter on the stage draw one's attention, and baffle the evocation, which needs all one's thought that it may call before one's eyes lovers escaping through a forest, or men in armour upon a mountain side. I have noticed too how elaborate costumes and scenery silence the evocation completely, and substitute the cheap effects of a dressmaker and of a meretricious painter for an imaginative glory.[82]

All should be suggestion, not a representation of nature.

> Sometimes a shadowy background, a pattern of vague forms upon a dim backcloth, would be enough, for the more the poet describes the less should the painter paint; and at the worst one but needs, as I think, enough of

scenery to make it unnecessary to look at the programme to find out whether the persons on the stage have met indoors or out of doors, in a cottage or in a palace.[83]

Yeats thought that such simple, suggestive scenery could be designed with a 'severe beauty' which would far surpass in aesthetic appeal the showy effects of expensive, realistic stage settings.

When Yeats attended a performance of Gordon Craig's production of *Dido and Aeneas* in the spring of 1901, he saw such scenery on the stage for the first time. He wrote to Craig: 'I thought your scenery to "Aeneas and Dido" the only good scenery I ever saw. You have created a new art.'[84] He asked Craig to dinner to discuss the principles of set design he had used. Craig wrote in his journal: 'If it had not been a poet, and Yeats that poet, one would have murmured: "And is it only scenery you saw?" '[85] But Gordon Craig was flattered by the attention given his art by a fellow artist whose genius he recognised and admired. They became close friends. Yeats frequented Craig's rehearsals, chipping away at the wall of secrecy with which Craig preferred to surround the technical details of his work. During the rehearsals of Craig's production of *Bethlehem* in 1902 he wrote:

I have learned a great deal about the staging of plays from 'the nativity', indeed I have learned more than Craig likes. His sister has helped me, bringing me to where I could see the way the lights were worked. He was indignant — there was quite an amusing scene. I have seen all the costumes too, and hope to get patterns. He costumed the whole play — 30 or 40 people I should say — for £25.[86]

Gordon Craig's sister, Edy, was a valuable ally. She and Pamela Smith agreed to do sketches for Yeats' play *Where there is Nothing*. As designers they had one great advantage. The exploitation of it did not please Craig.

Last Monday evening Pamela Smith brought round a big sketch book full of designs for the play made by herself and Edith Craig. They were particularly pleased because they know Gordon Craig's little stage dodges and are using them rather to his annoyance.[87]

In spite of Gordon Craig's irritation at the boldness of Yeats' artistic poaching their relationship remained a close one. Yeats constantly discussed with Craig problems of staging which came up in the course of his playwriting and his production work at the Abbey. When, in 1910, Craig developed an 'invention' which he thought would revolutionise stage technique he allowed Yeats to make the first use of it on the Abbey stage. He provided Yeats with a model stage on which to experiment and complete plans for constructing the 'invention' at the Abbey.

In the settings for the Purcell Society operas Yeats had seen what he called 'the only admirable stage scenery of our time'.

> . . . Mr. Gordon Craig has discovered how to decorate a play with severe, beautiful, simple effects of colour, that leave the imagination free to follow all the suggestions of the play. . . .[88] He created an ideal country where everything was possible, even speaking in verse, or speaking to music, or the expression of the whole of life in a dance . . .[89]

Such severely beautiful, simple and unobtrusive scenery seemed the only proper setting for verse drama, now that the platform stage of the Elizabethans was denied to modern producers.

> As we cannot, it seems, go back to the platform and the curtain, and the argument for doing so is not without weight, we can only get rid of the sense of unreality, which most of us feel when we listen to the conventional speech of Shakespeare, by making scenery as conventional.[90]

Yeats himself 'would have preferred to be able to return occasionally to the old stage of statue-making, of gesture', and indeed *On Baile's Strand* was originally written with such a stage in mind, but failing a return to the platform stage, the we must free the proscenium stage from the naturalistic trappings which hamper the imagination.

> We have made a prison-house of paint and canvas, where we have as little freedom as under our own roofs, for there is no freedom in a house that has been made with hands.

All art moves in the cave of the Chimaera, or in the more silent house of the gods, and neither cave, nor garden, nor house can show themselves clearly but to the mind's eye.[91]

With Craig's example before him Yeats set out to establish a tradition of non-realistic stage design for the Abbey. The main principles he wanted to establish were outlined as early as 1902 in a comment on George Russell's designs for Fay's production of Russell's *Deirdre*. The sets and costumes, while simple, were not in Yeats' opinion simple enough for poetic drama.

> I would like to see poetical drama, which tries to keep at a distance from daily life that it may keep its emotions untroubled, staged in but two or three colours. The background, especially in small theatres, where its form is broken up and lost when the stage is at all crowded, should I think be thought out as one thinks out the background of a portrait. One often needs nothing more than a single colour, with perhaps a few shadowy forms to suggest wood or mountain.[92]

In the early years of the Irish dramatic movement, Yeats himself kept a very close control over matters of design. Sets and costumes for *The Hour-Glass* and *Shadowy Waters* for instance were designed according to his principles by Robert Gregory with a colour scheme dictated by Yeats himself. Lady Gregory describes those early productions.

> As to our staging of plays, in 1903, the costumes for *The Hour-Glass* were designed by my son, and from that time a great deal of the work was done by him. *The Hour-Glass* dresses were purple against a green curtain. It was our first attempt at the decorative staging long demanded by Mr. Yeats. . . . His staging of *The Shadowy Waters* was almost more beautiful; the whole stage is the sloping deck of a galley, blue and dim, the sails and dresses are green, the ornaments all of copper.[93]

Although Robert Gregory, working under Yeats' guidance, managed to create on stage what Yeats characterised as 'a high grave dignity and that strangeness which Ben Jonson thought to be a part of all excellent beauty',[94] Annie

Horniman in her brief career as a stage designer was less successful. In 1903, Miss Horniman, who was about to provide the Irish dramatic movement the theatre on Abbey Street which would become its·permanent home, decided to participate in the movement in an artistic capacity as well. Her first endeavour in this area was to finance, design and manufacture the costumes for a production of Yeats' *The King's Threshold*. Although she followed Yeats' advice in using a grey background for the play, she used too many colours and too elaborate a style in the costuming itself to create a unified effect. The production design drew criticism, particularly from Frank Fay, who feared her forthcoming designs for *On Baile's Strand* might show similar defects. Yeats reassured him.

> Miss Horniman has to learn her work . . . and must have freedom to experiment. I think her *Baile's Strand* will prove much better. I had told her that old stages permitted elaborate dress though not elaborate scenes, and this combined with [the] fact of its being a Court misled her into overdoing colour and the like in certain parts.[95]

The situation required a great deal of tact since so much of the future of the movement depended on Miss Horniman's financial support. To prepare her for *On Baile's Strand* Yeats gave her a copy of Joyce's *Social Ireland* and suggested 'as delicately as I could that there ought not to be gorgeousness of costume'.[96] After *On Baile's Strand* Miss Horniman withdrew from active work as a stage designer.

As a matter of fact, the very form of *On Baile's Strand* cried out for strict simplicity of staging. ·As has been mentioned, Yeats had originally written it with a platform stage in mind. Thus

> the characters walk on to an empty stage at the beginning and leave that stage empty at the end, because I thought of its performance upon a large platform with a door at the back and an exit through the audience at the side, and no proscenium or curtain; and being intended for a platform and a popular audience — no other audience at the time caring a straw for us — is full of what I thought to be good round speeches.[97]

Yeats took an active part in planning the lighting and stage management of the play, watching the audience carefully on the opening night to see their reaction to each technical effect. After the first performance he wrote to Lady Gregory: 'I got a beautiful lighting effect in *Baile's Strand,* and the audience applauded the scene even before the play began. . . .'[98]

In *The Golden Helmet* (an early prose version of *The Green Helmet*) in 1908 Yeats experimented boldly with colour.

At the Abbey theatre the house is orange-red and the chairs and tables and flagons black, with a slight purple tinge which is not clearly distinguished from the black. The rocks are black with a few green touches. The sea is green and luminous, and all the characters except the Red Man and the Black Men are dressed in various shades of green, one or two with touches of purple which look nearly black. The Black Men all wear dark purple and have eared caps, and at the end their eyes should look green from the reflected light of the sea. The Red Man is altogether in red. He is very tall and his height is increased by horns on the Green Helmet. The effect is intentionally violent and startling.[99]

Yeats explained the principles on which this colour scheme had been worked out.

We staged the play with a very pronounced colour-scheme, and I have noticed that the more obviously decorative is the scene and costuming of any play, the more it is lifted out of time and place, and the nearer to faeryland do we carry it. One gets much more effect out of concerted movements — above all if there are many players — when all the clothes are the same colour. No breadth of treatment gives monotony when there is movement and change of lighting. It concentrates attention on every new effect and makes every change of outline or of light and shadow surprising and delightful. Because of this one can use contrasts of colour, between clothes and background or in the background itself, the complimentary colours for instance, which would be too obvious to keep the attention in painting. One wishes to make the movement of the action as important as possible, and the simplicity which gives depth of colour does this, just as, for precisely similar reasons, the lack of colour in a statue fixes the attention on the form.[100]

The strong emphasis that Yeats puts on the interplay of colour, movement and lighting in this passage shows how marked was the influence of Gordon Craig on Yeats' thinking at this time. In the first few years of their relationship, Yeats had been somewhat sceptical about the emphasis Craig placed on lighting in his work. In an article in *Samhain* in 1904, Yeats had observed:

If we remember that the movement of the actor and the gradation and the colour of the lighting, are the two elements that distinguish the stage picture from an easel painting, we may not find it difficult to create an art of the stage ranking as a fine art. Mr. Gordon Craig has done wonderful things with the lighting, but he is not greatly interested in the actor, and his streams of coloured direct light, beautiful as they are, will always seem, apart from certain exceptional moments, a new externality.[101]

And the experiments of the Swiss designer Appia, in which he used projected shadows of green boughs to 'show a man wandering through a wood, and not a man in the middle of it', Yeats dismissed as simply a more sophisticated form of naturalism.[102] But Yeats was by 1908 becoming more and more interested in new ways of using light on the stage. And Gordon Craig was soon to reveal to him a scenic invention which would shift the emphasis in production design entirely from colour co-ordination to lighting control.

Gordon Craig explained the principles of his invention after a dinner in Yeats' rooms on 7 January, 1910. Yeats was immediately enthusiastic, seeing in Craig's new scenic concept 'a means of staging everything that is not naturalistic', and even speculating that 'a completely new method even for . . . naturalistic plays' might grow from it.[103] Craig had developed a system of staging by which a single nonrepresentational set could be made to accommodate an endless variety of scenes. Denis Bablet describes Craig's invention.

[It] consisted chiefly of screens composed of four, six, eight, ten or twelve leaves which could be folded either forwards or backwards. All the leaves of a screen were the same height, but they might be different widths. . . . Any space and any atmosphere could be suggested by an appropriate arrangement of the screens. If the angle of the screen were altered, the appearance of the stage would change at once. This was, therefore, a single scene, which could take on many different aspects. . . .

For the foremost characteristic of this scene is that it is an architectonic construction with a life of its own. It is a solid, three-dimensional unit which adapts itself to the actor's movements, a group of screens which stand by themselves — they do not have to be hung from the flies, like old-fashioned scenery. They stand on the stage for what they are; they do not imitate nature, nor are they painted with realistic or decorative designs. They are monotone. . . . The screens can be moved about, folded and unfolded under the eyes of the audience, so that the transition from one scene to the next takes place gradually, like the changes in the play. . . . The screens were not to be lighted in the same way as ordinary scenery; the scene would come to life, and attain its full expressive power, through light. The light travelled over it, animating it, creating atmosphere and transforming it. Light coloured the screens and gradually changed their aspect.[104]

Craig was willing that the Abbey Theatre should be the first theatre in the world to use his 'scene', but only on the stipulation that Yeats should use it for all of his poetic works in the future. Yeats gladly agreed.[105] Craig presented Yeats with a model stage, equipped with screens, and lighting device. He suggested that Yeats not consider using the screens in actual production until he had played about with the model and mastered its effects. Throughout the summer of 1910 Yeats carried out experiments with the model stage.

All summer I have been playing with a little model, where there is a scene capable of endless transformation, of the expression of every mood that does not require a photographic reality. . . . Henceforth I can all but 'produce' my play while I write it, moving hither and thither little figures of cardboard through gay and solemn light and shade, allowing the scene to give the words and the words the scene.[106]

Craig himself demonstrated how the screens could be adapted to Yeats' heroic plays by two sketches: 'The Heroic Age — Morning' which suggested to Yeats the world of *On Baile's Strand* and 'The Heroic Age — Evening' which suggested *Deirdre*. Yeats' plans for a production of *Deirdre* played before Craig's screens illustrate the new enthusiasm for lighting effects his experimentation with the model had brought.

The barbarous dark-faced men, who have not hitherto been all I imagined (perhaps because our stage is shallow), will not show themselves directly to the eyes when they pass the door, nor will the dark-faced messenger when he comes to say that supper's ready, nor it may be Conchubar when he comes to spy and not to fight. I will see passing shadows and standing shadows only. Perhaps the light that casts them may grow blood-red as the sun sets, but of that I am not sure. . . . Should these shadows become a permanent part of the representation I will have to abandon the windows and doors through which one sees at present a wood and evening sky. But, perhaps, shadows of leaves seen on the wall beside the door under a shifting light will accompany the Musicians's opening speech.[107]

There has been a considerable alteration in Yeats' views since 1904 when he considered Craig's coloured light to be a new externality and Appia's projected shadows of leaves a misguided attempt to create a more perfect realism.

When Yeats produced *The Hour-Glass* at the Abbey Theatre in January 1911 using Craig's screens, he no longer depended entirely on colour but rather on the more subtle effects which could be produced by the play of lights and shadows on the ivory coloured surface of the screens. The difference between the old and the new production styles was striking.

> Up to the present year we always played it in front of an olive-green curtain, and dressed the Wise Man and his Pupils in various shades of purple (with a little green here and there); and because in all these decorative schemes, which are based on colour, one needs, I think, a third colour subordinate to the other two, we dressed the Fool in red-brown, and put touches of red-brown in the Wife's dress and painted the chair and desk the same colour. Last winter, however, we revived the play with costumes taken chiefly from designs by Mr. Gordon Craig, and with the screens he has shown us how to make and use. . . . and with the effects that depend but little on colour, and greatly upon delicate changes of tone.[108]

Craig's sketch of the Fool showed him dressed in a loose-fitting smock-like garment of a very light neutral colour and wearing a leather half-mask like that worn by the *zanni* of the *commedia dell 'arte* tradition. Yeats was delighted that the Abbey Theatre might be the first modern theatre to use the mask and talked of putting the fool and the blind man in *On Baile's Strand* into masks as well. 'It would give', he said, 'a wildness and extravagance that would be fine.'[109] However, it was some time before Craig could find time to supervise the making of the leather mask, so it was not ready for the 1911 production of *The Hour-Glass*.[110]

Although Yeats made a great deal of use of the model stage in revising earlier plays, and although he wrote *The Player Queen* particularly for Craig's scene, the actual collaboration of Yeats and Craig did not go beyond the design of the Abbey screens and the provision of sketches for *The Hour-Glass*. In 1913 Craig and Yeats talked of 'a big scheme of poetic drama' with Yeats as literary advisor.[111] Then Craig returned to Florence where he ran a School of Theatre in the Arena Goldoni, and from where he published *The Mask,* and the scheme was simply dropped. In the winter of 1913-14 Ezra Pound introduced Yeats to the Japanese

Noh play and Yeats' ideas about theatrical staging took another sharp turn.

The play form that Yeats and Edmund Dulac drew from a study of Ezra Pound's *Noh* materials brought a new asceticism to Yeats' stage-craft. Yet the elements used in staging *At the Hawk's Well* had in fact all been present in some form or another for some time in his own experiments and those of Gordon Craig. What was new was the extreme simplicity of the mounting — a patterned screen, a cloth unfolded and folded before the audience, three dancers and three musicians, masks and plain white light — and the emphasis which this simplicity threw on the human body engaged in ritual movement. Yeats had found a way to 'return . . . to the old stage of statue-making, of gesture',[112] but in a setting more intimate than the Elizabethan platform stage. The action of his play seemed to him to take place in 'a deep of the mind that had hitherto been too subtle for our habitation'. 'As a deep of the mind can only be approached through what is most human, most delicate, we should distrust bodily distance, mechanism, and loud noise.'[113]

In his introduction of the patterned screen, Yeats was returning to his old idea of 'decorative' staging. As early as 1904, Yeats had suggested to Robert Gregory that he consult Japanese prints to find the kind of stylised tree suitable to a decorative stage set.[114]

Yeats commented on the asceticism of the new staging.

I do not think of my discovery as mere economy, for it has been a great gain to get rid of scenery, to substitute for a crude landscape painted upon canvas three performers who before the wall or patterned screen describe landscape or event, and accompany movement with a drum and gong, or deepen the emotion of the words with zither of flute. Painted scenery, after all, is unnecessary to my friends and to myself, for our imagination kept living by the arts can imagine a mountain covered with thorn-trees in a drawing-room without any great trouble, and we have many quarrels with even good scene-painting.[115]

Edmund Dulac, who had recently illustrated an edition of *The Arabian Nights,* brought to the design of screen, masks and costuming a style that managed to combine primitive Aryan with Oriental elements. Yeats was delighted.

> I saw there the mask and head-dress to be worn in a play of mine by the player who will speak the part of Cuchulain, and who, wearing this noble, half-Greek, half-Asiatic face, will appear perhaps like an image seen in reverie by some Orphic worshipper.[116]

The nobility and strange beauty of Dulac's masks fired Yeats' imagination. The mask was already a central symbol for him of a duality in the human personality. He considered the possibility of assembling a collection of masks and writing plays for them. He wondered what effect the changing of a mask on stage would have, and began writing his second *Noh* play, *The Only Jealousy of Emer,* to find out. The mask would perhaps give him a simple means of representing on stage the phenomenon of 'the changeling' so frequently met with in Celtic legendry.

> I want to follow *The Hawk's Well* with a play on *The Only Jealousy of Emer* but I cannot think who should be the changeling put in Cuchulain's place when he is taken to the other world. There would be two masks, changed upon the stage. Who should it be — Cuchulain's grandfather, or some god or devil or woman?[117]

From *At the Hawk's Well* all of Yeats' plays, with one exception, take place as if 'in a deep of the mind', and use a simple non-realistic stage. *Words upon the Windowpane,* set in a Dublin rooming-house, was his only experiment with naturalism. In that play the naturalistic environment itself becomes a symbol and is placed in juxtaposition to the world of the spirits. In *The Death of Cuchulain* the Old Man opts for the ultimate in non-realistic staging.

> Emer must dance, there must be severed heads — I am old, I belong to mythology — severed heads for her to dance before. I had thought to have those heads carved, but no, if the dancer can dance properly no wood-carving can look as well as a parallelogram of painted wood.[118]

It is finally, not even the words, but the quality of the ritual pantomime that sets the scene.

V

Producers wishing to produce the Cuchulain plays as a continuous cycle may be given pause by Yeats' statement: '. . . they were so little planned for performance upon one evening that they should be at their best on three different kinds of stage'. But on close examination of the plays, Yeats' observation does not stand up.

On Baile's Strand was written for a bare platform stage; *At the Hawk's Well* and *The Only Jealousy of Emer* evoke their sense of place through poetry alone; *The Green Helmet's* gay and objective world may be created as well by lighting as by set painting; the expressionistic *The Death of Cuchulain* needs only a pillar-stone and good lighting control for its effect.

Gordon Craig's screens could provide a ritual place suitable for the production of all five Cuchulain plays. Or Craig's smooth, abstract, geometrical shapes could be replaced by huge textured, rock-like dolmen-shapes. On a circular platform stage, such shapes would suggest the great stone circles within which the prehistoric worshippers of sun god and moon goddess performed their rituals. There a tragic hero might

> . . . like a laughing string
> Whereon mad fingers play
> Amid a place of stone,
> Be secret and exult,
> Because of all things known
> That is most difficult.[119]

For other than drawing-room presentations, the folding and unfolding of the cloth is unnecessary. A ceremonial entrance to the place of ritual can be as effective. It is, I think, important that the presentation of *At the Hawk's Well* and *The Only Jealousy of Emer* be not obtrusively Japanese. Yeats took only the pattern of organisation from Japanese *Noh;* the materials are Celtic and it is an ancient Celtic ritual which he is attempting to restore. A study of what Yeats calls 'traditional Irish singing' and an investigation into the experimentation of Florence Farr on the psaltery will be more useful to the producer than a study of the exotic falsetto and discordant music of an actual Japanese *Noh* production. The spirits of Cuchulain and the others must seem to rise from the Irish soil and not be merely oriental imports.

In a production I staged at the University of Winnipeg in 1969, the cycle was played on a unit set of stone-like shapes. The musicians, druidical figures from some remote age, played sitar, tabla and recorder. Costuming was simple and limited to a few primary colours and careful attention was given to lighting control, particularly in scenes involving the supernatural, and scenes representing crisis points in the romance of Sun and Moon.

The Old Man who enters at the beginning of *The Death of Cuchulain* was dressed in a fairly modern suit and waistcoat. His make-up and physical bearing suggested the person of W. B. Yeats in his seventies. To see the figure of Yeats intrude upon the scene after we had sat immersed for two and a half hours in the Irish heroic age, to say that *he* came from mythology was an effect altogether startling, but, I think, right — for it sharpened the irony of that final most bitter and beautiful play.

6 The Sudden Cry of a Hawk

The action of *At the Hawk's Well* takes place amid those 'things discovered in the deep, when only body's laid asleep', which provided so much of the subject-matter of Yeats' early poetry.[1] *At the Hawk's Well* shows Cuchulain's first contact with those 'elemental creatures' who 'rant and rage in flood and wind',[2] the people of the Sidhe. Seeking a miraculous well whose waters give eternal life, Cuchulain spreads sail and, driven by a lucky wind over waves that seem charmed, comes at last to a rocky and barbarous shore. As he climbs the rocks, a great hawk swoops down on him from the air

> As though it would have torn me with its beak
> Or blinded me, smiting with that great wing.
> I had to draw my sword to drive it off . . .[3]

It is a masterful image, one 'to engross the present and dominate memory'.[4] There are others as powerful in the cycle of Cuchulain plays: Cuchulain, 'with shield before him and with sword in hand', fighting 'the deathless sea';[5] Cuchulain standing firm against the Red Man and the band of coal-black, cat-headed creatures he has gathered from the earth forts of the Connacht hills;[6] Cuchulain thrusting his sword into the ritual fire and addressing the flames themselves as those 'pure, glittering ones, that should be more than wife or friend or mistress'.[7] These are magical images, archetypal actions whose powerful effect on us ultimately defies intellectual analysis. Like all archetypal symbols, these images seem to stir directly the forces of the unconscious without a need for complete intellectual understanding. In an essay on William Morris in 1902, Yeats remarked that 'the important things, the things we must believe in or perish, are beyond argument', 'We can no more reason about them than can the pidgeon, come but lately from the egg, about the hawk whose shadow makes it cower among the grass.'[8]

The effect upon us of the great grey hawk whose shadow sweeps across the mountain side in *At the Hawk's Well* seems to be almost as much a matter of instinct. This observation applies equally to the other most striking images in the Cuchulain plays, for Yeats' method is such that it is always impossible to account in rational terms for the total effect of his symbols. However, if we study the 'fields of suggestiveness' they bring with them from the occult tradition and the other traditions from which he derives them, we shall certainly increase our understanding of the processes they set in motion.

The dominant images of the Cuchulain cycle — Cuchulain and the hawk, Cuchulain and the cat-heads, Cuchulain and the flames, Cuchulain and the waves — have roots in the doctrine of the elementals taught by Madame Blavatsky and by the Order of the Golden Dawn. Interpreting Celtic mythology according to occult doctrine, Yeats saw the people of the Sidhe as divided into four orders, each representing one of the four elements — air, earth, fire, and water. Cuchulain's contacts with the Sidhe in their various manifestations provide a series of rituals around which the Cuchulain plays are built.

The plot of each Cuchulain play is essentially simple but, as the plot unfolds, symbols 'set the mind wandering from idea to idea, emotion to emotion'.[9] As Yeats has remarked, 'there cannot be great art without the little limited life of the fable, which is always the better the simpler it is, and the rich, far-wandering, many-imaged life of the half-seen world beyond it.'[10] Before undertaking a detailed consideration of the text of the Cuchulain plays it might be useful for us to consider the primary associations some of his major symbols had for Yeats.

The wind, for instance, sweeps through *At the Hawk's Well* as relentlessly as it sweeps through the volume of lyrics Yeats published in the nineties under the title, *The Wind Among the Reeds*. A note from that volume may help us to understand the wind's symbolic significance in the play.

Yeats says:

I use the wind as a symbol of vague desires and hopes, not

merely because the Sidhe are in the wind, or because the wind bloweth as it listeth, but because wind and spirit and vague desire have been associated everywhere.[11]

In *At the Hawk's Well* the wind is from the West.

I follow much Irish and other mythology, and the magical tradition, in associating the North with night and sleep, and the East, the place of sunrise, with hope, and the South, the place of the sun at its height, with passion and desire, and the West, the place of sunset, with fading and dreaming things.[12]

Elsewhere, Yeats has identified the sea with the unconscious and with the mysterious, undifferentiated source from which all being emerges.

But a German psycho-analyst has traced the 'mother-complex' back to our mother the sea . . . to the loneliness of the first crab or crayfish that climbed ashore and turned lizard; while Gemistus Plethon not only substituted the sea for Adam and Eve, but ... made it symbolize the garden's ground or first original, 'that concrete universal which all philosophy is seeking.'[13]

The essay on William Morris cited above links imagery of Well and Tree to the stories of the Grail quest, 'the Heathen Grail that gave every man his chosen food, and not the Grail of Malory or Wagner'.[14] This Grail, a source of fertility and abundance, could be won only by 'men with lucky eyes and men whom all women love'.[15] Yeats comments on Morris' use of the symbols of Well and Tree.

In *The Well at the World's End* green trees and enchanted waters are shown to us as they were understood by old writers, who thought that the generation of all things was through water; for when the water that gives a long and fortunate life, and can be found by none but such a one as all women love, is found at last, the Dry Tree, the image of the ruined land, becomes green. To him indeed as to older writers Well and Tree are all but images of the one thing, of an 'energy' that is not the less 'eternal delight' because it is half of the body.[16]

In Morris' writings, the women who have 'prayed under the Shadow of the Green Tree and on the wet stones of the Well' and are 'worshippers of natural abundance' are good housewives and 'sit often at the embroidery frame'. They have wisdom in flocks and herds and they are before all fruitful mothers'.[17]

Yeats draws a sharp contrast between these lucky men and bountiful women who seek an earthly Paradise represented by the flowing Well and the Green Tree and those who, driven by spiritual desire, seek an unearthly Paradise. These are kin of the Wilderness and the Dry Tree. The idea that those who are driven by spiritual desire voluntarily chose the empty well and withered tree gives dramatic point to Cuchulain's decision at the climactic moment of *At the Hawk's Well*. It also makes clear the import of the song sung by the musicians at the end of the play.

II

At the beginning of *At the Hawk's Well* the musicians ceremoniously enter and prepare a place for the enactment of a ritual. They are poet-priests of the bardic tradition. By their opening song they evoke 'A Druid land, a Druid tune'![18] The subtle monotony of their music should produce in their hearers a state akin to that between sleeping and waking, a state wherein vision may take place. It is in the mind's eye that the real events of the play must be seen for the action takes place in some deep of the human mind.

> I call to the eye of the mind
> A well long choked up and dry
> And boughs long stripped by the wind . . .[19]

Since the generation of all things is through water, the well represents the source of life, the well-spring of existence. But the symbol opens up into another possible meaning, for the life-giving well of Celtic mythology and ancient ritual, long choked up and dry, is being called to the mind by Yeats. This is also Connla's well and associated with the gift of wisdom. Has the source of life, of wisdom, dried up? The purpose of

initiation ceremonies in magical orders as in primitive cults is
to reconnect the initiate with the source of his life. We are
about to take part in an initiation ritual. The boughs long
stripped by the wind are hazel boughs, associated in Irish
mythology with the Tree of Life. The leaves, symbols of
abundant life, have been stripped by the winds of desire —
particularly of spiritual desire as Yeats indicates in the Morris
essay.

> And I call to the mind's eye
> Pallor of an ivory face,
> Its lofty dissolute air . . .[20]

The ivory face is that of Cuchulain who, in the Dulac mask,
'will appear perhaps like an image seen in reverie by some
Orphic worshipper'.[21] Long pale faces are associated by Yeats
with the heroes of Celtic mythology as we see in the song at
the end of *The Death of Cuchulain.*[22] The word 'dissolute'
reminds us of the orgiastic nature of initiation rituals and the
sense of abandonment with which the hero must assume his
role. A 'lofty, dissolute air' was associated by Yeats with
Lionel Johnson, Ernest Dowson, Aubrey Beardsley and other
members of what Yeats described as his 'tragic generation'.
The alcoholism, sexual excesses, and so-called decadence
among the friends of Yeats' young manhood had seemed to
him to be a result of too great a spiritual desire.

> A man climbing up to a place
> The salt sea wind has swept bare.[23]

Cuchulain's quest takes him up out of life to a place made
desolate by the intensity of spiritual desire. Salt would seem
to be used here as a symbol of desire itself. In small
quantities it increases appetite, but it also kills vegetation and
stings the flesh.

   The musician now poses the central question of *At the
Hawk's Well.* Cuchulain comes apparently seeking immortality. Like 'those men with lucky eyes and men whom all
women love' he thinks of immortality as an infinite extension
of an earthly life filled with abundance. But all initiates into
traditions of ancient wisdom know that immortality is escape
from life and not an extension of it. The very value of
incarnation is questioned.

What were his life soon done!
Would he lose by that or win?
A mother that saw her son
Doubled over a speckled shin,
Cross-grained with ninety years,
Would cry, 'How little worth
Were all my hopes and fears
And the hard pain of his birth!'[24]

The quest which the hero faces is to some extent a search for that which gives meaning to life — that which would make a mother's hopes and fears worth something, that would justify the pain she endured in giving him birth. It is important to note that the image of 'a speckled shin' is not simply used to denote old age, but indicates a life spent in loyalty to the values of the hearth. The old man described is one who, as the musicians put it in the song at the end of the play, 'has married and stays/By an old hearth'.[25] Such a picture is in Cuchulain's mind in *On Baile's Strand* when he asks Conchubar, 'Are my shins speckled with the heat of the fire/Or have my hands no skill but to make figures/Upon the ashes with a stick?'[26]

The boughs of the hazel shake,
The sun goes down in the west.[27]

The Tree of Life trembles before a supernatural visitation. The sun, a symbol of consciousness, must go down before the contents of the unconscious become manifest.

The heart would be always awake,
The heart would turn to its rest.[28]

In this ritual, Yeats appears to see the figures on one level of meaning as representing heart, soul and intellect. The heart controls the rhythms of life, quickening, slowing down, in accord with the intensity of bodily experience. In *At the Hawk's Well*, it is the Old Man who moves to drum taps, who tries to stay awake but who sleeps. Oliver Gogarty has said that Yeats meant the Guardian of the Well to symbolise the intellect.[29] If this is so, is the Young Man (Cuchulain) then symbolic of the soul, that 'mouthful of sweet air' referred to in the song at the end of the play?

> Night falls;
> The mountainside grows dark;[30]

The dark night of the soul begins. Cuchulain faces an uphili climb into darkness.

> The withered leaves of the hazel
> Half choke the dry bed of the well;[31]

Access to the source of all being is stopped up by the remnants of a life which has been withered by desire.

> The guardian of the well is sitting
> Upon the old grey stone at its side
> Worn out from raking its dry bed,
> Worn out from gathering up leaves.[32]

If the Guardian does indeed symbolise intellect then the imagery here is most suggestive. The futility of raking the bed of a dry well, of gathering up leaves no longer living, causes her to sink into a state of stupor.

The Old Man enters through the audience, moving as if to drum taps. He uses fire-stick and socket to kindle a flame in the little heap of leaves and dry sticks which he makes.

> And now the dry sticks take the fire,
> And now the fire leaps up and shines
> Upon the hazels and the empty well.[33]

Memories and abandoned hopes recalled in sexual revery inflame the imagination and light up the barren tree of life and the dried up source of creativity. The heart gives one last cry to the winds of desire that it may be given peace at last.

> 'O wind, O salt wind, O sea wind!'
> Cries the heart, 'it is time to sleep;
> Why wander and nothing to find?
> Better grow old and sleep.'[34]

The Old Man turns to speak to the Guardian of the Well but she cannot hear him. He complains of her lack of responsiveness.

> You have not one word,
> While yesterday you spoke three times. You said:

'The well is full of hazel leaves.' You said:
'The wind is from the west.' And after that:
'If there is rain it's likely there'll be mud.'[35]

On the surface these are commonplaces, the kind of
conversation Yeats was likely to get from the spirit mediums
he sought in Soho flats. Actually they reiterate in symbolic
terms the main features of the human situation which the
play presents. The well-springs of life itself are stopped up
with personal memories and the debris of a personal life
made barren by intense desire. The most intense desires blow
in upon us from some half-realised region of our dreams. As
surely as rain produces mud, so the generative power which is
the source of all being produces 'the fury and the mire of
human veins'.[36]

> To-day you are as stupid as a fish,
> No, worse, worse, being less lively and as dumb.[37]

There is a strange inversion of mythological ideas here. It was
the salmon of knowledge that ate the berries or nuts of
wisdom in Connla's well and became bearer of wisdom to
Finn. The apparent stupidity of the Guardian is preparatory to
her possession by a supernatural force. The fish imagery is apt,
for the Sidhe are dexterous fishers and they fish for men with
dreams upon the hook.[38]

> Your eyes are dazed and heavy.[39]

Her condition is similar to that of a spirit medium just before
a seance.
  Complaining bitterly of her unresponsiveness, the Old Man
cries out:

> It is enough to drive an old man crazy
> To look all day upon these broken rocks
> And ragged thorns, and that one stupid face,
> And speak and get no answer.[40]

The madness of which the Old Man speaks would seem to be
akin to that Yeats was to call for in his own old age.

> Grant me an old man's frenzy,
> Myself must I remake

> Till I am Timon and Lear
> Or that William Blake
> Who beat upon the wall
> Till Truth obeyed his call . . .[41]

From such frenzy comes 'an old man's eagle mind'.[42]

In the midst of the Old Man's bitter complaints, Cuchulain enters, demanding that the Old Man speak to him.

> Then speak to me,
> For youth is not more patient than old age;
> And though I have trod the rocks for half a day
> I cannot find what I am looking for.[43]

Cuchulain has little patience and his belief in his luck is strong. He has no clear idea of the nature of what he seeks and no awareness of the cost of the quest. He has trod the rocks — that is, left behind the pleasant life among indolent meadows — for only half a day and is surprised he has not yet been rewarded with success.

The Old Man demands to know who speaks to him, who comes 'so suddenly' in this place where nothing thrives. After enduring fifty years of misfortune he is struck by the sharp contrast between the life Cuchulain has given up to undertake his quest and the life he will now be involved in.

> If I may judge by the gold
> On head and feet and glittering in your coat,
> You are not of those who hate the living world.[44]

The word *living* points to the extent of the renunciation which is required by all those who would undertake the quest Cuchulain has embarked on. Although at this point Cuchulain looks upon the immortality for which he searches as an extension of a happy and bountiful earthly life, he will soon become involved in pursuit of immortality of a different order. Ironically, an apparent lust for life has led Cuchulain to a point where he must give up the living world as mortals know it. This is the paradox which lies at the root of the Old Man's charge that the immortal dancers cheat those who pursue them.

Cuchulain identifies himself. 'I am named Cuchulain, I am

Sualtim's son.'[45] Cuchulain's is a name which will go about the world like wind, but here, coupled with that of his human parent, it seems curiously beside the point. The Old Man claims never to have heard the name, and the ancient house of Sualtim lies beyond the charmed waves of the sea. It is as though the candidate must divest himself of name and parentage before entering into the ritual of initiation. When we meet Cuchulain in *On Baile's Strand* he will claim as parent a 'clean hawk out of the air'.[46] The Old Man, noting Cuchulain's lofty, dissolute air, questions him as to what he is seeking. It is a kind of insanity voluntarily to become separated from the life of the indolent meadows. If it is not an ascetic hatred of the living world which has brought him here, is it blood lust or sexual desire?

> What mischief brings you hither? — you are like those
> Who are crazy for shedding of men's blood,
> And for the love of women.[47]

Cuchulain reveals that he has been summoned to this place by a story told over the wine cups before dawn.

> I rose from table, found a boat, spread sail,
> And with a lucky wind under the sail
> Crossed waves that have seemed charmed, and found this
>   shore.[48]

The waves that have seemed charmed constitute a separation from the experience of other mortals such as Yeats himself experienced when he began his magical experimentation. The Old Man's churlish replies lead Cuchulain to remark:

> You should be native here, for that rough tongue
> Matches the barbarous spot.[49]

This is a highly compressed dramatic statement. The Old Man has obviously penetrated to Cuchulain's sensibilities. The Old Man's contemptuous attitude has struck Cuchulain forcibly. As the Old Man has pointed out, there are no houses to sack or beautiful women to be carried off here. This is what makes the spot barbarous, and the Old Man's inhospitable attitude matches the inhospitable nature of the spot. But a barbarous tongue, in a different sense, is not inappropriate to words of

magical invocation. A barbarous tongue may mark one as
native to a magical setting. The Order of the Golden Dawn,
for instance, preserved foreign words and formulas in all their
rituals. Perhaps the old man can serve as a guide, just as
Connla the Druid served as a guide in the visions of Yeats and
his fellow experimenters in 1898. Cuchulain asks for the Old
Man's guidance.

> You can, it may be
> Lead me to what I seek, a well wherein
> Three hazels drop their nuts and withered leaves,
> And where a solitary girl keeps watch
> Among grey boulders. He who drinks, they say,
> Of that miraculous water lives for ever.[50]

Are the waters of which Cuchulain speaks to be considered
the waters of emotion and passion as Yeats suggested the
waters of Connla's well symbolised?[51] The immortality which
passion bestows is attested to in Yeats' essay on 'The Tragic
Theatre';[52] but it is an immortality which comes at the
expense of what we commonly call character. It removes us
from the 'casual comedy' and 'a terrible beauty is born'.[53]
The 'barren passion' for whose sake Yeats is childless at
forty-nine[54] itself seems appropriately symbolised by the dry
well, surrounded by stones. After all 'too long a sacrifice can
make a stone of the heart'.[55]

At any rate, the grey boulders, solitary girl and the hollow
among stones half-full of leaves are not what Cuchulain had
imagined he was seeking. Instead of a source of passionate
life he appears to have found a stony place, the repository of
memories of a life made bitter by desire. The old man scoffs
at Cuchulain's obvious disappointment.

> And do you think so great a gift is found
> By no more toil than spreading out a sail,
> And climbing a steep hill?[56]

Cuchulain's naïve underestimate of the sacrifices he must
make to complete the quest is typical of the mythological
hero. Yet even the Old Man does not fully comprehend the
paradoxical nature of the 'great gift' of which he speaks; that
the 'great gift' and the 'curse' he warns Cuchulain of should

be two aspects of the same thing he does not understand. Nor does he realise that, while the dancers cheat him and leave him with nothing, 'where there is nothing there is God'.[57]

> O, folly of youth,
> Why should that hollow place fill up for you,
> That will not fill for me?[58]

The words 'that hollow place' seem to open up the well symbol suggestively. Is there a hollow place surrounded by stones in every man's life capable of mysteriously filling itself with the divine presence? Why do such visitations come only fleetingly and while we sleep so that we awaken only dimly aware that something has transpired? Why are we left with only the evidence of slightly damp stones. The Old Man who has withdrawn from life and waited fifty years for this visitation cannot comprehend that there is another path to spiritual realisation, that of conflict, the way of the hero, the direct facing of one's daemon.

> I have lain in wait
> For more than fifty years, to find it empty,
> Or but to find the stupid wind of the sea
> Drive round the perishable leaves.[59]

Irrational desires emanating from the unconscious agitate old memories of past life.

Pressed for an answer by Cuchulain the Old Man admits that there is a moment when the water fills the well. But it is

> A secret moment that the holy shades
> That dance upon the desolate mountain know,
> And not a living man, and when it comes
> The water has scarce plashed before it is gone.[60]

Convinced of his great luck, Cuchulain declares that he will stand and wait.

> Why should the luck
> Of Sualtim's son desert him now? For never
> Have I had long to wait for anything.[61]

This unshakable belief in his own luck is a striking characteristic of Cuchulain at the beginning of the play cycle as it is

of Oedipus at the beginning of *Oedipus Rex*. All things have
come to Cuchulain 'with no more toil than spreading out a
sail'. It is as Sualtim's son that he has luck. Luck in this sense
is very much a thing of 'the living world'. Cuchulain has no
concept of the nature of that which he awaits. The Old Man
tries to drive him away.

> No! Go from this accursed place! This place
> Belongs to me, that girl there, and those others,
> Deceivers of men.[62]

Luck, in the sense that Cuchulain uses the term, is of no use
in the world Cuchulain has now entered. In this 'accursed
place' it may be turned into its opposite by those others,
'deceivers of men'. Surprised by the Old Man's bitter
denunciation of the immortals, Cuchulain asks:

> And who are you who rail
> Upon the dancers that all others bless?[63]

The ambiguity inherent in the concept of the people of the
Sidhe is brought out strongly here. The 'good people' are, in
fact, disasterous to the mortal lives with which they come
into contact. Infinitely desirable, the desire they enkindle in
human beings cannot be reconciled with human life. Witness
the folk stories of the 'faery touch', the 'stroke', the tale of
Red Hanrahan,[64] the man who dreamed of Fairyland,[65] and
others.

The Old Man tells of his fifty years of patient waiting and
of the bitter disappointment which has been his reward.
Three times the waters have risen but each time he has been
asleep. Cuchulain is not to be dissuaded.

> My luck is strong
> It will not leave me waiting, nor will they
> That dance among the stones put me asleep.[66]

Cuchulain's sense of having a special destiny is well founded,
but he does not yet comprehend that on this desolate
mountain, the destiny of the hero is a tragic destiny, that the
joy he seeks is a tragic joy, an exultation not of this world.

> If I grow drowsy I can pierce my foot.[67]

Cuchulain is close to realising the nature of his destiny here, although he does not realise the significance of what he says. A traditional mark of the hero victim in mythology has been some disfigurement of the foot. Self-inflicted, the wound becomes a symbol of the hero's conscious seeking of his own destiny. The Old Man cries out a warning.

> No, do not pierce it, for the foot is tender,
> It feels pain much.[68]

It is such considerations which have kept the Old Man from choosing the path of the hero. He once more warns Cuchulain to leave. Cuchulain forcibly declares that he will stay, and the air is rent by the sudden cry of a hawk.

III

In the conversation between Cuchulain and the Old Man which follows the hawk's cry we perceive that Cuchulain's quest is related not only to the waters of immortality but to the image of a great grey hawk as well. The hawk is Cuchulain's totem animal, his daemon, his external soul. If our analysis of the opening song of the musicians is correct, it is now beginning to take possession of the intellect. Primitive rites for the initiation of warriors involve a ritual coming to terms with the totem animal. The hawk spirit first manifest itself to Cuchulain in the form of an actual hawk which attacked him on the mountainside.

> I had to draw my sword to drive it off,
> And after that it flew from rock to rock.
> I pelted it with stones a good half hour
> And just before I had turned the big rock there
> And seen this place, it seemed to vanish away.
> Could I but find a means to bring it down
> I'd hood it.[69]

From his first contact with the hawk spirit, love and hatred are mixed for Cuchulain. Unity of being, which is a part of what the waters which rise in the well represent, would appear to be impossible of attainment at this extreme objective stage on the wheel of Cuchulain's fate. Here, at the beginning of Cuchulain's commitment to the heroic life,

Yeats makes use of the same image he uses to mark the end of one historical cycle and the beginning of another in his poem 'The Second Coming', the image of the circling hawk.

> Turning and turning in the widening gyre
> The falcon cannot hear the falconer;
> Things fall apart; the centre cannot hold;
> Mere anarchy is loosed upon the world,
> The blood-dimmed tide is loosed, and everywhere
> The ceremony of innocence is drowned;[70]

The situation in *At the Hawk's Well* is parallel. Although the waters of immortality, of wisdom, of unity of being (they are all the same in the magical tradition) bubble unseen at the centre of life even at this phase of extreme discord and objectivity in the life of Cuchulain, they will remain unattainable, and Cuchulain will find himself committed to a career of discord and violence.

The Old Man identifies the spirit which manifest itself as the hawk and which now is taking possession of the Guardian of the Well.

> The Woman of the Sidhe herself,
> The mountain witch, the unappeasable shadow.
> She is always flitting upon this mountainside,
> To allure or to destroy.[71]

By now the mountain has gained, through repeated mention in the same context, considerable power as a symbol of some mysterious realm of psychological experience. The term 'mountain witch' gains much of its effectiveness from this association. The word 'shadow' suggest the insubstantial nature of the image, its origin in darkness, the idea that it is the visible manifestation of something not directly visible. We are reminded also that Yeats has spoken of the evil that resides in the shadow of a certain indomitable kind of woman.[72] In the Cuchulain plays, the term 'witch' and the term 'goddess' are used to refer to the same order of being. The difference in the connotations of the two terms will become tremendously important for Cuchulain in *On Baile's Strand*. We should note that it is the Old Man who uses the term 'witch', and that he uses it to denote a spirit, not a human being who practises witchcraft. The Old Man notes the two aspects of the mountain witch, her capacity to allure and to destroy. When, at the end of the play, her image is projected on the woman Aoife, Aoife will take on these characteristics of the mountain witch. The tribes of female warriors led by Aoife worship the goddess in her most destructive form.

> When she has shown
> Herself to the fierce women of the hills
> Under that shape they offer sacrifice
> And arm for battle.[73]

The Old Man tells of a curse which falls on all those who dare to gaze into the goddess's unmoistened eyes.

> That curse may be
> Never to win a woman's love and keep it;
> Or always to mix hatred in the love;
> Or it may be that she will kill your children,
> That you will find them, their throats torn and bloody,
> Or that you will be so maddened that you kill them
> With your own hand.[74]

The problem of the interrelation of physical love and spiritual hate becomes acute when the hero decides consciously to face the images which issue from the shadows of his own unconscious.

When Cuchulain again refuses to heed the Old Man's warnings that he should withdraw, the cry of the hawk is heard once more. This time it clearly issues from the Guardian of the Well. Cuchulain exclaims:

> That cry!
> There is that cry again. That woman made it,
> But why does she cry out as the hawk cries?[75]

The ritual proper begins. The Guardian is possessed. It is not unlike the possession which overtakes the spirit medium at a seance. The emotional tone of the ensuing scene owes a great deal to Yeats' personal experience of supernatural phenomena.

The Old Man explains that the woman is merely a medium through which the hawk spirit manifests itself.

> It was her mouth, and yet not she that cried.
> It was the shadow cried behind her mouth;[76]

Again the reference is to a shadow. Is this shadow the projection of some force within Cuchulain? Does the shadow draw strength from the Old Man? He will lose consciousness completely as the hawk spirit gains strength. Now he watches in horror the early stages of possession.

> Look at her shivering now, the terrible life
> Is slipping through her veins. She is possessed.
> Who knows whom she will murder or betray
> Before she wakes in ignorance of it all,
> And gathers up the leaves?[77]

The 'terrible life' which slips through her veins is of a different order of being than that of the 'living world' referred to earlier by the Old Man.

> The water will have come and gone again;
> That shivering is the sign. O get you gone
> At any moment now I shall hear it bubble.
> If you are good you will leave it. I am old,
> And if I do not drink it now, will never;
> I have been watching all my life and maybe
> Only a little cupful will bubble up.[78]

The horrifying visitation and the coming of the miraculous water are related events. These two aspects of the supernatural are at this phase separate. This separation constitutes the curse. Unity of being is impossible. Cuchulain has a suggestion.

> I'll take it in my hands. We shall both drink,
> And even if there are but a few drops,
> Share them.[79]

This is a futile gesture towards concord at this discordant phase. Cuchulain will attempt a similar gesture in *The Green Helmet* with like results. The Old Man reads his own greed into Cuchulain's offer.

> But swear that I may drink the first;
> The young are greedy, and if you drink the first
> You'll drink it all.[80]

Ignoring all warnings, Cuchulain looks directly into the eyes of the hawk-woman. She fixes her eyes on him. He cries out to her.

> Why do you fix those eyes of a hawk upon me?
> I am not afraid of you bird, woman, or witch.[81]

It is Cuchulain's lack of fear which has brought about the initial contact with the hawk-woman, the curse. But it is his desire to possess her which will draw him from the well. She will allure him to destroy him.

> Do what you will, I shall not leave this place
> Till I have grown immortal like yourself.[82]

The irony of this is that the hawk-woman has gained immortality by being possessed by something which is not of the 'living world'. Cuchulain's idea of the nature of the immortality he seeks has changed though he is not yet aware of it. The Old Man has by now lost consciousness. The hawk-woman is moving into a hawklike dance. The voice of the musician cries out:

> O God, protect me
> From a horrible deathless body
> Sliding through the veins of a sudden.[83]

The irony of this, coming as it does immediately after Cuchulain's expressed desire to become immortal like the hawk, is sharp. It marks Cuchulain's possession by the hawk-spirit. The musician describes Cuchulain's state.

> The madness has laid hold upon him now
> For he grows pale and staggers to his feet.[84]

Cuchulain has grown immortal like the hawk-woman but a terrible price must be paid for this kind of immortality. He will now follow with desire, bodies that can never tire.[85]

> Run where you will
> Grey bird, you shall be perched upon my wrist.
> Some were called queens and yet have been perched there.[86]

The musician cries out:

> I have heard the water plash; it comes, it comes;
> Look where it glitters. He has heard the plash;
> Look he has turned his head.[87]

The waters rise as a reflex of Cuchulain's possession by the hawk-spirit. Immortality is present but he cannot take it in his hands. He does not possess it; it possesses him. Cuchulain has found what he was seeking but it is a curse, not a blessing. Unity of being is shattered. Now 'hatred will be sweet to the taste'.[88]

> He has lost what may not be found
> Till men heap his burial-mound
> And all history ends.[89]

> Only in death will unity be found.

> He might have lived at his ease,
> An old dog's head on his knees,
> Among his children and friends.[90]

Ordinary happiness and contentment are lost for ever to devotees of the hawk-goddess.

IV

When the Old Man awakens, he curses the 'shadows' who, he claims, have deluded him.

> The accursed shadows have deluded me,
> The stones are dark and yet the well is empty;
> The water flowed and emptied while I slept.
> You have deluded me my whole life through,
> Accursed dancers, you have stolen my life.
> That there should be such evil in a shadow.[91]

The Old Man's tendency to associate himself with the experience of Cuchulain opens up once again the question of his true identity. As I pointed out earlier, there is a sense in which the figures in the play — Old Man, Young Man, Guardian — each represent aspects of Cuchulain's being as he works out his relationship with that mysterious hawklike shadow which allures the threatens to destroy him. On a different level of meaning, the Old Man is one who pursues in fantasy the hawk-woman whom Cuchulain pursues in life. It is the dancers of his dreams who have stolen his life away.

Conculain re-enters after his unsuccessful pursuit of the hawk-woman. 'She has fled from me and hidden in the rocks.'[92] Cuchulain said 'run where you will grey bird', yet his pursuit has ended in the rocks which surround the dry well. The old man brings Cuchulain to a realisation of the significance of his experience.

> She has but led you from the fountain. Look!
> Though stones and leaves are dark where it has flowed,
> There is not a drop to drink.[93]

The battle-cry of Aoife's army is heard. The Old Man tells him:

> She has roused up the fierce women of the hills,
> Aoife and all her troop to take your life
> And never till you are lying in the earth
> Can you know rest.[94]

The Old Man has been Cuchulain's guide and interpreter through this spiritual experience. Cuchulain seems still entranced. He must now live out among the hills that fate he has already symbolically danced out on the mountain. But it will be long before he understands it. None the less his fate calls to him and he is 'doom-eager'.

> I will face them.
> He comes! Cuchulain, son of Sualtim, comes![95]

Like a man consumed by desire Cuchulain goes to battle. Later he will make love like one consumed by hate.

Like all magical rituals, this play gives symbolic expression to an inner drama close to the heart of human experience which in other than symbolic terms would be inexpressible. The ritual action in which Cuchulain participates in *At the Hawk's Well* is a symbolic representation of the pattern of his subsequent life. It is an initiation ceremony in which Cuchulain accepts his hawk nature, his tragic destiny and the heroic commitment on which that destiny is based. In a broader sense it is an acceptance of the human condition, of life and death, love and loathing.

As Cuchulain leaves, seeking the forces of Aoife, the musicians move us out of the trance state and back to an awareness of our own human world.

> Come to me, human faces,
> Familiar memories;
> I have found hateful eyes
> Among desolate places,
> Unfaltering, unmoistened eyes.[96]

The memory of the beauty and terror of the supernatural presence lingers on.

> Folly alone I cherish,
> I choose it for my share;
> Being but a mouthful of air,
> I am content to perish;
> I am but a mouthful of sweet air.[97]

It is the song of Cuchulain's soul, singing of the freedom which comes from a lighthearted acceptance of life and death. The bitterness of a life spent pursuing wisdom is pointed out.

> O lamentable shadows,
> Obscurity of strife!
> I choose a pleasant life
> Among indolent meadows;
> Wisdom must live a bitter life.[98]

The dry well and withered tree mock those who, driven by a mysterious spiritual desire, choose them over the possibility of an abundant life.

> 'The man that I praise',
> Cries out the empty well,
> 'Lives all his days
> Where a hand on the bell
> Can call the milch cows
> To the comfortable door of his house.
> Who but an idiot would praise
> Dry stones in a well?'

'The man that I praise',
Cries out the leafless tree,
'Has married and stays
By an old hearth, and he
On naught has set store
But children and dogs on the floor.
Who but an idiot would praise
A withered tree?'[99]

The man who gives up a comfortable life to pursue wisdom or to fulfil an heroic destiny is a fool, yet, as we shall see, folly itself is divine. We shall see more of this conflict between heroic values and the values of the hearth and threshold in *On Baile's Strand* when Cuchulain, a fool wandering 'passive, houseless and almost loveless', comes into conflict with the High King Conchubar.

7 A High, Wide, Foxy Man

In *The Green Helmet,* Cuchulain returns from Scotland to find his homeland ridden by strife and wracked by fear of a red giant who has risen from the sea to challenge the heroes of Ireland. In restoring harmony and honour to Ireland, Cuchulain displays the self-sacrificing and disinterested courage which Yeats thought of as the essence of nobility. Such courage lay at the heart of the ancient tradition that Yeats wanted to restore to modern Ireland.

> Here in Ireland we have come to think of self-sacrifice, when worthy of public honour, as the act of some man at the moment when he is least himself, most completely the crowd. The heroic act, as it descends through tradition, is an act done because a man is himself, because being himself, he can ask nothing of other men but room amid remembered tragedies; a sacrifice of himself to himself, almost, so little may he bargain, of the moment to the moment. I think of some Elizabethan play where, when mutineers threaten to hang the ship's captain, he replies: 'What has that to do with me?'[1]

It is just such a 'sacrifice of himself to himself' that Cuchulain makes in cheerfully offering his head to the Red Man. In so doing he finds his place as the true champion of all Ireland. His solitary heroism is in sharp contrast to the bravado of those who would merely lead the mob. Nor can he be turned from doing that which he must do to satisfy his own heroic nature.

> Would you stay the great barnacle goose
> When its eyes are turned to the sea and its beak to the
> salt of the air?[2]

The contrast between Cuchulain's heroic attitude and the pettiness, fear and bravado of his rivals gives rise to what Yeats calls 'heroic farce'. The tone of the play, like the set used in the Abbey production, is 'intentionally violent and startling'. Yeats' use of ballad metre, his emphasis on the rough and fearless gaiety of Cuchulain in the face of death, and his depiction of Celtic society as drunken, brawling and barbaric, create an effect quite unique in the Cuchulain plays. The spectacular exploits and tales of conquest which are the conventional trappings of heroism are treated ironically in *The Green Helmet,* so that emphasis may be placed on cheerful self-sacrifice as the only truly heroic act.

In the first part of the play, Conall and Laegaire engage in what appears to be a ritual of competitive lying upon clearly established traditional lines. The theme of their claims to recognition as Champions of Ireland is the story of a raid upon the raths or earth forts of Connault to capture a hoard of fairy gold guarded by monstrous cat-headed creatures. Such tales are, of course, frequently met in Irish folklore. It is a motif that such mythologists as John Rhys held to be a variation of the theme of the harrowing of hades by a culture hero. In Yeats' treatment the right of Conall and Laegaire to appropriate such a story to themselves is sharply questioned. They are in fact portrayed as types of what Yeats has called the 'melodious lying Irishman'.[3]

In the opening lines of the play Laegaire reveals himself to be haunted by the phantasmagoric shapes the stories of the raids on the fairy raths have conjured up. He also reveals that he himself does not believe in their literal existence.

> What is that? I had thought that I saw, though but in the
> wink of an eye,
> A cat-headed man out of Connacht go pacing and spitting
> by;
> But that could not be.[4]

Conall immediately asserts that any time Laegaire has seen the cat-heads he must have dreamed it, for it is Conall himself who killed them all. The heroes seem to be acutely aware of the part played by dreams and drunken fantasy in building up such stories — particularly those told by a competitor.

Cuchulain assumes that the story of the Red Man has a similar origin.

I have imagined as good when I've been as deep in the cup.
. . .   And believed it.[5]

Later in the play, after Laegaire has himself explicitly laid claim to the story of the defeat of the cat-heads, the wives of the heroes further undercut the credibility of such tales.

> *Laegaire's Wife.*   And go before me if you can.
>   My husband fought in the West.
> *Conall's Wife.* . . . . But what did he fight out there
>   But sidelong and spitting and helpless shadows of the
>   dim air?
>   And what did he carry away but straw and broken self?
> *Laegaire's Wife.* Your own man made up that tale
>   trembling alone by himself,
>   Drowning his terror.[6]

Yeats' ironic treatment of heroic materials provides one justification for his labelling the play an 'heroic farce'. This treatment also links *The Green Helmet* to Synge's *Playboy of the Western World*. It is interesting that the verse version of *The Green Helmet* was first presented at the Abbey in April 1910 as a curtain-raiser for the *Playboy*.

As a further means of undercutting conventional Irish attitudes towards heroism and of satirising the exaggerated and distorted sense of honour by which Irishmen excuse their quarrelsomeness, Yeats introduced into *The Green Helmet* a pattern of imagery drawn from the medieval beast fable. As a young man Yeats had been much taken with the cycle of stories and poems written about Reynard the Fox in the Middle Ages, and he noted that 'the tricks Reynard played upon the wolf and the lion and other beasts was a cover for much fantastical satire of the lords and priests'.[7] He once planned a long poem in imitation of the Reynard poems but later abandoned the project. Yeats also developed a deep interest in Chaucer. In 1905 he commented to A. H. Bullen that 'my imagination is getting so deep in Chaucer that I cannot get it down into any other well for the present . . .'[8] Chaucer's treatment of the beast fable in the Nun's Priest's Tale could not fail to attract his attention.

The imagery of *The Green Helmet* places the heroic world of Cuchulain in ironic juxtaposition with the mock-heroic world of Reynard and Chanticleer. While Cuchulain's attitude and actions are truly heroic and provide Yeats with one of his clearest statements of the nature of true nobility, the pettiness and quarrelsomeness of those who surround him are more appropriate to a crisis in a poultry yard than to a scene of epic heroism. Viewed in this way, Conall and Laegaire are seen as two quarrelsome roosters who vie with each other for the dominance of the poultry yard, each claiming to have conquered a number of mysterious and perhaps imaginary cats. Both however live in mortal terror of a fox which is preparing to visit the poultry yard for the third time. In Cuchulain's absence, Emer has been putting on airs inappropriate to an ordinary domestic fowl.

> And she makes light of us though our wives do all they can.
> She spreads her tail like a peacock and praises none but her man.[9]

Conall describes the Red Man to Cuchulain as 'a wide, high man' with a 'red foxy cloak' and with half-shut foxy eyes'.[10] Cuchulain is surprised to hear about the fox since he had expected to hear from Conall and Laegaire more tales of their adventures with the cats.

> I thought he had come for one of you
> Out of some Connacht rath, and would lap up milk and mew;
> But if he so loved water I have the tale awry.[11]

As it turns out, the test of heroism among the battling roosters is whether any of them is willing to stick his neck out to have it struck off by the fox.

This image pattern is confirmed by the charioteers in their argument over which of their masters is superior to the others.

> *Laeg.*   I am Laeg, Cuchulain's driver, and my master's cock of the yard.
>
> *Another Charioteer.* Conall would scatter his feathers.[12]

Laeg continues in the same metaphorical framework.

> *Laeg.*   You'd be dumb if the cock of the yard would but open his beak.
> *Another.* Before your cock was born, my master was in the fight.
> *Laeg.*   Go home and praise your grand-dad. They took to the horns for spite,
> For I said no cock of your sort had been born since the fight began.[13]

The question of who will rule the roost in Cuchulain's own household comes up briefly towards the end of the play. Cuchulain, however, is no Chanticleer. He is the great barnacle goose and will not be diverted by feminine arguments or pleading from directly flying towards his fate.

II

From the point of view of the Cuchulain cycle as a whole, one of the most interesting aspects of *The Green Helmet* is Yeats' treatment of Emer and the change that takes place in the nature of her love for Cuchulain. Long before her appearance on the scene we learn from Laegaire that her peacock ways have been a source of trouble among the wives of the heroes. Our first direct introduction to her is through the sound of her voice in sharp conflict with the other wives.

> *Laegaire's Wife* [without]. Mine is the better to look at.
> *Conall's Wife* [without]. But mine is better born.
> *Emer* [without]. My man is the pithier man.[14]

The women are distinguished from one another by the values they reveal in praising their men. To Emer, good looks and high birth are secondary to a man's character and courage (pith). The scene becomes one of pure physical farce as the women begin to wrestle to see who will enter the house first. It is obvious that Celtic queens derive their queenliness from their fierce pride and not from anything that later ages might characterise as decorum. Emer physically overcomes the other two queens and pushes herself to the front. It is Cuchulain who, in the interests of harmony, blocks her passage so that two additional doors can be made so that all three queens can enter at once.

As the new doors are being prepared, Emer describes in song the nature of her man's supremacy and the pride of her own love. It is not Cuchulain's deeds, or the quality of his mind, or of his body that is the basis of Emer's precedence over other women.

> Nothing that he has done;
> His mind that is fire,
> His body that is sun,
> Have set my head higher
> Than all the world's wives.
> Himself on the wind
> Is the gift that he gives . . .[15]

'Himself on the wind' means on the surface simply Cuchulain's reputation. In context, it implies his fame as reflected in the desire of women. Wind for Yeats is a symbol of desire as well as the carrier of the sound of a man's name.

> Therefore women-kind,
> When their eyes have met mine,
> Grow cold and grow hot,
> Troubled as with wine
> By a secret thought,
> Preyed upon, fed upon
> By jealousy and desire . . .[16]

Just as the envy Laegaire and Conall feel for Cuchulain is a tacit admission of his superiority, so the jealousy and desire all women feel in the presence of his wife give Emer supremacy among women.

> For I am moon to that sun,
> I am steel to that fire.[17]

Interpreted in terms of the beginning of Emer's song, the imagery of these lines implies: 'I am the reflection of the light of his body; my will is tempered by the heat of his mind'. Emer's song is a noble expression of the fierce and pride-filled love she bears Cuchulain at this point in the play. It is a love which allows little sympathy for Cuchulain's efforts to bring peace to the quarrelling factions. She tries to taunt him into contesting the championship.

> Cuchulain, put off this sloth and awake:
> I will sing till I've stiffened your lip against every
>   knave that would take
> A share of your honour.[18]

When this sets the women to quarrelling again, Cuchulain attempts to quell the tumult by flinging the helmet that is symbol of the championship of Ireland into the sea. The wives of Conall and Laegaire turn to attack him. Their husbands join the attack. This prompts Emer to draw a dagger and shout: 'Who is for Cuchulain?' When Cuchulain tries to silence her, she defies him and repeats her cry. The other wives draw daggers and a violent and confused brawl ensues. At the height of the tumult three figures 'coal-black and headed like cats' come up over the strand. They extinguish the torches which light the house and the moon goes into eclipse. When moonlight again streams into the room, the Red Man stands in the midst of the company. The cat-headed men crouch and stand about the door. The Red Man is the god of discord, the cat-headed men the enemies of light. Emer's song provides us with the key for unlocking the symbolic meaning of their action in this scene.

Emer's fierce pride and Cuchulain's rational desire for harmony have moments before come into direct opposition. In the ensuing din, the cat-heads manage to extinguish the light which has been provided throughout the play by Cuchulain's mind (as symbolised by the fire of the torches) and by Emer's love (as symbolised by the moon). The action of the cat-heads represents the confrontation between Cuchulain and Emer, just as the appearance of the Red Man represents the chaotic brawling of the mob.

When it becomes obvious that Cuchulain intends to give his head to the Red Man in satisfaction of the debt owed by Conall and Laegaire, Emer begins to keen his approaching death. Cuchulain points out that his lack of faithfulness to her in life has given her little but his fame to base her love upon. After his death, he points out, his fame will be even greater, and her supremacy among women will be unchallenged.[19] If Emer's love were still such as that which she described in her song, then this argument might bring her some comfort. But Emer, the momentary eclipse of her love now over, has undergone a remarkable change. She replies simply: 'It is you, not your fame that I love.'[20] If it is not fame that is important, Cuchulain thinks, then he will be easily replaced.

> You are young, you are wise, you can call
> Some kinder and comelier man that will sit at home in the
>   house.[21]

But it is not kindness, comeliness, or faithfulness that makes her love Cuchulain.

> Live and be faithless still.[22]

Emer's love has been purged of all elements except love itself. Nor does it need in any way to be reciprocated. The gift that Cuchulain gives her is still 'himself on the wind' but the image now has a deeper, more mysterious meaning.

Emer has one last fierce burst of pride. When Cuchulain refuses to be dissuaded from offering his head to the Red Man, she moves to kill herself so that she can join him. 'I too on the grey wing's path!'[23] By sheer masculine power, Cuchulain subordinates the will of the woman who moments before had seemed indomitable. He rejects any attempt to sentimentalise what he is about to do.

> Do you dare, do you dare, do you dare?
> Bear children and sweep the house.
> Wail but keep from the road.[24]

With a mocking jest, Cuchulain offers his head to the Red Man, leaving Emer with no comfort but the knowledge of her love itself.

The Green Helmet ends with Cuchulain declared champion of Ireland. His supremacy over the other heroes of Ireland is achieved by an act of sacrifice rather than of conquest. When Emer achieves supremacy over all other women it will be through an act of sacrifice as well. Her test will not come until, in *The Only Jealousy of Emer*, she is called upon to act out a love totally free of personal desire and hope of reciprocation. The change she undergoes in *The Green Helmet* is a preparation for that test.

8 Between a Fool and a Blind Man

The Fool and Blind Man of *On Baile's Strand* are key figures in the symbolic structure of the Cuchulain cycle. Beginning in the 1903 version of the play as Fintain and Barach, a lean blind man and a fat fool who acted as a chorus commenting on the main action, they evolved through much rewriting of the text into the symbolic figures of Fool and Blind Man, mysterious and masked personages who represent 'those combatants who turn the wheel of life'.[1] In Yeats' final version of the play, the Fool and Blind Man still provide chorus commentary. They are also in a sense the shadows of Cuchulain and Conchubar, and the sub-plot in which they are involved copies the main plot 'much as a shadow upon the wall copies one's body in the firelight'.[2] But the actions of the Fool and Blind Man do not just 'shadow' the action of the main plot, they 'foreshadow' it. In the opening scene of the play they appear to be working together to produce the fate of Cuchulain, whose life drifts 'between a fool and a blind man/To the end, and nobody can know his end'.[3] While it is true that the Fool represents those values held by Cuchulain at the beginning of the play and the Blind Man those values held by Conchubar, both figures may be taken on another level as symbolising principles operating in the mind of Cuchulain, the Fool symbolising Cuchulain's intuition and imagination, the Blind Man his critical and prudential intelligence. Yeats has prepared for this reading by having the Fool and Blind Man in the final version of the play appear to no other character except Cuchulain. They appear to the audience in the first scene, as if externalising an inner conflict of Cuchulain's as he prepares to meet Conchubar in debate. They appear to Cuchulain alone in the last scene as if providing an external symbol of the turmoil in Cuchulain's mind as he attempts to come to terms with the knowledge that he has slaughtered his own son. Seldom, outside of Shakespeare's similar use of the Fool in Lear, has a character's developing madness been given such powerful symbolic representation on the stage.

II

The relationship between Fool and Blind Man is established by the Fool's opening lines. 'What a clever man you are though you are blind! There's nobody with two eyes in his head that is as clever as you are.'[4] The Fool is related to that Fool of Faery who figures so prominently in folklore and who was so central to many of the visions of Yeats' friend George Russell (AE). Yeats commented in a letter to Russell about the Fool of Faery's connection with the Celtic God Aengus.[5] Certainly, the two eyes the Fool has in *On Baile's Strand* are those under whose gaze any trout may become 'a glimmering girl' and whose darting glance will always be on the lookout for 'the silver apples of the moon' and 'the golden apples of the sun'.[6] The Blind Man, lacking such vision, has 'got good sense'. He appears to represent practical intelligence and the prudential values, the Fool imagination and things of the spirit. Cleverness in the Blind Man is a direct result of spiritual blindness. No such visionary as the Fool could ever achieve the Blind Man's mastery of practical affairs. The Blind Man's kind of cleverness makes him an ideal chicken thief. 'Who but you could have thought that the henwife sleeps every day a little at noon? I would never be able to steal anything if you didn't tell me where to look for it.'[7] But the Blind Man deals with the fowl only after it is dead and stripped of its feathers.

> And what a good cook you are! You take the fowl out of my hands after I have stolen it and plucked it, and you put it into the big pot there, and I can go out and run races with the witches at the edge of the waves and get an appetite . . .[8]

A close reading of the Fool's speeches reveals their symbolic import. The sea suggests here as elsewhere the unconscious mind. The witches playing at the edge of the waves suggest those mysterious and disturbing images which obtrude into consciousness in that state between dreaming and waking, the state the Fool is perpetually in. Appetite is ambiguous. The Fool's stomach is pinched and hungry from lack of food but the appetite roused by running races with the witches is an appetite which leads the Fool to place a higher value on the feathers of the fowl than on the flesh, 'and when I've got it there's the hen waiting inside for me, done to the turn'.[9]

The Fool's admiration for the Blind Man's cleverness, a quality he knows he himself lacks, makes him particularly vulnerable to the Blind Man's treachery. The Blind Man replies, thinking of the plot to betray the Fool, not of the chicken itself. 'Done to the turn.'[10] The Fool, in a speech which is an accurate reflection of his own values, suggests a way of dividing the chicken. 'Come now, I'll have a leg, and you'll have a leg, and we'll draw lots for the wishbone.'[11] The Fool's assumption is that the meat will be evenly divided. On the really important question of who will get the wishbone, however, they will trust to luck. The Blind Man, whose values are quite different, will plot to get all the meat and to leave the Fool with the feathers and bones (including, one would assume, the wishbone on which the Blind Man places no value at all). The Fool envisions that the eating of the fowl will take place in a situation paralleling the court of Conchubar, with the Blind Man playing the part of High King and the Fool the part of a devoted courtier. 'I'll be praising you, I'll be praising you while we're eating it, for your good plans and for your good cooking. There's nobody in the world like you, Blind Man. Come, come.'[12] Suddenly the Fool remembers his friends of Faery.

> Wait a minute. I shouldn't have closed the door. There are some that look for me, and I wouldn't like them not to find me. Don't tell it to anybody, Blind Man. There are some that follow me. Boann herself out of the river and Fand out of the deep sea.[13]

It is as though the Fool's momentary consideration of the practical problem of dividing the chicken had closed the door on the images that are his almost constant companions. The Fool has been subject to the faery touch. His desire for the companionship of the supernatural beings is unequivocal.

Although he calls the faery-folk 'witches' the word holds none of the terror for him that it does for the Celtic warriors we are to meet in the next scene. The Fool's mention of the river goddess Boann and of Fand, brings to mind Cuchulain's meeting the hawklike goddess at the magic well in *At the Hawk's Well* and looks ahead to the meeting with Fand in *The Only Jealousy of Emer*. The goddesses who pursue the Fool are manifestations of the feminine principle, of the immortal moods, of human emotion.

> Witches they are, and they come by in the wind, and they cry, 'Give a kiss, Fool, give a kiss', that's what they cry. That's wide enough. All the witches can come in now. I wouldn't have them beat at the door and say, 'Where is the Fool? Why has he put a lock on the door?'[14]

So precious to the Fool are these images of vague desire that he is loathe to lock his heart against them. But practical considerations, an appetite for material things, causes him to betray those very 'witches' for whom he had just affirmed his devotion. 'Maybe they'll hear the bubbling of the pot and come in and sit on the ground. But we won't give them any of the fowl. Let them go back to the sea.'[15] The Fool's conflict here exactly parallels the conflict Cuchulain will face in the main plot of the play.

The Fool's reveries are interrupted by the Blind Man's exclamation: 'Ah! Ah —— ah ——.'[16] The Fool asks simply, 'why do you say 'Ah-ah?'[17] Much of the charm of the Fool consists in his naïve curiosity, the literalness of his perceptions, and his tendency to relate to life through mimicry rather than through analytic thought. The Blind Man explains. 'I know the big chair. It is today the High King Conchubar is coming. They have brought out his chair. He is going to be Cuchulain's master in earnest from this day out. It is that he's coming for.'[18]

By introducing the oath theme into the revised *On Baile's Strand* Yeats gave it an organic unity the first version lacked. In the revised version of the play Yeats displays a skill in the handling of exposition unknown in the 1904 version. The Fool is impressed by the news that Conchubar will be

Cuchulain's master. 'He must be a great man to be Cuchulain's master.'[19]

The link between the Blind Man and Conchubar is established by the Fool's praise of both of them. ('There's nobody in the world like you Blind Man.'[20]) The Blind Man agrees that Conchubar is great, for he is over all the rest of the kings of Ireland. The Fool is puzzled. 'Cuchulain's master! I thought Cuchulain could do anything he liked.'[21] In a state of freedom, Cuchulain is all-capable. External restraints set up to curb his will would be a violation of his nature. However, the Blind Man explains that the Hound of Ulster is to be denatured and domesticated.

> So he did, so he did. But he ran too wild, and Conchubar is coming today to put an oath upon him that will stop his rambling and make him as biddable as a housedog and keep him always at his hand. He will sit in this chair and put the oath upon him.[22]

We see now why the Blind Man said 'Ah — ah!' with such satisfaction when he noticed the great chair. The Fool, to whom all acts are acts of magic, particularly the capture of the spirit of Cuchulain, asks: 'How will he do that?'[23] The Blind Man, knowing that the political strategy by which Conchubar accomplishes his aims is of a world of experience foreign to the Fool, says: 'You have no wits to understand such things.'[24] If the Fool had such wits it would be less easy to cheat him of the chicken.

The scenes between Fool and Blind Man in the final version of the play are altogether masterful. As I have pointed out, Yeats has made the function of these figures in the play purposely ambiguous. We may consider that they are working out a comic parody of the main plot, or that they are engaged in a kind of ritual enactment that somehow determines the main plot. The Blind Man's play acting, like that of Falstaff, parodies and comments on real events, yet this enactment of future events by masked figures representing the combatants who turn the wheel of life has an air of magic about it.

The Blind Man assumes the role of Conchubar.

He will sit up in this chair and he'll say: 'Take the oath, Cuchulain. I bid you take the oath. Do as I tell you. What are your wits compared with mine, and what are your riches compared with mine? And what sons have you to pay your debts and to put a stone over you when you die? Take the oath, I tell you. Take a strong oath.'[25]

The Fool, falling into the role assigned him, crumples himself up and whines. 'I will not. I'll take no oath. I want my dinner.'[26] There seems, in the Fool's insistence on getting his dinner, to be much more at stake than the chicken which simmers in the pot. The appetite the Blind Man has promised to satisfy in the Fool goes beyond that which produces stomach pains. The Blind Man eventually will satisfy this hunger with feathers and not with the chicken. But, like the fate of Cuchulain, the Fool's dinner is not yet prepared. The Blind Man tries to silence the Fool's whining: 'Hush, hush! It is not done yet.'[27] The Fool objects: 'You said it was done to the turn.'[28] In a speech which might refer equally to the chicken in the pot or the destiny being prepared for Cuchulain, the Blind Man works to increase the Fool's appetite.

Did I, now? Well it might be done, and not done. The wings might be white, but the legs might be red. The flesh might stick hard to the bones and not come away in the teeth. But believe me, Fool, it will be well done before you put your teeth in it.[29]

In the light of the somewhat sinister tone of the Blind Man's speech, the Fool's reply is at once comic and chilling: 'My teeth are growing long with the hunger.'[30] This hunger of the Fool is related to the headlong passion with which the 'doom-eager' Cuchulain will seek his fate.

The irony of the scene that follows lies in the ambiguity of the Fool's appetite and the Blind Man's skill in playing upon this ambiguity. On the stage it is a very funny scene. But beneath the humour there is an awful sense that in some way these two are working together to produce the destiny of Cuchulain. The Blind Man begins to tell a story, apparently to take the Fool's mind off his appetite.

I'll tell you a story — the kings have story-tellers while

they are waiting for their dinner — I will tell you a story with a fight in it, a story with a champion in it, and a ship and a queen's son that has his mind set on killing somebody that you and I know.[31]

But, in another sense, the Fool's appetite is increased. 'Who is that? Who is he coming to kill?'[32]

> *Blind Man.* Wait, now, till you hear. When you were stealing the fowl, I was lying in a hole in the sand, and I heard three men coming with a shuffling sort of noise. They were wounded and groaning.
> *Fool.* Go on. Tell me about the fight.[33]

It is the action itself that fascinates the Fool. He is little interested in the detailed results of the action.

> *Blind Man.* There had been a fight, a great fight, a tremendous great fight. . . .[34]

This scene is mysteriously comic on stage and more than a little horrifying. Much of the irony rests in the fact that the Fool's promptings determine to a large extent the course the narrative takes. If the Fool's excitement symbolises Cuchulain's eagerness to play out his own destiny, then the implications of this are considerable. Comic irony and tragic irony are often two aspects of the same situation.

> . . . A young man had landed on the shore, the guardians of the shore had asked his name, and he had refused to tell it, and he had killed one, and the others had run away.
> *Fool.* That's enough. Come on now to the fowl. I wish it was bigger. I wish it was big as a goose.[35]

The fool tries to have the Blind Man break off the narrative at this point. Is he overcome by physical hunger or is he avoiding an area of dangerous knowledge?

> *Blind Man.* Hush! I haven't told you all. I know who that young man is. I heard the men who were running away say he had red hair, that he had come from Aoife's country, that he was coming to kill Cuchulain.[36]

Yeats' strategy in withholding the knowledge of the young man's parentage in this version of the play makes for a much stronger dramatic structure. The Fool's inability to grasp the significance of the clues the Blind Man gives him greatly increases his symbolic significance.

> *Fool.* Nobody can do that.[37]

The Fool seizes on the challenge to Cuchulain's prowess implied in the Blind Man's words rather than on the knowledge which if properly understood could prevent tragedy. This parallels Cuchulain's own reaction to the situation he finds himself in when the young man arrives at court to challenge him. Like the Fool he has all the elements of essential knowledge, but does not make the connections.

The Fool sings what we are obviously meant to take as a traditional song about Cuchulain's exploits. In the song, Cuchulain is portrayed as a semi-divine hero possessing great powers over the natural and the supernatural worlds. Thus, Yeats places the supernatural exploits attributed to Cuchulain in the old sagas in a kind of 'frame'. The Cuchulain we meet in the next scene is very much a mortal man, though he boasts to Conchubar and to the Young Man about his divine parentage.

> Cuchulain has killed kings,
> Kings and the sons of kings,
> Dragons out of the water,
> And witches out of the air,
> Banachas and Bonachas and people of the woods.[38]

It is partly his awareness of such legends as those sung of by the Fool that prompts Cuchulain to fight the Young Man, obviously the son of a king, when it is suggested that the Young Man has used witchcraft against him. The knowledge that they have already begun to leave names upon the harp sharpens the sense of honour of Celtic heroes. The Fool's mention of the slaying of a water dragon is interesting in light of Cuchulain's eventual fight with the sea. In Lady Gregory's book, the Banachas and Bonachas accompany Cuchulain when he goes into battle.[39] They are probably related to the *banshee* whose cry signals imminent death.

> Witches that steal the milk,
> Fomor that steal the children,
> Hags that have heads like hares,
> Hares that have claws like witches,
> All riding a-cock-horse
> Out of the very bottom of the bitter black North.[40]

The Fool's song is rich in the details of folk-belief. Witches were often thought to be responsible for the souring of milk, and the country people in Celtic countries were accustomed to put out milk to appease the faery-folk. Fomorians, according to Douglas Hyde, means 'men from under the sea'; every Samhain the Nemedians, according to the old sagas, had to deliver to the Fomorians of Tory Island two-thirds of their children, corn and cattle. The image of shape-changers taking the form or partial form of hares adds greatly to the horrifying phantasmagoria the Fool's songs evokes. The bitter black north referred to is the northern sea, the cock-horses a grotesque form of the horses of Mannannan, the sea god. We have seen that the sea symbolises the unconscious mind. The North for Yeats was associated with the night and with sleep. The world conjured up by the Fool's song is one in which horrifying images ride out of our sleep on very real nightmares. The images which ride those nightmares are of great significance to Cuchulain's destiny, having to do with the stealing of milk which is used to sustain the young and with the stealing of children. Though Cuchulain has slain such enemies as these images in the past, now in his confusion he will be overcome by them.

> *Blind Man.* Hush, I say!
> *Fool.* Does Cuchulain know that he is coming to kill him?
> *Blind Man.* How would he know that with his head in the
>   clouds. . . .[41]

This strongly suggests the parallel between the Fool and Cuchulain.

> He doesn't care for common fighting. Why should he put himself out, and nobody in it but the young man? Now if it were a white fawn that might turn into a queen before morning — [42]

The Blind Man rightly divines that Cuchulain, like the Fool, is a pursuer of the goddesses, that war for him must always be linked to love.

> *Fool.* Come to the fowl. I wish it was as big as a pig; a fowl with goose grease and pig's crackling.[43]

The goose and pig are both connected in Celtic mythology with heroic themes. Cuchulain, in *The Green Helmet,* referred to his approaching death as the flight of a great barnacle goose. The pig is also intimately connected with the theme of death in old stories. The more the Fool tries to bring the subject back to the fowl the closer we come to an exposition of Cuchulain's fate.

> *Blind Man.* No hurry, no hurry. I know whose son it is. I wouldn't tell anybody else, but I will tell you, — a secret is better to you than your dinner. You like being told secrets.
> *Fool.* Tell me the secret.[44]

The Blind Man's trickery brings such confusion to the Fool that his hunger for the chicken merges with a hunger for the tragic fate of Cuchulain.

> *Blind Man.* That young man is Aoife's son. I am sure it is Aoife's son. You have often heard me talking of Aoife, the great woman-fighter in the North?
> *Fool.* I know, I know. She is one of those cross queens that live in hungry Scotland.[45]

In view of what has gone on in this scene, the use of the adjective 'hungry' to describe the land of Aoife is interesting.

> *Blind Man.* I am sure it is her son. I was in Aoife's country for a long time.
> *Fool.* That was before you were blinded for putting a curse upon the wind.[46]

This mysterious reference invites us to question more deeply the identity of the Blind Man. In the early version of the play, when the Blind Man was individualised and named Fintain, the incident of the blinding was tied to an occurrence on shipboard and obviously related to the winds vital to navigation. Yeats has eliminated all details in this version of the play. In the context of the symbolism of the entire play cycle the curse upon the wind can only refer to the Blind Man's attitude towards the people of the Sidhe. Physical blinding would be a fitting punishment meted out by supernatural beings to one who had proven himself spiritually blind. When the plays of the Cuchulain cycle are played in sequence on a single night, the audience is drawn to associate the Blind Man with the Old Man in *At the Hawk's Well.* The Old Man did in fact deliver such a curse in that play. ('And who are you who rail/Upon those dancers all others bless?' Cuchulain asks, and when the Old Man returns to consciousness after the waters of the well have risen and fallen again he says: 'Accursed dancers, you have stolen my life./That there should be such evil in a shadow.') If the cycle is played with this connection in mind, the symmetry of Yeats' dramatic design is emphasised. The cycle opens with a conflict between Cuchulain and the Old Man; the middle play has a conflict between Fool and Blind Man; the final play ends with a scene between Cuchulain and the Blind Man.

The Blind Man tells the Fool that Aoife had in her house a boy who had her own red colour on him. He tells how this boy was brought up to kill Cuchulain. No motive is given for Aoife's antagonism to Cuchulain. In *The Death of Cuchulain* Aoife will tell Cuchulain she hated him because he left her. The real operative force is the curse which fell upon Cuchulain at the Hawk's Well. He can never know love unmixed with hate.

Cuchulain's step is heard outside and the Blind Man tells the Fool that Cuchulain is going to meet Conchubar, who has bidden him to take the oath. The sudden return to the idea of the oath Conchubar wants Cuchulain to take thoroughly confuses the Fool.

> What a mix-up you make of everything, Blind Man! You were telling me one story, and now you are telling me another story. . . . How can I get the hang of it at the end if you mix everything at the beginning? Wait till I settle it out.[47]

It is a mark of Yeats' skill at exposition that he is actually able to introduce a review here and turn it to comic purpose.

The Fool, in his confusion, speaks for the audience which is trying to cope with Yeats' highly condensed dramatic form. The Fool's comic recapitulation disarms the audience which might otherwise object to Yeats' underlining of the main issues. But how can *they* get everything straight at the end if everything is mixed up at the beginning? The Fool's objection that the Blind Man tells him one story and then tells him another would have been a valid criticism of Yeats' plotting in the first version of *On Baile's Strand*. In the revised version Yeats has managed to 'settle it out'. The two stories are now interconnected; the irony is that neither the Fool nor Cuchulain can see the connections.

The Fool sets up a primitive allegory in which one of his feet represents Cuchulain and one the Young Man. Conchubar is represented by the Fool's money bag. The Fool throws his hat up in the air to represent Aoife. But allegory is really of very little help. Making one thing stand for another in a mechanical and arbitrary fashion does not increase our knowledge of the things themselves or give us insight into their relationships. Symbolism, which operates on quite a different principle, does increase knowledge. It is to the symbolism of the entire scene between Blind Man and Fool that the audience must go if they would understand the meaning of what is about to happen. For a moment the Fool realises what the Blind Man is doing in distracting him from the chicken. 'It's many a time you cheated me before with your lies. Come to the cooking-pot, my stomach is pinched and rusty. Would you have it creaking like a gate?'[48]

The Fool shows his awareness of the treacherous tendency in the Blind Man. In the next scene Cuchulain will accurately describe Conchubar's motives and his strategy. Ironically, neither the Fool nor Cuchulain seems to be able to act upon such knowledge.

> *Blind Man.* Listen. I know who the young man's father is, but I won't say. I would be afraid to say. Ah, Fool, you would forget everything if you could know who the young man's father is.

> *Fool.* Who is it? Tell me now quick, or I'll shake you. Come, out with it, or I'll shake you.[49]

In exactly parallel circumstances Cuchulain will threaten the
Blind Man with physical violence in the last scene of the play.

> *Blind Man.* Wait, wait. There's somebody coming. . . . It is
> Cuchulain is coming. He's coming back with the High
> King. Go and ask Cuchulain. He'll tell you. It's little
> you'll care about the cooking pot when you have asked
> Cuchulain that . . .[50]

In the soliloquy that follows, Yeats achieves some of his
finest comic effects. Yet this is an important struggle, not
just a comic decoration. If the Fool is in some sense
Cuchulain's spirit or Cuchulain's imagination, his inability to
ask Cuchulain about the parentage of the Young Man is
highly significant. The Fool fails to ask Cuchulain this
all-important question because of cowardice. Is Cuchulain's
failure to ask himself the right questions a kind of spiritual or
imaginative cowardice? Does he avoid the knowledge that
could avert tragedy because of some strange failure of nerve?

> *Fool.* I'll ask him. Cuchulain will know. He was in Aoife's
> country. [*Goes up stage.*] I'll ask him. [*Turns and goes
> down stage.*] But no, I won't ask him, I would be afraid.
> [*Going up again.*] Yes, I will ask him. What harm in
> asking? The Blind Man said I was to ask him. [*Going
> down.*] No, no. I'll not ask him. He might kill me. I
> have but killed hens and geese and pigs. He has killed
> kings. [*Goes up again almost to big door.*] Who says I'm
> afraid? I'm not afraid. I'm no coward. I'll ask him. No,
> no, Cuchulain, I'm not going to ask you.[51]

The confusion and conflict here foreshadow the confusion
and conflict which will drive Cuchulain mad in the last scene
in the play. As he leaves, the Fool sings again the song of
Cuchulain's exploits.

> He has killed kings,
> Kings and the sons of kings,
> Dragons out of the water,
> And witches out of the air,
> Banachas and Bonachas and people of the woods.[52]

Ironically Cuchulain's entrance line points out that he has

been summoned before Conchubar to swear an oath of loyalty precisely because of such actions as have brought him fame.

> Because I have killed men without your bidding
> And have rewarded others at my own pleasure . . .
> You'd lay this oath upon me . . .[53]

And Cuchulain casts scorn upon the suggestion.

III

In the discussion between Cuchulain and Conchubar about the loyalty oath, Conchubar stresses such considerations as social responsibility, the desirability of a politically stable state and the need to maintain a sound system of defence. To Cuchulain such considerations are as pebbles when weighed against the value of personal freedom. The occasion which has prompted Conchubar's summoning of Cuchulain is the landing of the Young Man from Aoife's country on a shore which Cuchulain has left ill-guarded. Cuchulain's preference for the ecstatic life is in clear conflict with the interests of the state. Says Conchubar:

> He came to land
> While you were somewhere out of sight and hearing,
> Hunting or dancing with your wild companions.[54]

Cuchulain sees the Young Man's invasion as insufficient reason to place curbs on the freedom of his noble spirit.

> He can be driven out. I'll not be bound.
> I'll dance, or hunt, or quarrel or make love,
> Wherever and whenever I've a mind to.
> If time had not put water in your blood,
> You never would have thought it.[55]

Cuchulain's speeches are filled with references to conflict of the elements, the four basic substances — earth, air, fire and water — in terms of which man must work out his spiritual destiny. According to the magical tradition each element had associated with it a separate order of supernatural being. These four orders of 'elementals' are the people of the Sidhe, the shape-changers, the gods of the ancient Celts. Cuchulain's passionate nature and his association with the sun-god mark him as having a special relationship with the fire-spirits. Conchubar once also had fire in his blood but time has put water in it.

Conchubar pursues the precise line of argument the Blind Man predicted.

> I would leave
> A strong and settled country to my children.[56]

The fact that it is the oath which was to make life safe for the children of Conchubar and the other kings that robs Cuchulain of his own child is the central irony of the play. Cuchulain sees the oath as a device which will bring political subordination and humiliation to the one warrior whose very name has kept the country safe and who has protected Conchubar from foreign invasion and internal rebellion whenever the need arose. To take the oath would be to become like 'some cattle-raising king'.[57]

Cuchulain's distinction between cattle-raising and warrior kings is significant in the light of the final song of *At the Hawk's Well* and it helps to make clear the nature of Cuchulain's commitment in that play. Ironically, because Cuchulain has looked into the eyes of the hawk and cannot live all his days 'Where a hand on the bell/Can call the milch cows . . .', his swearing of an oath appropriate to a cattle-raising king will bring the hawk's curse down upon him. In his bitterness Cuchulain asks:

> Am I
> So slack and idle that I need a whip
> Before I serve you?[58]

In Cuchulain's view, what distinguishes man from beast is his recognition that 'a free gift is better than a forced', that he is capable of free will and thus of self-realisation. But from Conchubar's point of view, the problem with service offered as a free gift is that it may be withheld any time the giver loses respect for the receiver of the service. The gift of Cuchulain's loyalty is personal and does not relate to the office of High King. According to Conchubar his children fear that Cuchulain's loyalty will not be extended to them. They say to their father:

> How can we be at safety with this man
> That nobody can buy or bid or bind?
> We shall be at his mercy when you are gone;
> He burns the earth as if he were a fire,
> And time can never touch him.[59]

Cuchulain, whose ecstatic spirit relates to the condition of fire, is an obvious threat to those for whom the old fiery fountains are far off. The imagery here is appropriate to one who considers himself a son of the sun god and who may be a sun god himself. Cuchulain reacts to Conchubar's words with a scorn and caustic sarcasm that make him an altogether stronger character than he was in Yeats' first version of this play. He now conforms more consistently to the concept of him outlined in Yeats' letter to Frank Fay.

> The touch of something hard, repellent yet alluring, self assertive yet self immolating, is not all but it must be there. He is the fool —— wandering passive, houseless and almost loveless. Conchobhar is reason that is blind because it can only reason because it is cold. Are they not the cold moon and the hot sun?[60]

Yeats introduces the idea that Cuchulain is offspring of the sun god in a patronising and mocking speech of Conchubar.

> And you for all the wildness of your blood,
> And though your father came out of the sun,
> Are but a little king and weigh but light
> In anything that touches government,
> If put into the balance with my children.[61]

Cuchulain advises plain speech. Both he and Conchubar find their origin in some time when fire and earth were in greater contact. The noble and passionate nature that this has given them marks them as greater than other men. Therefore they should be more truthful to each other.

> We in our young days
> Have seen the heavens like a burning cloud
> Brooding upon the world, and being more
> Than men can be now that cloud's lifted up,
> We should be the more truthful.[62]

Mortality for a man like Cuchulain can be based only on loyalty to the laws of his own passionate nature. The truth is that Cuchulain simply does not like Conchubar's children.

> — they have no pith,
> No marrow in their bones, and will lie soft
> Where you and I lie hard.[63]

As the Blind Man predicted, Cuchulain's own childless state becomes the basis for one of Conchubar's principal arguments.

> You rail at them
> Because you have no children of your own.[64]

Cuchulain denies this, picking up the theme that the present generation bears little evidence of that 'condition of fire' which marked the heroic age which seems now to be past.

> I think myself most lucky that I leave
> No pallid ghost or mockery of a man
> To drift and mutter in the corridors
> Where I have laughed and sung.[65]

In the argument which follows, Conchubar puts forth the claims of family and race against Cuchulain's championing of the claims of the individual. It is a struggle between objectivity and subjectivity, between hunchback and hero. It is a central struggle of human experience. As Yeats said in a late poem:

> Many times man lives and dies
> Between his two eternities,
> That of race and that of soul,
> And ancient Ireland knew it all.[66]

Life, as the singing women will tell us, drifts between a Fool and a Blind Man to the end, and nobody can know his end.

Cuchulain claims that those who 'leave names upon the harp' have no longing for children. (Himself on the wind is the gift that he gives.) Conchubar disputes this. He reminds Cuchulain of the Scottish queen with 'stone-pale cheek and red-brown hair' and of Cuchulain's boast that he would sooner 'that fierce woman of the camp' bore him a son than any other.[67] Conchubar's choice of term prompts Cuchulain brilliantly to satirise the place held by women in the reasonable world of Conchubar.

> You call her 'fierce woman of the camp',
> For, having lived among the spinning-wheels
> You'd have no woman near that would not say,
> 'Ah! how wise!' 'What will you have for supper?'
> 'What shall I wear that I may please you, sir?'
> And keep that humming through the day and night
> For ever. A fierce woman of the camp![68]

Conchubar values women for the sake of service and flattery. Men of heroic temper value only women of spirit; for them love will always be conflict, love and hate inextricably mixed.

> But I am getting angry about nothing.
> You have never seen her. Ah! Conchubar, had you seen her
> With that high, laughing, turbulent head of hers
> Thrown backward, and the bowstring at her ear,
> Or sitting at the fire with those grave eyes
> Full of good counsel as it were with wine,
> Or when love ran through all the lineaments
> Of her wild body — although she had no child,
> None other had all beauty, queen or lover,
> Or was so fitted to give birth to kings.[69]

The autobiographical element is strong here and images from Yeats' own life come to mind. ('Maud Gonne at Howth station waiting a train,/Pallas Athene in that straight back and arrogant head.'[70])

Conchubar tries to end Cuchulain's revery.

> There's nothing I can say but drifts you farther
> From the one weighty matter.[71]

Conchubar accuses Cuchulain of being, like the Fool, unable to concentrate on the matter at hand. Ironically, what Cuchulain is discussing is relevant to the matter at hand. But the present line of discussion may lead Cuchulain into areas of insight not convenient to Conchubar.

> That very woman —
> For I know well that you are praising Aoife —

> Now hates you and will leave no subtlety
> Unknotted that might run into a noose
> About your throat, no army in idleness
> That might bring ruin on this land you serve.[72]

Cuchulain does not find the situation surprising.

> No wonder in that, no wonder at all in that.
> I never have known love but as a kiss
> In the mid-battle, and a difficult truce
> Of oil and water, candles and dark night,
> Hillside and hollow, the hot-footed moon —
> A brief forgiveness been opposites
> That have been hatred for three times the age
> Of this long-established ground.[73]

Sex is here seen as the archetypal division, the prototype of all the antinomies in the fallen world. Like Cuchulain's reference to a world falling away from a prior tradition of fire, this idea is one of the doctrines of the alchemical and kabbalistic traditions. The idea Cuchulain expresses here is closely related to the Nietzschean view of sexual relations. In *The Birth of Tragedy* Nietzsche says: 'Procreation depends on the duality of the sexes, involving perpetual strife with only periodically intervening reconciliations.'[74] William Blake also commented that 'sexual love is founded upon spiritual hate'.[75] In *Per Amica Silentia Lunae* related this to the conflict a man must engage in with his daemon in the working out of his destiny. His comments in this connection have particular relevance to the underlying action in the Cuchulain plays. Yeats writes:

> Then my imagination runs from Daemon to sweetheart, and I divine an analogy that evades the intellect. I remember that Greek antiquity has bid us look for the principal stars, that govern enemy and sweetheart alike, among those that are about to set, in the Seventh House as the astrologers say; and it may be 'sexual love', which is 'founded upon spiritual hate,' is an image of the warfare of man and Daemon; and I even wonder if there may not be some secret communion, some whispering in the dark between Daemon and sweetheart.[76]

Conchubar is less concerned with the spiritual inevitability
of the enmity of of Aoife for Cuchulain than with its
practical consequences.

> Aoife makes war on us, and every day
> Our enemies grow greater and beat the walls
> More bitterly, and you within the walls
> Are every day more turbulent; and yet,
> When I would speak about these things, your fancy
> Runs as it were a swallow on the wind.[77]

Accused of the Fool's tendency to let his mind wander,
Cuchulain is actually the one capable of seeing the situation
in its true light. The frame of reference of his thinking is
mythological and not political. He sees every event in the
context of a total metaphysical pattern. This breadth of
vision makes it impossible for him to concentrate on those
elements in a situation which to the spiritually blind
Conchubar constitute reality.

Conchubar points to the door where the other kings have
gathered to await Cuchulain's decision. Both the old counsel-
lors who constitute Conchubar's party and the younger kings,
dancers and harp-players who follow Cuchulain, are represented. All, says Conchubar, wait anxiously for news that
Cuchulain will be bound into obedience and so make the land
safe for them and their children.

> You are but half a king and I but half;
> I need your might of hand and burning heart,
> And you my wisdom.[78]

Conchubar has already rejected Cuchulain's burning heart,
and will confirm that rejection later. Conchubar's 'wisdom'
without warmth of heart is a cold thing indeed. Cuchulain's
son will be destroyed by Conchubar's cold mind and
Cuchulain's mighty hand, while Cuchulain's burning heart
will drive him mad.

In imagery which brings to mind Cuchulain's commitment
at the Hawk's Well Cuchulain addresses his followers. He
depends on their being as fully committed to the hawk's life
as he is.

> Nestlings of a high nest,
> Hawks that have followed me into the air
> And looked upon the sun, we'll out of this
> And sail upon the wind once more.[79]

Confident that they will follow him he prepares to resume the ecstatic life.

> This king
> Would have me take an oath to do his will,
> And having listened to his tune from morning,
> I will no more of it. Run to the stable
> And set the horses to the chariot-pole,
> And send a messenger to the harp-players,
> We'll find a level place among the woods,
> And dance awhile.[80]

Cuchulain has been tricked into surrendering his aristocratic will to the demands of a democratic voice vote, and of course the jury has been fixed by Conchubar. All of the kings shout out that Cuchulain should take the oath. Cuchulain has talked about 'sailing upon the wind'. His followers, now settled men, speak of their dread of 'this turbulence'.

Conchubar has stolen the chicken. Having cleverly manipulated Cuchulain into a position where he is faced with extreme disappointment at what he considers betrayal by his followers, he will now press the oath upon him. In his bitterness, Cuchulain loses all will to resist.

> It's time the years put water in my blood
> And drowned the wildness of it . . .[81]

We return to the theme of the opposition of fire and water. Cuchulain realises he is out of phase in a world run by Conchubar. He betrays his own nature in trying to adjust.

> for all's changed,
> But that unchanged.[82]

Only Cuchulain's blood remains in the condition of fire, true to the fiery cloud in which he was conceived.

> I'll take what oath you will:
> The moon, the sun, the water, light or air,
> I do not care how binding.[83]

In the magical tradition, the most potent rituals are those
which invoke the sun, the moon and the elements.
Cuchulain's oath will be sworn on his own element, fire. But
it is a fire lighted from the hearth, fire brought into the
service of domestic values, not the fire of the fiery cloud, the
sun, or of the old fiery fountains which are the source of all
life. Conchubar will attempt to use flames from the hearth
fire magically to subdue the flames of Cuchulain's burning
heart and to make them too serve domestic values.
Conchubar says:

> On this fire
> That has been lighted from your hearth and mine;
> The older men shall be my witnesses,
> The younger yours. The holders of the fire
> Shall purify the thresholds of the house
> With waving fire, and shut the outer door,
> According to the custom; and sing rhyme
> That has come down from the old law-makers
> To blow the witches out.[84]

The Fool's words come back to us: 'I wouldn't have them
beat at the door and say, "Where is the Fool? Why has he put
a lock on the door?" '[85] Conchubar continues:

> Considering
> That the wild will of man could be oath-bound,
> But that a woman's could not, they bid us sing
> Against the will of woman at its wildest
> In the Shape-Changers that run upon the wind.[86]

We see now how thoroughly Cuchulain has been tricked by
Conchubar, how little the debate we have heard has really
been about unguarded borders. The central issue has really
been Cuchulain's spiritual allegiance. Shall his burning heart
owe allegiance to the fiery cloud or to the hearth? Shall he sit
among the spinning wheels or continue to play at hazard with
the will of woman at its wildest, whether it manifest itself in
the Shape-changers or in the indomitable spirit of a woman
such as Aoife? Three women, keepers of the sacred fire, sing
these words as the oath-taking ceremony proceeds:

> May this fire have driven out
> The Shape-changers that can put
> Ruin on a great king's house
> Until all be ruinous.[87]

The spirits of the wind are driven out by the flames of the
hearth fire. The spirits of the wind are seen as the source of
all tragedy, bringing general calamity through the destruction
of dynasties.

> Names whereby a man has known
> The threshold and the hearthstone,
> Gather on the wind and drive
> Women none can kiss and thrive,
> For they are but whirling wind,
> Out of memory and mind.[88]

Only the spirits of the hearth and home can drive from a
man's mind images of the 'pale windy people', women whose
kiss is disastrous to mortals.

> They would make a prince decay
> With light images of clay
> Planted in the running wave;[89]

This is a somewhat obscure reference. I think the most likely
meaning in context would involve the shape-changing ability
of the Sidhe. When a man looks into the water he seems to
see human shapes, in longing for which he may go mad. Or in
the case of Cuchulain 'light images of clay' in the likeness of
Conchubar may cause him to take arms against the waves
themselves.

> Or, for many shapes they have,
> They would change them into hounds
> Until he had died of his wounds,
> Though the change were but a whim;[90]

The following of the faery hounds led inevitably to disaster,
as in the case of Red Hanrahan.[91] Yeats has told us that when
the faery hounds appear in mythology in pursuit of the faery
deer, the hounds represent the desire of man for woman and
the deer the desire of woman for the desire of man.[92]

> Or they'd hurl a spell at him,
> That he follow with desire
> Bodies that can never tire
> Or grow kind, for they anoint,
> All their bodies joint by joint
> With a miracle-working juice
> That is made out of the grease
> Of the ungoverned unicorn.[93]

In *The Only Jealousy of Emer,* Emer says of the woman of the Sidhe

> 　　　　　　I know her sort.
> They find our men asleep, weary with war,
> Lap them in cloudy hair or kiss their lips;
> Our men awake in ignorance of it all,
> But when we take them in our arms at night
> We cannot break their solitude.[94]

The unicorn, Yeats has said, represents 'a type of masterful and beautiful life.'[95] The Sidhe can never tire or grow kind because of their total commitment to a masterful and beautiful life. This commitment is shared by such indomitable women as Aoife. That is why she casts an 'evil shadow' on any man who would love her.[96]

> But that man is thrice forlorn,
> Empty, ruined, wracked, and lost,
> That they follow, for at most
> They will give him kiss for kiss
> While they murmur, 'After this
> Hatred may be sweet to the taste'.[97]

'No wonder in that, no wonder at all in that,' Cuchulain has said, accepting a love which is 'a brief forgiveness between opposites/That have been hatreds for three times the age/Of this long-'stablished ground.'[98]

> Those wild hands that have embraced
> All his body can but shove
> At the burning wheel of love
> Till the side of hate come up.[99]

The use of this wheel image by the singing women is

significant. Taken together with Yeats' comment that the Fool and Blind Man represent 'those combatants who turn the wheel of life', it establishes the prominence of cyclical patterns in Yeats' thought long before his wife's automatic writing began to dictate the details of the system outlined in *A Vision*. This wheel of love, which is also the wheel of Cuchulain's life, provides a framework for the whole Cuchulain cycle.

> Therefore in this ancient cup
> May the sword-blades drink their fill
> Of the home-brew there, until
> They will have for masters none
> But the threshold and hearthstone.[100]

In a ritual replete with sexual significance, the symbols of conflict and domesticity are united.

Cuchulain addresses his followers:

> I'll take and keep this oath, and from this day
> I shall be what you please, my chicks, my nestlings.
> Yet I had thought you were of those that praised
> Whatever life could make the pulse run quickly,
> Even though it were brief, and that you held
> That a free gift was better than a forced.—[101]

He briefly remembers the heroic values by which he has heretofore lived. 'But that's all over.—'[102] Cuchulain sees the oath, not as a simple affirmation of allegiance, but as a renunciation of the values which are the laws of his very nature.

> I will keep it to;
> I never gave a gift and took it again.[103]

The very surrender of his freedom has become a noble act, since he sees it not as a concession to Conchubar but as a gift to his followers. His sense of honour will make him keep the oath. When an impulse more basic than honour causes him to attack the High King, he will be thrown into confusion and assume he must be bewitched.

> If the wild horse should break the chariot-pole,
> It would be punished. Should that be in the oath?[104]

Cuchulain's bitterness at what his followers have asked him to do is still apparent. He points out to his followers the full implications of the servitude he is entering into for their sake. The humiliating punishments which must be inflicted during the breaking of a wild horse provides an appropriate image for the process of subduing a warrior of Cuchulain's spirit.

> I swear to be obedient in all things
> To Conchubar, and to uphold his children.[105]

Ironically, obedience to Conchubar will rob him of his own child.

Conchubar assumes control of the ceremony. 'We are one being, as these flames are one.'[106] The fire has been lit from Conchubar's and Cuchulain's hearth fire. The concept of interdependence put forth by Conchubar is not unlike that by which the Blind Man will try to calm the Fool after the chicken has been stolen. 'I give my wisdom, and I take your strength.'[107]

There is an ironic ambiguity in the phrase 'and I take your strength.'

> Now thrust the swords into the flame, and pray
> That they may serve the threshold and the hearthstone
> With faithful service.[108]

The opposition between the values represented by the Sidhe and those represented by threshold and hearthstone is a central issue throughout the entire play cycle. It provides the theme of the final song of *At the Hawk's Well*.

> 'The man that I praise',
> Cries out the empty well,
> 'Lives all his days
> Where a hand on the bell
> Can call the milch cows
> To *the comfortable door of his house*.
> Who but an idiot would praise
> Dry stones in a well?'
>
> 'The man that I praise',
> Cries out the leafless tree,
> 'Has married and stays

>   By *an old hearth*, and he
>   On naught has set store
>   But children and dogs on the floor
>   Who but an idiot would praise
>   A withered tree?'[109]

The conflict reaches its crisis in the climax of *On Baile's Strand*. Emer, in *The Only Jealousy of Emer*, expresses the hope that Cuchulain will return to the hearth in his old age, but is able to save him from merging entirely with the Sidhe only by giving up that hope.

Cuchulain looks into the flames and appears to achieve mystical contact with those fiery spirits which are so much a part of his own nature.

>   O pure, glittering ones
>   That should be more than wife or friend or mistress,
>   Give us the enduring will, the unquenchable hope,
>   The friendliness of the sword!—[110]

One wonders if Cuchulain is taking part in the same ritual as Conchubar. Is he perhaps, 'in the rout/Of the fire-born moods',[111] affirming allegiance to something deeper than Conchubar guesses? His speech seems more an affirmation of his own passionate nature than of loyalty to Conchubar.

Suddenly a cry is heard, demanding that the outer door be opened. Conchubar, proud to exhibit the wild stallion whose will he has subdued, orders that the caller be let in. It is the Young Man from Aoife's country. During the fire ceremony, the outer door had been shut against the witches. Now the influences of the 'will of woman at its wildest' re-enter the assembly, to do battle with Conchubar for the allegiance of Cuchulain.

IV

On entering the assembly house, the Young Man announces that he has come to weigh his sword against Cuchulain's sword. Conchubar demands that he first prove that he is of noble lineage, but the Young Man is under bonds not to reveal his name. His courage must serve as proof of his nobility. Cuchulain recognises the signs of nobility in the youth's hawklike nature and prepares to take up the challenge. The prospect of noble combat makes Conchubar's promise of wisdom seem of little account.

> What's wisdom to the hawk, when that clear eye
> Is burning nearer up in the high air?[112]

Leading the Young Man into the light, Cuchulain detects his strong resemblance to Aoife. The truth almost passes the threshold of his consciousness. But he dismisses it.

> You are from the North,
> Where there are many that have that tint of hair —
> Red-brown, the light red-brown.[113]

Like the Fool, Cuchulain is still unable to make the connections which would avert tragedy.

> Come nearer, boy,
> For I would have another look at you.
> There's more likeness — a pale, a stone-pale cheek.
> What brought you, boy? Have you no fear of death?[114]

The Young Man closely resembles the Cuchulain of *At the Hawk's Well* as well as his mother, Aoife. He professes the noble fatalism of the aristocratic warrior. 'Whether I live or die is in the gods' hands.'[115]

Cuchulain, whose own boasting has been noted by Conchubar, recognises when a professed indifferences to death is backed by real knowledge of what death is like. 'That is all words, all words; a young man's talk.'[116] He gently puts aside the Young Man's profession of courage and speaks in mythological terms of his own great luck and strength. If the outcome of the battle is in the gods' hands, then the Young Man should realise he has challenged a favourite of the gods.

> I am their plough, their harrow, their very strength;
> For he that's in the sun begot this body
> Upon a mortal woman, and I have heard tell
> It seemed as if he had outrun the moon
> That he must follow always through waste heaven,
> He loved so happily.[117]

Cuchulain's account of his supernatural origin is here not

qualified by such expressions as 'as men say' as it was when he spoke of it to Conchubar. In some versions of the old stories of Cuchulain he is the son of the Celtic sun god Lugh. In the overall pattern of Yeats' play cycle, Cuchulain himself represents the sun who must follow the moon always through waste heaven.

> He'll be but slow
> To break a tree that was so sweetly planted.[118]

Tree imagery and hawk imagery are related in the play cycle, as we have seen in *At the Hawk's Well*. Later the Fool will sing

> When you were an acorn on the tree-top,
> Then was I an eagle-cock;
> Now that you are a withered old block,
> Still am I an eagle-cock.[119]

Cuchulain asks to see the Young Man's arm and compares it with his own.

> That arm had a good father and a good mother
> But it is not like this.[120]

The irony of the scene increases as Cuchulain's words become more and more appropriate to a reality he does not recognise. The Young Man is angry at what he takes to be Cuchulain's patronising tone.

> You are mocking me;
> You think I'm not worthy to be fought,
> But I'll not wrangle but with this talkative knife.[121]

Actually it is the Young Man's very worthiness that makes Cuchulain want to put off the moment of conflict.

> Put up your sword; I am not mocking you.
> I'd have you for my friend, but if it's not
> Because you have a hot heart and a cold eye,
> I cannot tell the reason.[122]

The Young Man has his father's heart and mother's eye, but, though he finds the combination attractive, Cuchulain does not recognise its source.

> He has got her fierceness,
> And nobody is as fierce as those pale women.
> But I will keep him with me, Conchubar,
> That he may set my memory upon her
> When the day is fading.—[123]

In a very real sense, Cuchulain is bewitched. In spite of his oath, devotion to hearth and threshold is forgotten in the presence of this reminder of 'woman's will at its wildest'. The very fierceness of the Young Man's determination to kill Cuchulain makes him attractive. Hatred is sweet to the taste.

> You will stop with us,
> And we will hunt the deer and the wild bulls;
> And when we have grown weary, light our fires
> Between the wood and water, or on some mountain
> Where the Shape-Changers of the morning come.[124]

Cuchulain's lyrical description of the ecstatic life belies the fact that he has just said: 'But that's all over'. He is still a devotee of the Shape-Changers, the 'women none can kiss and thrive'.

> The High King would make a mock of me
> Because I did not take a wife among them.[125]

Cuchulain's reference to his confrontation with Conchubar shows little awareness that its outcome has altered his entire situation. The oath is far from his mind at this point. The Young Man is embarrassed by Cuchulain's intimate tone. Cuchulain asks:

> Why do you hang your head? It's a good life:
> The head grows prouder in the light of the dawn,
> And friendship thickens in the murmuring dark
> Where the spare hazels meet the wool-white foam.[126]

The mystic atmosphere of a place of natural magic is evoked.

> But I can see there's no more need for words
> And that you'll be my friend from this day out.[127]

The nobility of Cuchulain's words has won the friendship of the Young Man. This friendship would now be sealed if

Conchubar did not interrupt to remind Cuchulain of the demands of the political world Cuchulain has sworn allegiance to.

> He has come hither not in his own name
> But in Queen Aoife's and has challenged us
> In challenging the foremost man of us all.[128]

Cuchulain seems not to comprehend the implications of this.

> Well, well, what matter?[129]

Cuchulain is, as far as the subtleties of politics are concerned, the Fool. Conchubar points out his folly.

> You think it does not matter,
> And that a fancy lighter than the air,
> A whim of the moment, has more matter in it,
> For, having none that shall reign after you,
> You cannot think as I do, who would leave
> A throne too high for insult.[130]

All of Conchubar's efforts on behalf of his children seem somehow abstract in comparison to Cuchulain's instinctive response to his own unrecognised child. Cuchulain's folly is true wisdom because unlike Conchubar's cleverness it is not cold. Cuchulain is unimpressed by Conchubar's argument.

> Let your children
> Re-mortar their inheritance, as we have,
> And put more muscle on.[131]

He turns to the Young Man to initiate an exchange of gifts, a ritual by which an immediate contest may be avoided without loss of honour.

> I'll give you gifts,
> But I'd have some thing too — that arm-ring, boy.
> We'll have this quarrel out when you are older.[132]

The Young Man is drawn to Cuchulain but fears he may be dishonoured if he abandons his mission.

> There is no man I'd sooner have my friend
> Than you, whose name has gone about the world
> As if it had been the wind; but Aoife'd say
> I had turned coward.[133]

Cuchulain points out that the exchange of gifts eliminates any dishonour that might be associated with a decision not to fight.

> I will give you gifts
> That Aoife'll know and all her people know,
> To have come from me. My father gave me this.
> He came to try me, rising up at dawn
> Out of the cold dark of the rich sea.
> He challenged me to battle, but before
> My sword had touched his sword, told me his name,
> Gave me this cloak, and vanished.[134]

In the old sagas, the details of Cuchulain's meeting with his father Lugh were quite different. Yeats has created a ritual for the acknowledgement of parenthood. Apparently Lugh, like Cuchulain, would not own as his son anyone who would not meet even himself in battle. The gift of the cloak becomes an acceptance of Cuchulain as his son. By proposing that he re-enact this ritual with the Young Man Cuchulain is tacitly accepting him as his son, even though he is not consciously aware of their relationship.

> It was woven
> By women of the Country-under-Wave
> Out of the fleeces of the sea.[135]

If the 'nine forsaken sea queens' who fling shuttles to and fro in the Country-under-Wave are the Fates of Celtic mythology, then the magic cloak is itself the web of destiny which joins Cuchulain to the sun god and the Young Man to Cuchulain.

For Cuchulain such artificial concepts as 'honour' carry little weight when compared to the urgency of his attraction to the Young Man.

> O! tell her
> I was afraid, or tell her what you will.[136]

In a very deep sense Cuchulain is being true to the sacred oath he has sworn to the 'pure glittering ones' of his own hearth fire. But the disregard for his own reputation he shows here, while noble in the context of Cuchulain's loyalty to his instincts, is not conducive to the success of Conchubar's plan to leave his own children 'a throne too high for insult'.

Cuchulain realises that Aoife is more apt to believe that he heeded a supernatural omen than that he declined to fight through physical cowardice.

> No; tell her I heard a raven croak
> On the north side of the house, and was afraid.[137]

To the kings who have been watching Cuchulain's behaviour towards the Young Man it seems that a witch of the air has troubled Cuchulain's mind. Cuchulain points out that it is not witchcraft that has made him attempt to avoid the fight. It is merely that the Young Man's head is like a woman's head he had a fancy for. In a sense it is the same thing — two different ways of talking about human emotion.

Conchubar, showing the dislike of the practical man for all that cannot be brought under the control of the will and the intellect, describes the workings of man's emotional nature in terms of witchcraft.

> A witch of the air
> Can make a leaf confound us with memories.
> They run upon the wind and hurl the spells
> That make us nothing, out of the invisible wind.
> They have gone to school to learn the trick of it.[138]

Cuchulain, anxious to complete the exchange of gifts, replies.

> No, no — there's nothing out of common here;
> The winds are innocent. — That arm-ring, boy.[139]

Two worlds are at war here. Cuchulain does not deny the existence of vague, irrational desires (the winds), but they are a natural part of life (nothing out of common) to be accepted and integrated. However, he lacks the one piece of information, his family connection with the Young Man, which would make his feelings comprehensible and acceptable to Conchubar's world.

The other kings offer to take up the challenge of the Young Man. The offer is an affront to Cuchulain's pride and sense of honour.

Back! back! Put up your swords! Put up your swords!
There's none alive that shall accept a challenge
I have refused. Laegaire, put up your sword![140]

But the Young Man is ready to meet them.

No, let them come. If they've a mind for it,
I'll try it out with any two together.[141]

The Young Man's every word draws Cuchulain closer to him.

That's spoken as I'd have spoken it at your age.
But you are in my house. Whatever man
Would fight with you shall fight it out with me.
They're dumb, they're dumb. How many of you would
    meet
This mutterer, this old whistler, this sand-piper,
· This edge that's greyer than the tide, this mouse
That's gnawing at the timbers of the world,
This, this ——[142]

It is as though Cuchulain has moved into some hypnotic
battle chant with the praising of his sword. The other kings
are struck dumb by it. We now see the full extent of that
desire for a son that caused Cuchulain to cry out in the night.

Boy, I would meet them all in arms
If I'd a son like you. He would avenge me
When I have withstood for the last time the men
Whose fathers, brothers, sons, and friends I have killed
Upholding Conchubar, when the four provinces
Have gathered with the ravens over them.[143]

In what far different terms do Cuchulain and Conchubar see
the value of having offspring. Cuchulain holds to the ancient
and heroic belief that a warrior must have sons to avenge his
death and to preserve the honour of the family name.
Conchubar would sacrifice the present to the future and
create a state where his children may lie soft where his
generation has lain hard. There is irony in Cuchulain's listing
of the families he has destroyed upholding Conchubar. He
will destroy one more in the same cause.

But I'd need no avenger. You and I
Would scatter them like water from a ditch.[144]

The hawk is no longer sleepy. The Young Man accepts Cuchulain's proffered friendship.

> We'll stand by one another from this out.
> Here is the ring.[145]

As usual, Cuchulain will be first among equals.

> No, turn and turn about.
> But my turn's first because I am older.[146]

He spreads the cloak.

> Nine queens out of the Country-under-Wave
> Have woven it with the fleeces of the sea
> And they were long embroidering it.[147]

The cloak is the tapestry of Cuchulain's fate, long in preparation and complex in its interwoven strands.

> —Boy,
> If I had fought my father he'd have killed me,
> As certainly as if I had a son
> And fought with him, I should be deadly to him;[148]

It is as though Cuchulain is commenting on the interwoven patterns on the embroidered cloak.

> For the old fiery fountains are far off
> And every day there is less heat o' the blood.[149]

Cuchulain returns to the myth of origin of man's spirit in the condition of fire. It was on fire that Cuchulain swore his oath. The ambiguous nature of that oath is brought to mind.

Cuchulain's ceremonial exchange of gifts against his express wishes is too much for Conchubar. He intervenes.

> No more of this. I will not have this friendship.
> Cuchulain is my man, and I forbid it.
> He shall not go unfought, for I myself —[150]

This brings Cuchulain into direct confrontation with the High King. 'I will not have it.'[151] Conchubar is astonished. 'You lay commands on me?'[152] Cuchulain seizes Conchubar. 'You shall not stir, High King. I'll hold you there.'[153]

Their relationship, as Conchubar has pointed out, is like

that of head and heart of the same being. Their relationship is untroubled as long as 'these flames are one', that is as long as the mind and the emotions agree. Now, when the promptings of the heart overcome the dictates of the head, the process will be attributed to witchcraft. As Cuchulain lays hands on the High King, the kings about them murmur of Cuchulain's conquest by the witches. An old king shouts:

> Some witch has worked upon your mind, Cuchulain.
> The head of that young man seemed like a woman's
> You'd a fancy for. Then of a sudden
> You laid your hands on the High King himself![154]

This is an accurate description of the 'witchcraft' that has worked on Cuchulain. There is still nothing out of common here, if Cuchulain were properly to interpret his feelings. But the sense of otherness he experiences and his horror at finding himself attacking the High King in defiance of his oath confuse him and make him fearful of the irrational force which has gripped him. 'And laid my hands on the High King himself?'[155]

Cuchulain now turns away from those forces in life which he has always served, away from the laws of his own nature. He accuses the Young Man of being responsible for the witchcraft. The Young Man, totally bewildered by the turn things have taken, denies that he has done any such thing. But Cuchulain is determined. It is now sword on sword. They leave, to meet in combat on the strand.

The full horror of the situation emerges as we realise how fully Cuchulain has betrayed the Young Man in the process of betraying himself. The Young Man has been robbed of the honour which would have come from the clean acceptance of a direct challenge. And one would imagine that he is now much less prepared psychologically for the fight than he might otherwise have been.

As the fight goes on outside, the three keepers of the sacred fire gaze into the ashes of the bowl. They are alone.

First Woman. I have seen, I have seen!
Second Woman.   What do you cry aloud?
First Woman. The Ever-living have shown me what's to
    come.[156]

The ambiguous nature of the fire ritual of the previous scene is emphasised by the mystery which surrounds the identity of the three Women. They themselves, the tenders of the fire, seem here to be in the service of those forces Conchubar meant them to expel. Are they, like the nine sea queens, related to the Fates? Do they represent past, present and future? What relation have they to the Weird Sisters who appear in *Macbeth*? It is in the ashes of the bowl that Cuchulain's fate is seen, the remains of that fire Cuchulain has talked about so ceaselessly, and it is the destruction of his house that is predicted. The hearth fire, blown by the winds of ungoverned emotion, shall consume the threshold.

> *Third Woman.* How? Where?
> *First Woman.*   In the ashes of the bowl.
> *Second Woman.* While you were holding it between your hands?
> *Third Woman.* Speak quickly!
> *First Woman.*   I have seen Cuchulain's roof-tree
> Leap into fire, and the walls split and blacken.[157]

The image is of the destruction of the dynasty Cuchulain might have established through the Young Man.

> *Second Woman.* Cuchulain has gone out to die.[158]

In a very real sense this is true.

> *Third Woman.*   O! O!
> *Second Woman.* Who could have thought that one so great as he
> Should meet his end at this unnoted sword![159]

The three Women, like many seers, do not recognise the full import of the visions that they see.

> *First Woman.* Life drifts between a fool and a blind man
> To the end, and nobody can know his end.[160]

The idea that Fool and Blind Man do not just parody the main plot but somehow determine it is confirmed. They symbolise certain of the life-forces which determine Cuchulain's fate. As 'combatants who turn the wheel of life', they would seem to me to be an early version of the Fool and

Hunchback who appear in *A Vision*. Hunchback and Fool are Phases 26 and 28 respectively on the Great Wheel of lunar phases. Between them is the Saint, passively accepting his fate. Yeats will make considerable use of this symbolism in *The Death of Cuchulain*.

> *Second Woman.* Come, look upon the quenching of this
> greatness.[161]

The opposition of fire and water again.

> *First Woman.* No crying out, for there'll be need of cries
> And rending of the hair when it's all finished.[162]

The final cry will be that of the *banshee*. It will be heard of course by the Fool.

V

After the modulated grief of the three Women, the rage of the Fool is a distinct shock. He enters, dragging the Blind Man with him. He throws the Blind Man down by the big chair.

> *Fool.* You have eaten it, you have eaten it! You have left
> me nothing but the bones.[163]

How horrifying the double meanings make this scene, coming as it does immediately upon the last. Conchubar, magpie (thief) or maggot (corpse-chewer) has stolen and devoured the only thing Cuchulain ever cared deeply for. Now Cuchulain is left with nothing but the bones of what was once his son.

> *Blind Man.* O, that I should have to endure such a plague!
> O, I ache all over! O, I am pulled to pieces! This is the
> way you pay me all the good I have done you.[164]

As if in a dream, the issues of Cuchulain's relationship with Conchubar are worked out in the dispute between Blind Man and Fool.

> *Fool.* You have eaten it! You have told me lies. I might
> have known you had eaten it when I saw your slow
> sleepy walk.[165]

The horrifying picture of the cannibalistic Conchubar is made vivid by the detailed picture given by the Fool of the slow, sleepy walk of the Blind Man.

> Lie there till the kings come. O, I will tell Conchubar
> and Cuchulain and all the kings about you![166]

Indeed it is the Fool who gives Cuchulain the clue to interpret Conchubar's betrayal of him.

The debate continues, point by point reviewing the issues between Conchubar and Cuchulain.

> *Blind Man.* What would happen to you but for me, and you
> without your wits? If I did not take care of you, what
> would you do for food and warmth?
> *Fool.* You take care of me? You stay safe, and send me
> into every kind of danger. You sent me down the cliff
> for gull's eggs while you warmed your blind eyes in the
> sun; and then you ate all that were good for food. You
> left me the eggs that were neither egg nor food.[167]

The egg symbolism scarcely requires comment. It is as though we are being taken into some strange scene of conflict, deep in the mind of Cuchulain.

> Keep quiet now, till I shut the door. There is some noise
> outside — a high vexing noise, so that I can't be listening to
> myself.[168]

The door that the Fool once unlocked to let the witches in is now locked to keep out the cry of the *banshee*. The Fool's inability to listen to himself in the presence of death symbolises the state of confusion Cuchulain is in on his entrance. 'Why can't they be quiet? Why can't they be quiet?'[169] We have here a foretaste of Cuchulain's madness.

The Blind Man tries to get away.

> Ah! you would try to get away, would you. [*Follows
> Blind Man and brings him back.*] Lie there! lie there! No,
> you won't get away! Lie there till the kings come. I'll tell
> them all about you. I will tell it all. How you sit warming
> yourself, when you have made me light a fire of sticks,
> while I sit blowing it with my mouth. Do you not always

make me take the windy side of the bush when it blows, and the rainy side when it rains.[170]

The Blind Man warms himself by the Fool's fire just as Conchubar makes use of Cuchulain's burning heart.

> *Blind Man.* O, good Fool! listen to me. Think of the care I have taken of you. I have brought you to many a warm hearth, where there was a good welcome for you, but you would not stay there; you were always wandering about.[171]

The accusation is one that could be made by Conchubar against the homeless Cuchulain.

> *Fool.* The last time you brought me in, it was not I who wandered away, but you that got put out because you took the crubeen out of the pot when nobody was looking. Keep quiet now.[172]

A symbolic description of the trickery of Conchubar which robbed Cuchulain of the chance of a home.

> *Cuchulain.* [*Rushing in*]. Witchcraft! There is no witchcraft on the earth, or among the witches of the air, that these hands cannot break.[173]

Cuchulain's destruction has come through his turning away from the Shape-changers of the morning to whom he was formerly devoted.

> *Fool.* Listen to me Cuchulain. I left him turning the fowl at the fire. He ate it all, though I had stolen it. He left me nothing but the feathers.[174]

Feathers become a symbol of the strange reward of those who face defeat. They symbolise the secret exultation of the tragic hero. In *The Death of Cuchulain,* Cuchulain's soul will take on a 'soft, feathery shape'.

> *Cuchulain.* Fill me a horn of ale!

> *Blind Man.* I gave him what he likes best. You do not know how vain this Fool is. He likes nothing as well as a feather.[175]

To the Blind Man as to Conchubar, feathers and what they
represent are vanity.

> *Fool.* He left me nothing but the bones and feathers.
> Nothing but the feathers, though I had stolen it.
> *Cuchulain.* Give me that horn. Quarrels here, too!
> [*Drinks.*] What is there between you two that is worth a
> quarrel? Out with it![176]

Life drifts between a Fool and a Blind Man — and Cuchulain
asks them what there is between them worth a quarrel.

> *Blind Man.* Where would he be but for me? I must be
> always thinking — thinking to get food for the two of us,
> and when we've got it, if the moon is at the full or the tide
> on the turn, he'll leave the rabbit in the snare till it is
> full of maggots, or let the trout slip back through his
> hands into the stream.[177]

Conchubar has commented earlier on Cuchulain's attitude
towards affairs of state.

> You think it does not matter,
> And that a fancy lighter than the air,
> A whim of the moment, has more matter in it.[178]

The Fool, now playing with the feathers, has begun to sing.

> *Fool* [*singing*].
> When you were an acorn on the tree-top,
> Then was I an eagle-cock;
> Now that you are a withered old block,
> Still am I an eagle-cock.[179]

This traditional rhyme, collected by Douglas Hyde in Country
Dublin,[180] plays on the legendary longevity of the eagle by
comparing it with the oak. In using it in this context, Yeats
seems to equate the eagle with the spiritual aspect of man (as
represented by the Fool) and the oak with the material
aspect of man. Cuchulain, by rejecting his eagle- or hawk-like
nature has identified with the material aspect of his being.
('He'll be but slow/To break a tree that was so sweetly
planted.'[181]) The feathers the fool plays with represent the
life that Cuchulain has forsaken — his eagle nature — but to
which his spirit as represented by the Fool is still loyal.

Blind Man. Listen to him now. That's the sort of talk I
have to put up with day out, day in.

[*The fool is putting the feathers into his hair.
Cuchulain takes a handful of feathers out of the heap
the Fool has on the bench beside him, and out of the
Fool's hair, and begins to wipe the blood from his
sword with them.*

Fool. He has taken my feathers to wipe his sword. It is
blood that he is wiping from his sword.[182]

The contact of the feathers with the blood of the Young Man
brings about a connection that Cuchulain will soon make
consciously.

Cuchulain [*goes up to door at back and throws away
feathers*]. They are standing about his body. They will
not awaken him, for all his witchcraft.

Blind Man. It is that young champion that he has killed.
He that came out of Aoife's country.[183]

The trap is set.

Cuchulain. He thought to have saved himself with witchcraft.

Fool. That Blind Man there said he would kill you. He
came from Aoife's country to kill you. That Blind Man
said they had taught him every kind of weapon that he
might do it. But I always knew that you would kill
him.[184]

An incredible concentration of effect is attained. It is as
though Cuchulain's psychology has been externalised. The
Fool gives him one idea at a time from what the Blind Man
has said. It is as if Cuchulain's spirit is selecting for him facts
and ideas from an intellect from which he has become
alienated and now deeply distrusts.

Cuchulain [*to the Blind Man*]. You knew him, then?

Blind Man. I saw him, when I had my eyes, in Aoife's
country.

Cuchulain. You were in Aoife's country?

Blind Man. I knew him and his mother there.

Cuchulain. He was about to speak of her when he died.

> *Blind Man.* He was a queen's son.
> *Cuchulain.* What queen? what queen? [*Seizes Blind Man, who is now sitting upon the bench.*] Was it Scathach? There were many queens. All the rulers were queens.
> *Blind Man.* No, not Scathach.
> *Cuchulain.* It was Uathach, then? Speak! speak!
> *Blind Man.* I cannot speak; you are clutching me too tightly. [*Cuchulain lets him go.*] I cannot remember who it was. I am not certain. It was some queen.[185]

Is this the representation of a man bullying his own intellect, trying in his confusion to remember, to make those connections which will make the situation clear? With determination Cuchulain seeks the knowledge which will destroy him. The scene closely parallels Oedipus' cross-examination of the blind Theresias.

> *Fool.* He said a while ago that the young man was Aoife's son.
> *Cuchulain.* She? No, no! She had no son when I was there.
> *Fool.* That Blind Man there said that she owned him for her son.
> *Cuchulain.* I had rather he had been some other woman's son. What father had he? A soldier out of Alba? She was an amorous woman — a proud, pale amorous woman.[186]

We are reminded of the connection in Cuchulain's mind between Aoife and the women none can kiss and thrive.

> *Blind Man.* None knew whose son he was.
> *Cuchulain.* None knew! Did you know, old listener at doors?
> *Blind Man.* No, no; I knew nothing.
> *Fool.* He said a while ago that he heard Aoife boast that she'd never but the one lover, and he the only man that had overcome her in battle.[187]

The connection is made.

> *Blind Man.* Somebody is trembling, Fool! The bench is shaking. Why are you trembling? Is Cuchulain going to hurt us? It was not I who told you, Cuchulain.[188]

Cuchulain gets the message, not from his mind, but from his

emotional or intuitive nature (his spirit). Yeats' skill in setting up this recognition scene makes the suspense and horror almost unbearable.

> *Fool.* It is Cuchulain who is trembling. It is Cuchulain who
> is shaking the bench.
> *Blind Man.* It is his own son he has slain.[189]

In the speech that follows, Cuchulain's new knowledge brings him to re-examine the whole question of his allegiance to the 'witches' and to reconsider the nature of evil. As he moves into that madness which is a form of true wisdom, he sees Conchubar as the source of his tragedy and not the 'pale windy people'.

> *Cuchulain.* 'Twas they that did it, the pale windy people.
> Where? where? where? My sword against the thunder![190]

For a moment Cuchulain is ready to make war against the gods.

> But no, for they have always been my friends;
> And though they love to blow a smoking coal
> Till it's all flame, the wars they blow aflame
> Are full of glory, and heart-uplifting pride,
> And not like this. The wars they love awaken
> Old fingers and the sleepy strings of harps.[191]

Cuchulain is restored to his adoration of the Sidhe and the life they engender.

> Who did it them? Are you afraid? Speak out!
> For I have you under my protection
> And will reward you well.[192]

We recall with horror that he also put the Young Man under his protection.

>   Dubthatch the Chafer?
> He'd an old grudge. No, for he is with Maeve.
> Laegaire did it! Why do you not speak?
> What is this house?[193]

Madness takes hold on him as he grasps at a truth that cannot be held in a sane mind.

Now I remember all.

[*Comes before Conchubar's chair, and strikes out with
his sword, as if Conchubar was sitting upon it.*]
'Twas you who did it — you who sat up there
With your old rod of kingship, like a magpie
Nursing a stolen spoon. No, not a magpie,
A maggot that is eating up the earth!
Yes, but a magpie, for he's flown away.
Where did he fly to?
Blind Man.   He is outside the door.
Cuchulain. Outside the door?
Blind Man.   Between the door and the sea.
Cuchulain. Conchubar, Conchubar! The sword into your
heart![194]

In the original saga material, Conchubar arranged that his
Druids should bewitch Cuchulain into mistaking the sea for
the assembly of Red Branch kings. Yeats chooses to make
Cuchulain's fight with the sea a function of his madness — a
symbolic act representing Cuchulain's struggle against his fate
before it overwhelms him. Cuchulain does literally what
Hamlet speaks of doing figuratively. He takes arms against a
sea of troubles. The Fool creeps to the big door and watches.

Fool. He is going up to King Conchubar. They are all
about the young man. No, no, he is standing still. There
is a great wave going to break, and he is looking down to
the sea, but he is holding up his sword as if he were
going into a fight. [*Pause.*] Well struck! Well struck![195]

The image is much more powerful described through the eyes
of the Fool than it could ever be if represented on the stage.
It is a mysteriously moving archetypal image, a companion to
that picture we are given of Cuchulain beating off the attack
of the great grey hawk on the mountainside.

In the revised version of the play, Yeats brings about a
remarkable transformation of the final dialogue between
Blind Man and Fool simply by having the Blind Man repeat
his command of 'Come here' to the Fool three times. In the
final version, the Fool is much more than a mere reporter of
the events which are happening on the shore. During the fight

with the waves, he becomes deeply identified with the mad hero. When Cuchulain is overcome all the excitement drains from the Fool and he passively does the will of the Blind Man. Only by playing the scene this way can the delicate balance between tragedy and comedy be preserved.

> *Blind Man.* What is he doing now?
> *Fool.* O! he is fighting the waves!
> *Blind Man.* He sees King Conchubar's crown on every one of them.
> *Fool.* There, he has struck at a big one! He has struck the crown off it; he has made the foam fly. There again, another big one!
> *Blind Man.* Where are the kings? What are the kings doing?
> *Fool.* They are shouting and running down to the shore, and the people are running out of the houses. They are all running.
> *Blind Man.* You say they are running out of the houses? There will be nobody left in the houses. Listen, Fool![196]

Just as Conchubar may be even now planning his next political move in the light of Cuchulain's behaviour, so the Blind Man plots a raid on the ovens of the empty houses. The tragic joy of Cuchulain in that final intense moment when all is unmixed passion is reflected in the excitement of the Fool.

> *Fool.* There, he is down! He is up again. He is going out in the deep water. There is a big wave. It has gone over him. I cannot see him now. He has killed kings and giants, but the waves have mastered him, the waves have mastered him!
> *Blind Man.* Come here, Fool!
> *Fool.* The waves have mastered him.
> *Blind Man.* Come here!
> *Fool.* The waves have mastered him.
> *Blind Man.* Come here I say.
> *Fool* [*coming towards him, but looking towards the door*]. What is it?
> *Blind Man.* There will be nobody in the houses. Come this way; come quickly! The ovens will be full. We will put our hands into the ovens.[197]

The final scene of *On Baile's Strand* remained vivid in Yeats' imagination throughout his life.

> And when the Fool and Blind Man stole the bread
> Cuchulain fought the ungovernable sea;
> Heart-mysteries there . . .[198]

The heart mysteries grow even deeper in the next play in the cycle, *The Only Jealousy of Emer.*

9 The Fifteenth Night

I

The flaming passions which envelop Cuchulain's burning
heart are quenched by the waters of the sea. His soul 'begins
to tremble into stillness,/To die into the labyrinth of itself'.[1]
Robartes describes the experience in 'The Phases of the
Moon'.

> All thought becomes an image and the soul
> Becomes a body: that body and that soul
> Too perfect at the full to lie in a cradle,
> Body and soul cast out and cast away
> Beyond the visible world.[2]

Aherne points out:

> All dreams of the soul
> End in a beautiful man's or woman's body.[3]

In *The Only Jealousy of Emer* Cuchulain, in some strange
region beyond the visible world, meets the goddess Fand,
pure beauty, an image of his own soul in its pure subjective,
feminine form.

At the beginning of the play, the musicians of *At the
Hawk's Well* return. The First Musician sings of the nature
and origin of feminine beauty.

> A woman's beauty is like a white
> Frail bird, like a white sea-bird alone
> At daybreak after stormy night
> Between two furrows upon the ploughed land . . .[4]

The simile invites an interpretation of all of its elements.
'White frail bird' suggests the purity and delicacy of beauty.
'White sea-bird alone' suggests the isolation of beauty and its
origin in the absolute, in *anima mundi*, the unconscious, or
the undifferentiated source of all being to which souls return

between incarnations. 'At daybreak after stormy night' suggests the violence of incarnation. 'Between two furrows upon the ploughed land' suggests that beauty is out of place in man's workaday world. In other words, such manifestations of beauty as we find in this life have their origin in some other life. Beauty as found in this life seems stranded in a setting foreign to it. It is therefore fragile and lonely. Back of this treatment of beauty is the belief that physical beauty is the result of emotional toil in past lives.

> A sudden storm, and it was thrown
> Between dark furrows upon the ploughed land.[5]

'A sudden storm' refers to the violence of incarnation.

> How many centuries spent
> The sedentary soul
> In toils of measurement . . .[6]

The soul is pictured as labouring through incarnation after incarnation in sedentary toil (like the artist) to produce beauty.

> Beyond eagle or mole . . .[7]

Beyond the world of our experience (that is, the physical world which we know whose uppermost limits are marked by the flight of eagles and whose lower limits by the digging of moles).

> Beyond hearing or seeing . . .[8]

In a world which is beyond the reach of our senses.

> Or Archimedes, guess . . .[9]

In a world which is beyond the understanding of science.

> To raise into being
> That loveliness.[10]

The soul is pictured as engaging in purposeful toil to bring forth the physical beauty which its present incarnation exhibits. Yeats has said that a saint will have one incarnation as a beautiful man or a beautiful woman.

> A strange, unserviceable thing,
> A fragile, exquisite, pale shell . . .[11]

Yeats points out that beauty is of no practical use in the world of ploughed furrows. Changing the figure, the musician sings of beauty as a delicate shell which has been produced by a living creature, just as beauty has been produced by the emotional toil of past lives. It has been thrown up on the shore. Though of no apparent usefulness, it strikes one as 'strange', having some significance or power beyond the practical.

> That the vast troubled waters bring . . .[12]

This is the 'gong-tormented' sea of the Byzantium poems which is the source of all images.

> To the loud sands before day has broken.[13]

Sound here seems to be a symbol of the clamour of the world of consciousness. The Country-under-Waves is a silent world. It is on the shore that the sounds of the storm are clearly heard.

> The storm arose and suddenly fell
> Amid the dark before day had broken.[14]

Is this storm connected with Cuchulain's battle with the sea? Emer later says the other kings stood 'like cattle in a gale'.

> What death? What discipline?[15]

This clearly refers to that emotional toil in past lives. But it is also connected with the fate which has overtaken Cuchulain.

> What bonds no man could unbind,
> Being imagined within
> That labyrinth of the mind . . .[16]

Aherne says, in 'The Phases of the Moon',

> > The song will have it
> That those that we have loved got their long fingers
> From death, and wounds, or on Sinai's top,
> Or from some bloody whip in their own hands.
> They ran from cradle to cradle till at last

Their beauty dropped out of the loneliness
Of body and soul.[17]

The musician asks:

What pursuing or fleeing,
What wounds, what bloody press,
Dragged into being
This loveliness?[18]

After the extremity of emotion which Cuchulain has undergone, after the violent killing of his own son, the attempt to
unbind the bonds of remorse in which this has placed him,
the willing of his own destruction in his fight with the sea,
Cuchulain meets in the labyrinth of his own mind, Fand,
image of peace and beauty. For the moment at least love has
been separated from that bodily desire which inevitably
associates it with pain and conflict. As Blake has said: 'Sexual
love is founded upon spiritual hate'. And as the Women sing
in *On Baile's Strand,* speaking of witches who ride upon the
wind, those symbols of desire,

Those wild hands that have embraced
All his body can but shove
At the burning wheel of love
Till the side of hate comes up.[19]

The Ghost of Cuchulain, experiencing in his meeting with
Fand a love almost devoid of desire, approaches a state of
pure subjectivity and almost escapes the workings of the
wheel. The Figure of Cuchulain, possessed by Bricriu, god of
discord, symbolises pure desire unmixed with other elements.
He plots to bring Cuchulain's soul back towards objectivity
once more. In her meeting with Bricriu Emer's love for
Cuchulain is tested. The terms of that test go right to the
heart of the mystery of what constitutes womanly beauty,
courage, desire and love.

II

The musicians, like the priests in some strange ritual, evoke
the scene. They bring before the eyes an image consisting,
like a Japanese painting, of a few suggestive symbols.

> I call before the eyes a roof
> With cross-beams darkened by smoke;
> A fisher's net hangs from a beam,
> A long oar lies against the wall.
> I call up a poor fisher's house . . .[20]

Here the body of Cuchulain is stretched, his state the ambiguous one of those who have struggled with the elementals.

> A man lies dead or swooning,
> That amorous man,
> That amorous, violent man, renowned Cuchulain . . .[21]

In the light of Cuchulain's relations with the Sidhe, the word 'amorous' begins to take on a special meaning. We remember too that it was the mixture of violence and love in the affair with Aoife that involved him in the fate which has overtaken him.

> Queen Emer at his side,
> At her bidding all the rest have gone . . .[22]

Emer has dismissed all others in preparation for the ritual of recalling Cuchulain from the spirit world.

> But now one comes on hesitating feet,
> Young Eithne Inguba, Cuchulain's mistress.[23]

Eithne's timidity shows that she lives on a plane of experience below that which Emer, through her nobility and resignation, has attained. That the strength and nobility of her love places her above sexual jealousy we have already seen in *The Green Helmet*. ('Live and be faithless still.'[24])

> She stands a moment in the open door.
> Beyond the open door the bitter sea,
> The shining bitter sea, is crying out . . .[24]

Yeats has written:

> Some neo-platonist, I forget who, describes the sea as a symbol of the drifting indefinite bitterness of life, and I believe there is like symbolism intended in the many Irish voyages to the islands of enchantment, or that there was,

at any rate, in the mythology out of which these stories have been shaped.[25]

In the song the sea sings, the two images which symbolised beauty in the opening song — shell and bird — are brought together.

> White shell, white wing!
> I will not choose for my friend
> A frail unserviceable thing
> That drifts and dreams, and but knows
> That waters are without end
> And that wind blows.[26]

It is the song the bitter sea sings to beauty. The image of beauty has been cast ashore from the sea of man's bitterness. The sea has cast it out because beauty is delicate and without practical value, being related to a sense of the eternal and to vague desires.

Emer speaks:

> Come hither, come sit down beside the bed;
> You need not be afraid, for I myself
> Sent for you Eithne Inguba.[27]

Because Eithne thinks of love in terms of physical desire she finds difficulty in accepting that Emer feels no jealousy towards her. Emer, however, has almost given up desire and is left only with a single hope. That hope does not put her in competition with Eithne.

Emer plans to use the magic of Eithne's youth and sexuality to draw the spirit of Cuchulain back to the world of the living. Ironically, it is not by such ties that Cuchulain is bound to the world. It is rather to Emer he is bound as 'men are bound to women by the wrongs/They do or suffer'.[28] Eithne herself recognises this.

> He loves me best,
> Being his newest love, but in the end
> Will love the woman best who loved him first
> And loved him through the years when love seemed lost.[29]

This is the one hope which has sustained Emer through the

years of Cuchulain's unfaithfulness. Before she attains totally selfless love, this hope too must be renounced. Using an image which provides an ironic parallel to the sea shell of the opening song, Eithne predicts her own fate.

> Women like me, the violent hour passed over,
> Are flung into some corner like old nut-shells.[30]

Before Eithne begins to call the spirit of Cuchulain, Emer throws new logs upon the fire and stirs the half-burnt logs until they break in flame. The flames of the hearth fire, used to cleanse the house against the 'witches of the air' in *On Baile's Strand,* are used here against the influence of the sea.

> Old Manannan's unbridled horses come
> Out of the sea, and on their backs his horsemen;
> But all the enchantments of the dreaming foam
> Dread the hearth-fire.[31]

In this play the 'elementals' we are concerned with are the 'enchantments of the dreaming foam', that is, the water spirits. Emer's hope that Cuchulain will return to the hearth fire and to her implies that he will eventually give up entirely his relations with the Sidhe.

Emer gives Eithne her instructions.

> Bend over him;
> Call out dear secrets till you have touched his heart,
> If he lies there; and if he is not there,
> Till you have made him jealous.[32]

Emer's ability to use desire and jealousy as weapons in her fight with the Sidhe is mark of the extent to which she is no longer dominated by either. Eithne says, 'Cuchulain, listen'.[33] But this is not exactly what Emer had in mind.

> Those words sound timidly; to be afraid
> Because his wife is but three paces off,
> When there is so great need, were but to prove
> The man that chose you made but a poor choice . . .[34]

Emer's pride and nobility allow her to love Cuchulain with a love which carries her beyond such pettiness as human jealousy. She tries to stir a similar pride in Eithne. She puts the matter clearly and simply: 'We're but two women struggling with the sea'.[35] The contest is the feminine equivalent of Cuchulain's battle with the sea. Eithne takes heart.

> O my beloved, pardon me, that I
> Have been ashamed. I thrust my shame away.[36]

This thrusting away of her shame gives Eithne what power she has over the supernatural forces, just as Emer's thrusting away of her hope makes her eventually able to conquer Fand. Emer has stirred the sexual pride of Eithne.

> I have never sent a message or called out,
> Scarce had a longing for your company
> But you have known and come; and if indeed
> You are lying there, stretch out your arms and speak;
> Open your mouth and speak, for to this hour
> My company has made you talkative.[37]

The desire of the man is for a woman, the desire of a woman is for the desire of the man.

> Our passion had not chilled when we were parted
> On the pale shore under the breaking dawn.[38]

Eithne, confident now of her sexual power, is certain that if Cuchulain does not heed her voice then he must be unreachable.

> He cannot speak; or else his ears are closed
> And no sound reaches him.[39]

Emer advises physical contact.

> Then kiss that image;
> The pressure of your mouth upon his mouth
> May reach him where he is.[40]

Cuchulain's body is treated like an image of the hero, into which Cuchulain's spirit may be drawn as it is said the spirits of gods were drawn into images made by Egyptian priests. Eithne kisses the lifeless lips, then starts back.

> It is no man.
> I felt some evil thing that dried my heart
> When my lips touched it.[41]

Eithne's sexual confidence turns to terror as she realises her
desire has called forth something beyond the human. Emer
believes they have succeeded.

> No, his body stirs;
> The pressure of your mouth has called him home;
> He has thrown the changeling out.[42]

Emer's confidence is unshaken. She sees the restoring of
Cuchulain as the calling home of a wandering spirit. Eithne,
more sensitive to physical attributes, cries out:

> Look at that arm;
> That arm is withered to the very socket.[43]

The deformed hunchback is opposite the hero on the Great
Wheel and provides the hero with his Mask. And 'there's no
deformity but saves us from a dream'.[44]

> The thirteenth moon but sets the soul at war
> In its own being, and when that war's begun
> There is no muscle in the arm . . .[45]

Emer is unafraid, though Eithne moves far off. Emer's noble
pride asserts itself in indignation that a stranger should dare
to lie in great Cuchulain's bed, usurp his image.
     The changeling identifies himself.

> I am named Bricriu — not the man — that Bricriu,
> Maker of discord among gods and men,
> Called Bricriu of the Sidhe.[46]

The spirit who has usurped Cuchulain's image is the same
spirit who, as the Red Man, sowed discord in *The Green
Helmet*. Emer asks for what purpose Bricriu has come.

> I show my face, and everything he loves
> Must fly away.[47]

Eithne runs out but Emer stands firm.

> You people of the wind

Are full of lying speech and mockery:
I have not fled your face.[48]

Bricriu says, 'You are not loved'.[49]

As the symbol of the discordant phase upon the Great Wheel which provides the hero with his Mask, Bricriu himself represents the violent destiny of Cuchulain. He may also be seen as the twisted face of pure desire unmixed with other elements, or of the hate which in the life of Cuchulain has always been mixed with love but which in this phase is now split from it. In any case, Bricriu has no power over Emer because the ties which bind her to Cuchulain are almost free of the element of desire. Unfrightened by Bricriu's gaze, Emer demands that Cuchulain be brought back. Bricriu says that if Emer is willing to pay the price Cuchulain will be freed. The Sidhe may return those they have kidnapped, accepting as ransom 'a less valued thing'. Bricriu gives examples of this practice. The details are from Celtic faery stories and folk belief.

> The fisher, when some knowledgeable man
> Restores to him his wife, or son, or daughter,
> Knows he must lose a boat or net, or it may be
> The cow that gives his children milk; and some
> Have offered their own lives.[50]

A very specific price has been set on Cuchulain's life.

> I do not ask
> Your life, or any valuable thing;
> You spoke but now of the mere chance that some day
> You'd be the apple of his eye again
> When old and ailing, but renounce that chance
> And he shall live again.[51]

'You spoke but now.' Has Bricriu been summoned by Eithne's kiss or Emer's words? For Emer, what Bricriu asks is probably more valuable than her own life. The question will be whether it is more important to her than Cuchulain's life.
Emer replies,

> I do not question
> But you have brought ill-luck on all he loves;

> And now, because I am thrown beyond your power
> Unless your words are lies, you come to bargain.[52]

Because Emer has accepted the fact that Cuchulain does not reciprocate her love, yet continues to love him, she is beyond Bricriu's power to do her harm. Unlike desire, which may be thwarted by bad luck, hope must be voluntarily renounced if it is to be destroyed. Bricriu can have no power over Emer unless she wills it. Bricriu recalls Emer's pride of mastery in the early years of her marriage.

> You loved your mastery, when but newly married,
> And I love mine for all my withered arm;
> You have but to put yourself into that power
> And he shall live again.[53]

Emer refuses voluntarily to put herself under the curse which submission to Bricriu's will involves. Bricriu taunts her: 'You dare not be accursed, yet he has dared.'[54] There is a difference between the curse which falls on men and that which falls on women. The curse for a man is the thwarting of desire, for a woman the abandonment of hope.

> I have but two joyous thoughts, two things I prize,
> A hope, a memory, and now you claim that hope.[55]

The memory Emer speaks of is shared by Cuchulain. The Ghost of Cuchulain in this play has been so purified of desire and other elements productive of discord that it moves almost into a state of pure subjectivity. Its only ties with this life are memories of Emer, of wrongs done by her and to her. Emer brings back Cuchulain from the Sidhe, but at the price of accepting a curse equivalent to that which fell upon Cuchulain in *At the Hawk's Well*. It is such emotional toil that creates beauty. Emer at the end of the play is like a white sea bird alone, cast up upon ploughed land after a storm. Having renounced even hope, she has moved beyond the place where she seems at home in this world. She is, in a sense, purer than Fand who longs and therefore is not complete.

Bricriu at first points out how futile and therefore valueless the hope is. But Emer refuses to renounce it. Bricriu asks if she knows the consequences of loving the Sidhe.

> You've watched his loves and you have not been jealous
> Knowing that he would tire, but do those tire
> That love the Sidhe?[56]

It has been her single hope that has kept Emer from jealousy. But can the hope of rewinning Cuchulain be sustained in the face of Cuchulain's love of the Absolute? If Cuchulain escapes the Wheel of Life (or Love) altogether at the phase of total subjectivity by kissing the goddess Fand, he will not return.

Bricriu grants Emer second-sight so that she may see Cuchulain's Ghost and the Woman of the Sidhe.

> I have dissolved the dark
> That hid him from your eyes, but not that other
> That's hidden you from his.[57]

It is not a general darkness that hides the souls of others from us, but is personal to us — a kind of blindness. Bricriu has given Emer 'insight' into Cuchulain's soul. Her's remains dark to Cuchulain.

> He cannot hear — being shut off, a phantom
> That can neither touch, nor hear, nor see;
> The longing and the cries have drawn him hither.[58]

Cuchulain, the curse of his incarnation momentarily disentangled from his soul, is indeed a phantom. There can be no life at the fifteenth phase. Bricriu outlines a process of 'dreaming back' similar to that described in *A Vision*. Yeats' view of the history of the soul after death was rooted in the philosophy of Swedenborg.

> He heard no sound, heard no articulate sound;
> They could but banish rest, and make him dream,
> And in that dream, as do all dreaming shades
> Before they are accustomed to their freedom,
> He has taken his familiar form; and yet
> He crouches there not knowing where he is
> Or at whose side he is crouched.[59]

Emer sees a woman beside her husband. It is the moon goddess, now in her fifteenth phase, the phase of the full moon. She appears as Fand, whose name means 'tear'. This is the same goddess Cuchulain met in *At the Hawk's Well* in the form of a hawk, the shape in which she apparently manifests herself at Phase 1 of her cycle.

> She has hurried from the Country-under-Wave
> And dreamed herself into that shape that he
> May glitter in her basket; for the Sidhe
> Are dexterous fishers and they fish for men
> With dreams upon the hook.[60]

Shape-changers apparently dream themselves into the shapes they assume just as the souls of the dead assume the shapes of their dreams. The practice of the Sidhe in fishing for men with dreams upon the hook has been a constant theme of the entire play cycle, particularly evident in *At the Hawk's Well* and *On Baile's Strand*.

Emer shows her developing jealousy of Fand by an attack which is based on the unsubstantial nature of dreams.

> And so that woman
> Has hid herself in this disguise and made
> Herself into a lie.[61]

Bricriu refutes her materialism. The surface of life is not the sole reality.

> A dream is body;
> The dead move ever towards a dreamless youth
> And when they dream no more return no more . . .[62]

A clear statement of the doctrine of *A Vision* concerning the fate of the soul after death. It is of such memories Cuchulain must clear himself before he reaches the stage where he will return no more.

> And those more holy shades that never lived
> But visit you in dreams.[63]

All spirits are not spirits of the dead. Some spirits (the Sidhe) who have never taken mortal form visit us in dreams. These are the images that Carl Jung calls 'archetypes of the unconscious'. Emer speaks of the effect on mortal man of commerce with the Sidhe.

> I know her sort.
> They find our men asleep, weary with war,
> Lap them in cloudy hair or kiss their lips;
> Our men awake in ignorance of it all,
> But when we take them in our arms at night
> We cannot break their solitude.[64]

The term 'solitude' seems to imply that the 'holy shades' with whom some men form alliance have their origin within the minds of the men themselves. Dr Jung has discussed this relationship in terms of a man's relating to the Anima image which emerges from his unconscious.

> No knife
> Can wound that body of air. Be silent; listen;
> I have not given you eyes and ears for nothing.[65]

The elemental nature of the Sidhe who appear in this play seems to be shifting or at least ambiguous. Fand comes from the Country-under-Wave, yet her body is of air. Probably this is just a way of indicating her spiritual (non-material) nature.

The Ghost of Cuchulain addresses Fand:

> Who is it that stands before me there
> Shedding such light from limb and hair
> As when the moon, complete at last
> With every labouring crescent past,
> And lonely with extreme delight
> Flings out upon the fifteenth night.[66]

Fand is referred to directly as the moon goddess here. She is seen as the full moon on the Great Wheel of lunar phases in *A Vision*. The word 'labouring' links this speech with the opening song of the play. The beauty of the full moon has been created by the emotional toil of the first fourteen incarnations of the moon. Fand becomes a symbol of feminine beauty. Eithne and Emer are partial incarnations of Fand just as the Guardian and Aoife were partial manifestations of the Mountain Witch in *At the Hawk's Well*.

> Because I long I am not complete.[67]

Desire makes the heart impure. Fand lacks completeness by

an hour or so. When the moon goddess achieves total fullness she will no longer experience desire, being totally fulfilled by the light of the sun. Yeats also makes use of the old idea that certain elemental spirits need union with a mortal before they themselves gain immortality. The idea expressed here also applies to Emer. The longing which expresses itself in her one hope makes her impure.

> What pulled your hands about your feet,
> Pulled down your head upon your knees,
> And hid your face?[68]

What, in other words, binds you to your old self, to your old life, robbing you of the opportunity for freedom?

> Old memories:
> A woman in her happy youth
> Before her man had broken troth,
> Dead men and women. Memories
> Have pulled my head upon my knees.[69]

In the final version of the play the emphasis is clearly on Cuchulain's memories of Emer, Cuchulain having been cleansed of memories of his son's death by the fight with the sea. In an earlier version Cuchulain had listed among his memories:

> A dying boy, with handsome face
> Upturned upon a beaten place;
> A sacred yew-tree on a strand.[70]

It is memories of Emer which hold him back from merging with the Sidhe. In the earlier version Yeats included the lines:

> A man is held to those whom he has loved
> By pain they gave, or pain that he has given —
> Intricacies of pain.[71]

These lines do not appear in the final version though the idea they represent is alluded to in the term 'intricacies of blind remorse' which Cuchulain uses.

Fand, who represents the moon one hour before the full, calls upon Cuchulain to give her his love. He has loved many beautiful mortals of Phase 14. Fand needs his kiss to be complete. Cuchulain recognises her now.

> I know you now, for long ago
> I met you on a cloudy hill
> Beside old thorn-trees and a well.
> A woman danced and a hawk flew,
> I held out arms and hands; but you,
> That now seem friendly, fled away
> Half woman and half bird of prey.[72]

The hawk spirit Cuchulain met in *At the Hawk's Well* is obviously an incarnation of the moon goddess at an opposite phase to that represented by her incarnation as Fand. In terms of bird imagery, the goddess appears as a hawk at Phase 1 on the Great Wheel, a white sea bird at Phase 15 and as a crow as we move towards Phase 1 again in *The Death of Cuchulain*. Fand pleads with Cuchulain to give her his love.

> Hold out your arms and hands again;
> You were not so dumbfounded when
> I was that bird of prey, and yet
> I am all woman now.[73]

The movement from the total objectivity of Phase 1 on the Great Wheel to the total subjectivity of Phase 15 is also a movement from masculine to feminine values. Cuchulain replies:

> I am not
> The young and passionate man I was,
> And though that brilliant light surpass
> All crescent forms, my memories
> Weigh down my hands, abash my eyes.[74]

Yeats has gained considerable power by being able to assume the myth of *A Vision* behind his ritual drama. Allusions to the myth give structure to the scene. Once we understand the moon imagery the meaning of the lines of the scene become quite clear. Although absolute beauty, as represented by Fand, far surpasses the beauty of any of the women that he has loved, he is somehow mysteriously bound by memory to those 'crescent forms', beauty as it manifest itself in those earthly women.

> Then kiss my mouth. Though memory

> Be beauty's bitterest enemy
> I have no dread, for at my kiss
> Memory on the moment vanishes:
> Nothing but beauty can remain.[75]

Total obliviousness is the condition of those who embrace the beauty which is beyond the human. Cuchulain asks:

> And shall I never know again
> Intricacies of blind remorse?[76]

A reference to the human condition. Remorse and the 'intricacies of pain' bind us to life. To be lifted from the intricacies of blind remorse is to be lifted from life itself. The term 'intricacies' as used here seems related to the idea of the 'labyrinth of the mind' in the musician's song and the 'labyrinth of himself' mentioned in 'The Phases of the Moon'.

Fand says, 'Time shall seem to stay his course . . .'[77] This is the experience of all who are transported by the Sidhe.

> When your mouth and my mouth meet
> All my round shall be complete
> Imagining all its circles run . . .[78]

The word 'imagining' is significant. Fand has 'dreamed herself' into her present shape. In a sense eternity is the imagination. Fand tells Cuchulain:

> And there shall be oblivion
> Even to quench Cuchulain's drouth,
> Even to still that heart.[79]

The use of the thirst image to represent desire for oblivion is fittingly applied to Cuchulain who, doomeager, fought the waves and was overwhelmed by them.

Yeats skilfully prepares for the remarkable ambiguity of the final song of the play. The song begins: 'Why does your heart beat thus?' Since Emer has had direct experience of the supernatural and since Eithne is in the presence of her loved one in the last scene, the question might naturally be taken to apply to them. But Yeats has carefully introduced the matter of heartbeats in relation to both Fand and Cuchulain. Fand is spoken of as 'one that though her heart can beat' and

Cuchulain is referred to in the phrase 'even to still that heart'. Thus the final song may be read as applying to any one of the principal characters.

Thirsting for oblivion, Cuchulain is about to kiss Fand's mouth when memory of Emer draws him back. Hearing Cuchulain call out his wife's name, Fand says:

> So then it is she
> Made you impure with memory.[80]

Memories flood in upon Cuchulain.

> O Emer, Emer, there we stand;
> Side by side and hand in hand
> Tread the threshold of the house
> As when our parents married us.[81]

Fand says:

> Being among the dead you love her
> That valued every slut above her
> While you still lived.[82]

Cuchulain cries: 'O my lost Emer!'[83]

The main difference between the final version of *The Only Jealousy of Emer* and the earlier verse version is a number of cuts which Yeats has made in the text. In the earlier version Yeats included more dialogue between Cuchulain and Fand and a dialogue between Bricriu and Fand which he has cut altogether from the final edition as published in *Collected Plays* in 1934. In the final version much less emphasis is placed on the reasons for Cuchulain's hesitancy, on Fand's feelings and on the background quarrel between Fand and Bricriu. The cuts tend to throw the emphasis on to Emer's decision and away from other elements in the play. Now everything builds towards the climax of Emer's story. In the meantime there is great simplicity and economy in handling Cuchulain's hesitancy to kiss Fand. For Cuchulain to give up remorse is to give up the only meaning life has had. In the earlier version of the play Cuchulain had accused Fand of being in ignorance 'of all whereby a lover's quiet is rent'[84] and had said of her face, 'That face, though fine enough, is a fool's face/And there's folly in the deathless Sidhe/Beyond

man's reach.'[85] Reluctance to merge totally with that divine
folly, to plunge all that has made him human into total
oblivion, remains in the final version the main reason for his
hesitancy though the matter is more briefly treated.

Fand taunts him.

> And there is not a loose-tongued schemer
> But could draw you, if not dead,
> From her table and her bed.
> But what could make you fit to wive
> With flesh and blood, being born to live
> Where no one speaks of broken troth,
> For all have washed out of their eyes
> Wind-blown dirt of their memories
> To improve their sight?[86]

Fand presses Cuchulain to accept the full implications of his
relations with the Sidhe which have been mentioned in every
play. Cuchulain cries, 'Your mouth, your mouth!'[87]

Bricriu urges Emer to cry out that she renounces
Cuchulain's love before he has given Fand the kiss.

> I am Fand's enemy come to thwart her will,
> And you stand gaping there. There is still time.
> Hear how the horses trample on the shore,
> Hear how they trample! She has mounted up.
> Cuchulain's not beside her in the chariot.
> There is till a moment left; cry out, cry out!
> Renounce him, and her power is at an end.
> Cuchulain's fool is on the chariot-step
> Cry—[88]

Emer makes her decision: 'I renounce Cuchulain's love for
ever.'[89] Eithne returns:

> Come to me, my beloved, it is I.
> I Eithne Inguba. Look! He is there.
> He has come back and moved upon the bed.
> It is I that have won him from the sea.
> That brought him back to life.[90]

Eithne's professions of pride in her sexual power seem ironic
to us now that we are acquainted with the intricacies of blind

remorse which are the essence of the human condition, now that we know that the powerful magic which has brought Cuchulain back has not been Eithne's desire but Emer's renunciation of desire. The figure on the bed has replaced the twisted mask of Bricriu with the Cuchulain mask. Emer, exhausted from emotional toil, reports without excitement the revival of Cuchulain: 'Cuchulain wakes.'[91] The fifteenth phase having passed, Cuchulain returns, attempting now to lose his sense of otherness in the arms of Eithne Inguba.

> Your arms, your arms! O Eithne Inguba,
> I have been in some strange place and am afraid.[92]

III

As I mentioned earlier, Yeats appears to have left the final song purposely ambiguous. However, it seems to me to yield the most coherent meaning dramatically if it is taken to be the thoughts of Emer after her experience, addressed to Eithne Inguba, who is overjoyed at the return of Cuchulain to her.

The musicians sing:

> Why does your heart beat thus?
> Plain to be understood,
> I have met in a man's house
> A statue of solitude,
> Moving there and walking;
> Its strange heart beating fast
> For all our talking.
> O still that heart at last.[93]

Why is your heart beating so rapidly in the excitement of Cuchulain's return? To speak plainly I have had a vision of Fand, goddess of beauty appearing in the image of a beautiful solitary woman. No matter what we say about the nature of such a goddess, her heart beat like yours in desire for Cuchulain. May she cease to desire him.

> O bitter reward
> Of many a tragic tomb![94]

How bitter it must be for Fand to be thwarted in her love

after the many incarnations which have gone to produce her almost absolute beauty.

> And we though astonished are dumb
> Or give but a sigh and a word,
> A passing word.[95]

Such a thing strikes us dumb with awe or else we pass it off with a sigh or an insignificant remark.

> Although the door be shut
> And all seem well enough,
> Although wide world hold not
> A man but will give you his love
> The moment he has looked at you,
> He that has loved the best
> May turn from a statue
> His too human breast.[96]

Never be secure in your love, even when you and your love are behind closed doors, even though you may be so beautiful that all men immediately fall in love with you. Remember that even so amorous a man as Cuchulain may turn away from the goddess of beauty herself.

> What makes your heart so beat?
> What man is at your side?
> When beauty is complete
> Your own thought will have died
> And danger not be diminished;
> Dimmed at three-quarter light,
> When moon's round is finished
> The stars are out of sight.[97]

This is a reminder to Eithne that her relationship with Cuchulain is temporary. In the presence of absolute beauty itself, her light will fade as the stars fade in the light of the full moon.

10 What Stood in the Post Office?

The old man 'looking like something out of mythology' who introduces *The Death of Cuchulain* speaks directly for W. B. Yeats in the last year of his life. His speech takes its place as the last of a long series of 'curtain speeches' which Yeats began in the early days of the Irish dramatic movement and continued throughout his career as a playwright. In the Old Man's introduction to this final play, Yeats returns to those ideas about theatre which his addresses to the early audiences of the Irish dramatic movement had introduced. In the person of the Old Man Yeats looks back over a lifetime devoted to the attempt to re-establish ritual verse drama in the modern theatre, in the face of public preference for melodrama, realism and sãtire. At seventy-three Yeats has lost none of his belligerence and none of the delight in mob-baiting which was always an essential part of his platform style. The Old Man wears with pride the charge that he is out of fashion and out of date.

> I have been asked to produce a play called *The Death of Cuchulain.* It is the last of a series of plays which has for theme his life and death. I have been selected because I am out of fashion and out of date like the antiquated romantic stuff the thing is made of.[1]

Elsewhere Yeats has written:

> We have been succeeded by a school of satire that has for its subject the actual life of the village and the slum, and more recently by what may grow into a school of psychological drama; but we might, if the Irish Government at the establishment of the Free State had done something no revolution of strong farmers, clerks and lawyers would permit, have founded a school that could have substituted, as only literature without satirical or

realistic prepossessions could, positive desires for the negative passion of a national movement beaten down into party politics, compelled for a century to attack everything, to suspect everybody.[2]

The Old Man's prologue reflects Yeats' bitterness at the rejection by modern Ireland of those ideals which were the first ambitions of the Irish dramatic movement. The play itself marks a return to those positive values which could have saved Ireland from apparently endless partisan conflict.

Like the founders of the Irish dramatic movement, the Old Man affirms his relation to classical literature and to that school of acting exemplified by the eighteenth-century tragedian Talma, 'which permits an actor . . . to throw up an arm calling down the thunderbolts of Heaven, instead of seeming to pick up pins from the floor . . . '[3] The Old Man says: 'I am so old I have forgotten the name of my father and mother, unless indeed I am, as I affirm, the son of Talma, and he was so old that his friends and acquaintances still read Virgil and Homer.'[4]

The Old Man's inability to remember his parentage (though he affirms he is the son of Talma) in a sense defines the nature of Yeats' last play. Though it is clearly related to the tradition of heroic tragedy, it is in a form considerably removed from the plays of Sophocles, Shakespeare, Racine, or even Japanese *Noh*. In a letter written on 1 January, 1939, twenty-seven days before his death, Yeats said: 'I think my play is strange and the most moving I have written for some years. I am making a prose sketch for a poem — a kind of sequel — strange too, something new.'[5]

Yeats' life-long involvement in theatrical journalism and propaganda is recalled in the Old Man's words. 'When they told me that I could have my own way, I wrote certain guiding principles on a bit of newspaper.'[6] The writing of 'certain principles on a bit of newspaper' was a practice of Yeats' very common in the early days of the Abbey, as witness such occasional publications as *Samhain,* and the *Arrow,* designed to acquaint the audience with the principles and ideals of the Irish dramatic movement. 'I wanted an audience of fifty or a hundred, and if there are more, I beg them not to shuffle their feet or talk when the actors are speaking.'[7]

Although Yeats never entirely gave up the early dream of a theatre which would be a powerful force in shaping the Irish national life, he recognised that a theatre which depended on popularity with the mob could never have the artistic freedom to forge the soul of Ireland. With his discovery of the Japanese *Noh* form, Yeats began consciously to write for the few. He could see no opportunity to create an allusive theatre of beauty, appealing to cultivated minds, if the mass audience needed always to be satisfied. In notes to *The Only Jealousy of Emer* he said:

> While writing these plays, intended for some fifty people in a drawing-room or a studio, I have so rejoiced in my freedom from the stupidity of an ordinary audience that I have filled 'The Only Jealousy of Emer' with those little known convictions about the nature and history of a woman's beauty, which Robartes found in the *Speculum* of Gyraldus and in Arabia Deserta among the Judwalis.[8]

The Old Man reveals Yeats' idea of what constitutes an aristocratic theatre. The playwright works only for the people he likes; the audience is small because the playwright is select in choosing his friends, not because only a few people like his kind of theatre. Such a theatre Milton had in mind when he wrote *Comus.* 'I am sure that as I am producing a play for people I like, it is not likely in this vile age, that they will be more in number than those who listened to the first performance of Milton's *Comus.*'[9]

The cultivation required involves knowledge of the preceding plays in the play cycle, for *The Death of Cuchulain* is not an isolated work. 'On the present occasion they must know the old epics and Mr. Yeats' plays about them; such people, however poor, have libraries of their own.'[10]

It is not an aristocracy of wealth that Yeats seeks for his audience; nor has he any patience with dogmatic, intellectual *parvenus*.

> If there are more than a hundred I won't be able to escape people who are educating themselves out of the Book Societies and the like, sciolists all, pickpockets and

opinionated bitches. Why pickpockets? I will explain that,
I will make it all quite clear.[11]

Those who fake an air of cultivation by putting forth
second-hand opinion and stolen cultural tags, earn the
contempt of the aristocratic artist.

The sound of drum and pipe interrupts the Old Man.
'That's from the musicians; I asked them to do that if I was
getting excited. If you were as old you would find it easy to
get excited.'[12] The Old Man here accurately reports what
Yeats had found to be a characteristic of old age. In a letter
to Edith Heald written in December 1938, Yeats commented:

> For two days I have been tired — that is my one
> impediment. I have tired myself finishing the play and
> writing a lyric that has risen out of it, and also talk-
> ing. . . . Dorothy goes home early in February and you and
> I will be alone here, and I, despite all this pleasant
> excitement which gives me subject for poems, will be glad
> of it. Indeed that quiet will be a necessity for me. My
> whole mind has changed, it is more sensitive, more
> emotional.[13]

With the aid of a singer, a piper and a drummer, picked up
here and there about the streets, the Old Man proposes to
re-establish the music of Homer. Yeats has returned to the
high hopes of those early experiments on the psaltery with
Florence Farr. 'I promise a dance. I wanted a dance because
where there are no words there is less to spoil.'[14] This may
seem to be a curious position for a poetic playwright to take.
The reference is to the musical part of drama, or at least to
that ritual portion that tends towards music. On the stage,
Yeats has found that music and dance merge more success-
fully than music and lyric. Yeats' irritation with the tendency
of musicians and singers to 'spoil' the words of his lyrics is
well documented. As he comments in an essay: 'What was the
good of writing a love-song if the singer pronounced love
"lo-o-o-o-o-ve," or even if he said "love", but did not give it
its exact place and weight in the rhythm?'[15]

It is Emer who must perform the ritual dance. 'Emer must
dance, there must be severed heads — I am old, I belong to

mythology — severed heads for her to dance before.'[16] The dance the Old Man refers to is similar to that which Yeats used in *The King of the Great Clock Tower*. About that dance, Yeats has written:

> The dance with the severed head, suggests the central idea of Wilde's *Salome*. Wilde took it from Heine who has somewhere described Salome in hell throwing into the air the head of John the Baptist. Heine may have found it in some Jewish religious legend for it is part of the old ritual of the year: the mother goddess and the slain god.[17]

The staging of the dance in *The Death of Cuchulain* is to be symbolic and non-naturalistic.

> I had thought to have had those heads carved, but no, if the dancer can dance properly no wood-carving can look as well as a parallelogram of painted wood. But I was at my wit's end to find a good dancer; I could have got such a dancer once, but she has gone; the tragicomedian dancer, the tragic dancer, upon the same neck love the loathing life and death.[18]

This is a reference to Ninette de Valois who danced the part of Fand in *Fighting the Waves*. The Old Man's insistence that the dancer dancing the part of Emer (like the dancer who danced the part of Fand) represent both 'love and loathing', 'life and death', identified Emer with the nature goddess who appears at the centre of the play cycle and with the harlot of the final song. The harlot sings:

> But that the flesh my flesh has gripped
> I both adore and loathe[19]

and asks:

> Are those things that men adore and loathe
> Their sole reality?[20]

The Old Man expresses his contempt for the theatre of sentimentality and realism represented for him by the unheroic, non-symbolic dancers painted by Degas. Realism has turned from an art which should be timeless to one which at most merely chronicles the trivia of history. The degeneration of the dance is symbolic of the abandonment of the heroic ideal in all the arts.

I spit three times, I spit upon the dancers painted by Degas. I spit upon their short bodices, their stiff stays, their toes whereon they spin like peg-tops, above all upon that chambermaid face. They might have looked timeless, Rameses the Great, but not the chambermaid, that old maid history. I spit! I spit! I spit![21]

At the end of the Old Man's prologue, the stage darkens and the final play of the Cuchulain cycle begins.

II

The lights come up on a bare stage. Eithne Inguba seeks Cuchulain. In her hand is a message from Emer warning Cuchulain to avoid battle until the next morning when Conall Caernach will arrive with an army to support him. On her tongue is a message from Maeve urging him in Emer's name to do battle immediately. Emer's message is meant to save his life, Maeve's to bring his death.

The twin aspects of the feminine deity appear to manifest themselves in the figures of Emer and Maeve in this play. Emer representing love, tries to save Cuchulain's life; Maeve, representing hate, plots his death. Each tries to use Eithne for her own purpose. The war goddess Morrigu, in the meantime, speaks only to the dead, and she speaks out of neither love nor hatred. She has *arranged* the dance — the dance which itself represents both love and loathing.

Emer, in this play, is so far beyond sexual jealousy that she sends Eithne Inguba to be Cuchulain's bedfellow, so that love may keep him from seeking death on the battlefield. She seems in fact to take on more the function of the goddess of love than of Cuchulain's human wife. Perhaps this is the end result of a process which began in *The Only Jealousy of Emer* when she seemed to move beyond Fand in perfection of her love by freeing herself entirely of desire.

Cuchulain discovers Emer's note, but none the less chooses to go out to battle, facing great odds and almost certain death. In the scene which follows Cuchulain's discovery of the note the relationships become clear. Emer and Maeve, as positive and negative aspects of the female deity, attempt to use Eithne in their struggle for Cuchulain. The Morrigu, summoned by Cuchulain's warlike words, appears between Cuchulain and Eithne. Her presence makes the entire situation suddenly intelligible to Eithne.

We have witnessed in the play cycle the change in the form the goddess takes at the different phases on the wheel which marks the cycle of a man's life. At Phase 1, as he accepts his heroic destiny, the goddess appears in the form of a hawk. At Phase 15, she is a white, frail bird. As the wheel moves round towards the death of the hero at Phase 1, the goddess takes the form of a carrion crow.

Eithne senses the presence of the Morrigu.

> Morrigu, war goddess, stands between.
> Her black wing touched me upon the shoulder, and
> All is intelligible.[22]

Eithne has been divided between her desire for Cuchulain to go out and seek glory in mortal combat and her desire to keep him with her. It is this ambivalence that the contradictory messages from Maeve and Emer symbolise. Now all is intelligible to her. In neither case can Cuchulain's decision have any effect on her, for whatever course of action he decides to follow, his decision will not be made for her sake. She has lost him to the war goddess herself. Cuchulain is doom-eager. All other desires have drained from him. Morrigu has come between them.

The dazed Eithne continues.

> 　　　　　　　　Maeve put me in a trance.
> Though when Cuchulain slept with her as a boy
> She seemed pretty as a bird, she has changed,
> She has an eye in the middle of her forehead.[23]

As if in a dream, the female figures in Cuchulain's life seem to fade into one another. Eithne's description of Maeve seems first to suggest Aoife, then Badb — a variant of the Morrigu. Eithne's attempt to convince Cuchulain that they are both in the grips of forces greater than human draws from Cuchulain a scornful reply.

> But she that put those words into your mouth
> Had nothing monstrous; you put them there yourself . . .[24]

In this intensely powerful scene Cuchulain lashes out at
Eithne with a savage cynicism. He has passed into the first of
the three final phases in the journey of the human soul — the
phase of the Hunchback. He accuses Eithne of betraying him
because she now loves some younger man, yet he proposes to
take no action against her. Everything sublunary must
change. Eithne recognises the cynicism of the phase of the
Hunchback as a sign of Cuchulain's approaching death.

> You're not the man I loved,
> That violent man forgave no treachery.
> If thinking what you think, you can forgive,
> It is because you are about to die.[25]

Cuchulain detects the strange exultation of Eithne's feminine
nature at his approaching death, though she is but a shadow
of the goddess to whom he will be sacrificed.

> Spoken too loudly and too near the door;
> Speak low if you would speak about my death,
> Or not in that strange voice exulting in it.
> Who knows what ears listen behind the door?[26]

We recall the last scene of *On Baile's Strand* and the terms in
which Cuchulain addressed the Blind Man: 'Did you know
old listener at doors?'[27]

Eithne is stirred to a magnificent show of pride. She
prepares to suffer an heroic death to vindicate the honour of
her love. She tells Cuchulain that when he is gone she will
denounce herself to his·servants so that they, in their anger,
will put her to death in whatever foul way should please their
fancy. Her speech is artfully contrived to taunt Cuchulain
into showing some passion at her alleged treason. She flings
into his teeth the charge that the basest servant would show
more passion in the circumstances than he does. Her attempt
to arouse Cuchulain's passion is fruitless. The phase of the
Hunchback marks the death of passion. Only the cynical view
of life of a Conchubar or a Blind Man remains. Cuchulain
says simply, 'Women have spoken so, plotting a man's
death.'[28]

A servant enters to tell Cuchulain his great horse is bitted. Cuchulain asks the servant's advice as to how he should treat Eithne. With the craft of a Conchubar or a Blind Man, he plants in the servant's mind a false picture of Eithne's situation which will serve to thwart any attempt at heroics on her part. The servant suggests she be drugged with poppy-juice.

> What herbs seem suitable, but protect her life
> As if it were your own, and should I not return
> Give her to Conall Caernach because the women
> Have called him a good lover.[29]

This extremely painful scene ends with Eithne's statement that the fact that the Morrigu is her witness would bring her comfort if it were not for Cuchulain's approaching death.

> I might have peace that know
> The Morrigu, the woman like a crow,
> Stands to my defence and cannot lie,
> But that Cuchulain is about to die.[30]

As Eithne mourns, not her own fate, but Cuchulain's, the stage darkens.

III

When the stage lights up again, it is empty. Cuchulain enters wounded. As he tries to fasten himself to a piller-stone with his belt, Aoife, erect and white-haired, enters. In the scene with Aoife, Cuchulain moves into the second last phase on the Great Wheel, the phase of the Saint. As he nears his death, figures from the past appear before him. The appearance of the Blind Man from *On Baile's Strand* will mark Cuchulain's entrance into the final phase, the phase of the Fool. Cuchulain will begin to talk of a 'soft feathery shape' as the Blind Man prepares to steal his head just as the Blind Man stole the chicken long ago leaving the Fool to babble about the feathers.

In the present scene Cuchulain and Aoife re-live that love scene near the Hawk's Well in which he conquered her in all his masculine pride. Now, as he assumes more and more of the feminine quality of the Saint, she wraps her veil aroung him. In a scene in which they appear to have shifted roles, she prepares to plunge a sword into his passive, receiving body. But she does not complete the act. There is one more phase to go.

Cuchulain recognises Aoife.

> You fought with a sword,
> It seemed that we should kill each other, then
> Your body wearied and I took your sword.[31]

Aoife tells him to look again. 'Your hair is white.'[32] The theme of the changing goddess again. Aoife says:

> That time was long ago,
> And now it is my time. I have come to kill you.[33]

Cuchulain asks: 'Where am I? Why am I here?'[34] Cuchulain's confusion as he approaches death gives the whole scene an air of strangeness, as all distinction between what is inside and what is outside of Cuchulain's mind is lost. Gently Aoife explains.

> You asked their leave,
> When certain that you had six mortal wounds,
> To drink out of the pool.[35]

There is a strange parallel between *At the Hawk's Well* and *The Death of Cuchulain*. The Cuchulain cycle opens with the Old Man and Cuchulain beside an empty well over which a hawk spirit presides. It ends with the Blind Man and Cuchulain beside a pool over which a crow-headed Woman presides. Dry hazels have been replaced by a pillar-stone. Aoife's ritual with veil and sword seems to be a reversal of the love scene at the Hawk's Well. Does Cuchulain at last drink from the Pool of Death the Waters of Immortality?

Cuchulain asks Aoife's help in fastening himself to the pillar-stone.

> I have put my belt
> Upon this stone and want to fasten it
> And die upon my feet, but am too weak.
> Fasten this belt.[36]

Cuchulain, bound to the pillar-stone and ceremonially prepared for death by Aoife, suggests a sacrificial victim at some
midsummer ritual. Prometheus also comes to mind.

> And now I know your name,
> Aoife, the mother of my son. We met
> At the Hawk's Well under the withered trees.
> I killed him upon Baile's Strand, that is why
> Maeve parted ranks that she might let you through.
> You have the right to kill me.[37]

Thus *The Death of Cuchulain* is skilfully linked to the rest of
the cycle. Cuchulain, at the edge of death, seems in the
presence of his entire life, just as Yeats in the last year of his
life found himself plunged into the midst of old themes, old
responsibilities — as a reading of his last poems reveals.

Aoife declares that she *has* a right to kill Cuchulain, but
that was not the reason the army parted ranks.

> The grey of Macha, that great horse of yours
> Killed in the battle, came out of the pool
> As though it were alive, and went three times
> In a great circle round you and that stone,
> Then leaped into the pool; and not a man
> Of all that terrified army dare approach,
> But I approach.[38]

Cuchulain adds, 'Because you have the right.'[39] It is a
strangely moving image. The incident is drawn from the old
saga materials. As Yeats presents it, it seems to tap our
unconscious, taking on a meaning which is beyond rational
analysis.

The ritual begins. Like the Japanese sword which Yeats
kept on his writing table — that masculine symbol wrapped in
a piece of feminine silk embroidery — Cuchulain is ceremoniously wrapped round with Aoife's veil. The horse went three
times round; the veil is wound about his body. The gyre
winds towards its extreme. The tincture soon will change.

> *Aoife.* But I am an old woman now, and that
> Your strength may not start up when the time comes
> I wind my veil about this ancient stone
> And fasten you to it.

Cuchulain.   But do not spoil your veil.
Your veils are beautiful, some with threads of gold.
Aoife. I am too old to care for such things now.
[*She has wound the veil about him.*]
Cuchulain. There was no reason so to spoil your veil:
I am weak from loss of blood.[40]

The reversal of the sexes has begun. The winding of the veil has done its work. Cuchulain becomes more feminine as Aoife becomes more masculine.

Aoife.   I was afraid,
But now that I have wound you in the veil
I am not afraid. But — how did my son fight?[41]

We hear again the story of the fight at Baile's Strand. In an exchange of remarkable tenderness, Cuchulain and Aoife re-live the scenes which have dominated their lives. The tenderness is made sharply dramatic and most moving by the knowledge that Aoife's mission is to kill Cuchulain and that both accept this. It appears that the curse of the Hawk's Well is about to be resolved in an heroic scene which would invest Cuchulain's death with great meaning. But Yeats has more ironies in store.

Cuchulain. Age makes more skilful but not better men.
Aoife. I have been told you did not know his name
And wanted, because he had a look of me,
To be his friend, but Conchubar forbade it.
Cuchulain. Forbade it and commanded me to fight;
That very day I had sworn to do his will,
Yet refused him, and spoke about a look;
But somebody spoke of witchcraft and I said
Witchcraft had made the look, and fought and killed
him,
Then I went mad, I fought against the sea.[42]

It is with great economy that Yeats now gets his effects. The stark simplicity of this places before the mind's eye an image of great power and beauty. We get a strong sense of the mystery of life as Aoife's reminiscence is juxtaposed with that of Cuchulain.

> *Aoife.* I seemed invulnerable; you took my sword,
>   You threw me on the ground and left me there.
>   I searched the mountain for your sleeping-place
>   And laid my virgin body at your side,
>   And yet, because you had left me, hated you,
>   And thought that I would kill you in your sleep,
>   And yet begot a son that night between
>   Two black thorn-trees.
> *Cuchulain.*   I cannot understand.
> *Aoife.* Because about to die![43]

On the edge of death, the common words by which we relate
such things one to the other have slipped from Cuchulain's
grasp. He sees now beyond the surface of life to a greater
mystery. He is now the Fool. He 'would know all wisdom if
he could know anything'.[44] As Cuchulain moves into this
phase, the Blind Man from *On Baile's Strand* appears.

> *Aoife.*   Somebody comes,
>   Some countryman, and when he finds you here,
>   And none to protect him, will be terrified.
>   I will keep out of sight, for I have things
>   That I must ask questions on before I kill you.[45]

IV

The Blind Man's first utterance reminds us of *On Baile's
Strand.* Laying down his stick, he stoops and touches
Cuchulain's feet. Then he feel Cuchulain's legs.

> *Blind Man.* Ah! Ah![46]

We think of the Fool's question in the earlier play: 'Why do
you say "Ah! Ah!" '[47]

> *Cuchulain.*   I think you are a blind old man.
> *Blind Man.* A blind old beggarman. What is your name?
> *Cuchulain.* Cuchulain.
> *Blind Man.*   They say that you are weak with wounds.
>   I stood between a Fool and the sea at Baile's Strand
>   When you went mad.[48]

The Blind Man is identified. We are reminded of the Fool
who was his constant companion.

> What's bound about your hands
> So that they cannot move? Some womanish stuff.[49]

Cuchulain's first speech in the presence of the Blind Man in *On Baile's Strand* was: 'Witchcraft! There is no witchcraft on the earth or among the witches of the air, *that these hands cannot break.*'[50] The Blind Man says:

> I have been fumbling with my stick since dawn
> And then heard many voices. I began to beg.
> Somebody said I was in Maeve's tent,
> And somebody else, a big man by his voice,
> That if I brought Cuchulain's head in a bag
> I would be given twelve pennies . . .[51]

There is a strong suggestion of solar symbolism here. A Blind Man extinguishes Cuchulain for twelve pennies. Twelve is the number of months in the year. The Blind Man appears to be a representative of the forces of darkness.

> I had the bag
> To carry what I get at kitchen doors . . .[52]

Cuchulain's head is thus associated with that chicken stolen long ago. ('I might have known you had eaten it when I saw your slow, sleepy walk.'[53])

> Somebody told me how to find the place;
> I thought it would have taken till the night,
> But this has been my lucky day.[54]

The striking parallels between this play and *At the Hawk's Well* come to our attention. It is difficult to escape the suggestion that the Blind Man is somehow connected with the Old Man of *At the Hawk's Well*. There is an ironic reversal of roles here. In *At the Hawk's Well* it was Cuchulain who, with strong faith in his luck, came upon what he sought after tredding the rocks only half a day.

Cuchulain.   Twelve pennies!
Blind Man. I would not promise anything until the woman,
The great Queen Maeve herself, repeated the words.
Cuchulain. Twelve pennies! What better reason for killing
a man?
You have a knife, but have you sharpened it?[55]

Cuchulain, subjectivity almost totally gone, discusses his death as though it had nothing to do with him. It is the kind of folly Pearse talks about in his poem *The Fool*.

> *Blind Man.* I keep it sharp because it cuts my food.
> [*He lays bag on ground and begins feeling Cuchulain's body, his hands mounting upward.*]
> *Cuchulain.* I think that you know everything, Blind Man.
> My mother or my nurse said that the blind
> Know everything.
> *Blind Man.*   No, but they have good sense.
> How could I have got twelve pennies for your head
> If I had not good sense?[56]

The practical man, materialistic and concerned about cutting his food, has good sense but is blind to those qualities of life which make for nobility. His speciality is betrayal.

> *Cuchulain.*   There floats out there
> The shape that I shall take when I am dead,
> My soul's first shape, a soft feathery shape . . .[57]

We remember the Blind Man's words in *On Baile's Strand*. 'I gave him what he likes best. You do not know how vain this Fool is. He likes nothing so well as a feather.'[58]
Cuchulain continues:

> And is not that a strange shape for the soul
> Of a great fighting-man?[59]

The voice of the Fool echoes in our memories: 'Still I am an eagle-cock.'[60]
Like the darkness creeping over the sun during an eclipse, the hands of the Blind Man move over Cuchulain's body.

> *Blind Man.*   Your shoulder is there,
> This is your neck. Ah! Ah! Are you ready, Cuchulain!
> *Cuchulain.* I say it is about to sing.
> [*The stage darkens.*
> *Blind Man.* Ah! Ah![61]

There is music of pipe and drum.

V

When the lights come up it is on a bare stage. A woman with

a crow's head stands on the stage. It is the Morrigu. She stands towards the back holding a black parallelogram the size of a man's head. There are six other parallelograms near the backcloth. The Morrigu speaks: 'The dead can hear me and to the dead I speak.'[62] It is only those who have been carried beyond the sensual music of life who can understand life in its entirety, seeing it whole and from outside the constant war of love and loathing, life and death, male and female. The Morrigu displays the head of Cuchulain, now a black parallelogram. He has passed beyond Phase 28 and has become that unkneaded dough Robartes speaks about in 'The Phases of the Moon'.[63] The heads of the six men who gave Cuchulain mortal wounds are also presented in the form of black parallelograms. Cuchulain has received one wound for each of the six phases the soul passes through from Phase 22 (the Breaking of Strength) through Phase 28. The Morrigu's statement at the end of her speech that she arranged the dance refers both to the dance that Emer dances in the play and the entire dance of Cuchulain's life and death. As I have mentioned, three female figures, three manifestations of the goddess, predominate in this play. Maeve plots the death of Cuchulain. Emer dances a dance of resurrection. The Morrigu presides over the entire process.

As we have seen, Yeats associated the dance of the severed heads with the dance that Salome danced before the head of John the Baptist. This in turn was associated in his mind with the dance of some nature goddess before the head of her victim. This association must have been greatly enriched by Yeats' occult studies, for John the Baptist figured as a powerful magical figure in early gnostic sects. It should be noted that there is a festival associated with John the Baptist held three days after midsummer, the date we have fixed for the death of Cuchulain when we consider it as a seasonal ritual.

In a note on *The King of the Great Clock Tower,* Yeats speaks of an old Gaelic legend in which 'a certain man swears to sing the praise of a certain woman, his head is cut off and the head sings'.[64] When Yeats made use of this plot in *The King of the Great Clock Tower* the man whose head was cut off became 'a stroller and a fool'. A line of the song which he sang ('O, what is life but a mouthful of air?'[65]) echoes the words of the final song of *At the Hawk's Well.* The idea of the severed head of a fool singing to a dancing woman was one that appeared to haunt Yeats. Emer's dance ends on the sound of bird notes.

The dance described by Yeats is highly ritualistic. Emer runs in after the exit of the Morrigu. When she begins to dance, she seems to rage against the heads of those who wounded Cuchulain. She makes motions as if to strike them, going three times around the circle of the heads. The head of Cuchulain is raised above the others on a pedestal. Emer moves towards it as if in adoration or triumph. She prostrates herself before it, then rises listening. She stands motionless, as if hesitating between the head and what she hears. In the silence a few faint bird notes are heard. The stage slowly darkens.[66]

VI

When the stage brightens we are at an Irish Fair of our own day. Three musicians in street-singers' clothes occupy the stage. Two of them begin to pipe and drum. The third begins to sing.

> The harlot sang to the begger-man.
> I met them face to face,
> Conall, Cuchulain, Usna's boys
> All that most ancient race . . .[67]

The harlot, modern Ireland, has met face to face the heroes of Ireland's heroic age.

> Maeve had three in an hour, they say.
> I adore those clever eyes,
> Those muscular bodies, but can get
> No grip upon their thighs.[68]

The harlot is much taken by the passion and the sexual prowess of Ireland's legendary heroes. But the romantic dream of Ireland's past is unsubstantial and ultimately unsatisfying.

> I meet those long pale faces,
> Hear their great horses, then
> Recall what centuries have passed
> Since they were living men.[69]

Romantic Ireland's dead and gone.

> That there are still some living
> That do my limbs unclothe,
> But that the flesh my flesh has gripped
> I both adore and loathe.[70]

The real lovers, the living men of modern Ireland, she both loves and hates. But this is, after all, the human situation. Love and loathing have always been interwoven for those who would love the goddess. Her present incarnation as a prostitute does not alter that situation.

> Are those things that men adore and loathe
> Their sole reality?[71]

The question seems ambiguous. Does it mean: 'Is material existence the sole reality?' Or does it mean: 'Are those things that engage a man's emotion his sole reality?'

> What stood in the Post Office
> With Pearse and Connolly?
> What comes out of the mountain
> Where men first shed their blood?
> Who thought Cuchulain till it seemed
> He stood where they had stood?[72]

Cuchulain's next incarnation was in the Easter Uprising of 1916.

> No body like his body
> Has modern woman borne,
> But an old man looking back on life
> Imagines it in scorn.[73]

Yeats, at seventy-three, is scornful of the physical perfection that Cuchulain's body represents. It is the spirit that is important. Ironically, the statue of Cuchulain that commemorates the rebels is intensely physical.

A statue's there to mark the place,
By Oliver Sheppard done.
So ends the tale that the harlot
Sang to the beggar-man.[74]

The Cuchulain cycle closes on this note of ironic ambiguity. The 'tale that the harlot sang to the beggar-man', the ballad which ends in an image of a statue of Cuchulain, stands at once for the play cycle itself, the history of Ireland, and Yeats' own life. Yeats, like the Easter rebels, met death with the image of Cuchulain dominating his mind.

Notes

Introduction

1. W. B. Yeats, *The Variorum Edition of the Plays of W. B. Yeats,* ed. Russell K. Alspach (New York: Macmillan, 1966) p. 526.
2. Ibid., p. 454.
3. Ibid., p. 1305.
4. Ibid., p. 568.
5. W. B. Yeats, *The Letters of W. B. Yeats,* ed. Allan Wade (London: Rupert Hart-Davis, 1954) p. 922.
6. T. S. Eliot, "Yeats", *The Norton Anthology of English Literature,* Vol. 2 (New York: W. W. Norton & Co. Inc., 1968) p. 1834.
7. T. S. Eliot, "Ulysses, Order, and Myth", ibid., p. 1825.

1 The Ritual of a Lost Faith

1. W. B. Yeats and T. Sturge Moore, *Correspondence 1901-1937,* ed. Ursula Bridge (New York: Oxford University Press, 1953) p. 156.
2. W. B. Yeats, *Autobiographies* (London: Macmillan, 1966) pp. 253-4.
3. Ibid., p. 255.
4. Ibid., p. 64.
5. W. B. Yeats, *Explorations* (London: Macmillan, 1962) p. 7.
6. *Autobiographies,* p. 72.
7. Ibid.
8. *Explorations,* p. 13.
9. W. B. Yeats, *Memoirs,* ed. Denis Donoghue (London: Macmillan, 1972) pp. 123-4.

10. W. B. Yeats, *The Collected Plays of W. B. Yeats* (London: Macmillan, 1962) pp. 266-7.
11. Virginia Moore, *The Unicorn* (New York: Macmillan, 1954) p. 27.
12. *Memoirs*, p. 124.
13. W. B. Yeats, *Uncollected Prose 1*, ed. John P. Frayne (New York: Columbia University Press, 1970) pp. 130-37.
14. *Memoirs*, p. 27.
15. Israel Regardie, *The Golden Dawn* (River Falls: Hazel Hills Corporation, 1970) p. 23.
16. Ibid., p. 28.
17. Ibid.
18. For a concise account of the Jungian view of "individuation" see Carl Jung, *et al.*, *Man and his Symbols* (New York: Dell Publishing Co, 1968) pp. 157-254.
19. *Autobiographies*, pp. 185-6.
20. *Memoirs*, p. 125.
21. John Rhys, *Lectures on the Origin and Growth of Religion as Illustrated by Celtic Heathendom* (London: Williams & Norgate, 1892) pp. 553-4.
22. *Letters*, p. 297.
23. Ibid., p. 264.
24. Ibid., p. 293.
25. Ibid., pp. 293-4.
26. Birgit Bjersby, *The Interpretation of the Cuchulain Legend in the Works of W. B. Yeats* (Upsala: A. B. Lundequista Bokhandeln, 1950) p. 43.
27. Richard Ellman, *Yeats — The Man and the Masks* (New York: E. P. Dutton, 1948) pp. 124-5.
28. *Memoirs*, p. 125.
29. *Letters*, p. 324.
30. Ibid.
31. Ellman, op. cit., p. 126.
32. W. B. Yeats, *Essays and Introductions* (London: Macmillan, 1961) pp. 167-8.
33. *Autobiographies*, pp. 455-6.
34. *Essays and Introductions*, p. 232.
35. Ibid.
36. W. B. Yeats and T. Sturge Moore, op. cit., p. 156.

37. Morton Irving Seiden, *William Butler Yeats - The Poet as A Mythmaker* (East Lansing: Michigan State University Press, 1962) pp. 46-7.
38. Joseph Hone, *W. B. Yeats, 1865-1939* (London: Macmillan, 1962) p. 470.

2 That Famous Man Cuchulain

1. *Variorum Plays*, p. 567.
2. Phillip L. Marcus, *Yeats and the Beginning of the Irish Renaissance* (Ithaca: Cornell University Press, 1970) p. 235.
3. *Uncollected Prose*, p. 350.
4. Ibid.,
5. Quoted by Marcus, op. cit., p. 234.
6. *Letters*, p. 308.
7. W. B. Yeats, *Letters to the New Island*, ed. Horace Reynolds (Cambridge: Harvard University Press, 1934) p. 159.
8. Cf. Thomas P. O'Neill, "The Springs of 1916", Goddard Lieberson (ed.), *The Irish Uprising: 1916-1922* (New York: CBS Records, 1966) p. 1.
9. *Uncollected Prose*, p. 256.
10. Ibid.
11. O'Neill, op. cit., p. 1.
12. Ibid., p. 4.
13. Padraic H. Pearse, *Collected Works of Padraic H. Pearse — Political Writings and Speeches* (Dublin: Phoenix Publishing Co., 1917) p. 91.
14. Giles W. L. Telfer, "Yeats's Idea of the Gael", Liam Miller (ed.), *The Dolmen Press Yeats Centenary Papers MCMLXV* (Dublin: Dolmen Press, 1968) p. 101.
15. Padraic H. Pearse, *Collected Works of Padraic H. Pearse — Songs of the Irish Rebels, etc.* (Dublin: Phoenix Publishing Co., 1917) pp. 229-30.
16. *Collected Plays*, pp. 704-5.
17. Marcus, op. cit., p. 224.
18. *Variorum Plays*, p. 572.
19. *Collected Plays*, p. 276.

20. Ibid., p. 225.
21. *Uncollected Prose*, p. 359.
22. *Essays and Introductions*, p. 513.
23. *Uncollected Prose*, pp. 189-90.
24. Ibid., p. 190.
25. *Letters*, pp. 249-50.
26. Seiden, op. cit., p. 16.
27. Myles Dillon (ed.), *Irish Sagas* (Cork: Mercier Press, 1968) p. 17.
28. *Variorum Plays*, p. 573.
29. *Letters to the New Island*, p. 101.
30. David Greene, "Táin Bó Cúalnge", Dillon, op. cit., p. 98.
31. Lady Gregory, *Cuchulain of Muirthemne* (London: John Murray, 1902) p. 38.
32. Ibid., p. 49.
33. Ibid.
34. Ibid., pp. 78-9.
35. Ibid., p. 81
36. *Collected Plays*, p. 287.
37. Gregory, op. cit., p. 313.
38. Ibid., p. 316.
39. Ibid., p. 319.
40. Ibid.
41. *Collected Plays*, p. 215.
42. Gregory, op. cit., p. 280.
43. Ibid., pp. 289-90.
44. Ibid., pp. 290-91.
45. Ibid., p. 293.
46. *Variorum Plays*, p. 550.
47. Gregory, op. cit., pp. 326-7.
48. Ibid., p. 340.
49. *Collected Plays*, p. 696.
50. Ibid., p. 694.
51. Ibid., pp. 219-20.
52. Padraic H. Pearse, *Collected Works of Padraic H. Pearse — Plays, Stories, Poems* (Dublin: Phoenix Publishing Co., 1917) p. 334.
53. *Letters*, p. 425.
54. *Essays and Introductions*, p. 515.

3 The Burning Wheel of Love

1. Quoted by Ellman, op. cit., p. 129.
2. A. Norman Jeffares, *W. B. Yeats — Man and Poet* (London: Routledge & Kegan Paul, 1949) p. 140.
3. *Letters,* p. 391.
4. Ibid.
5. Ibid., p. 396.
6. Peter Ure, *Toward A Mythology* (New York: Russell & Russell, 1967) p. 16.
7. Leonard E. Nathan, *The Tragic Drama of William Butler Yeats* (New York: Columbia University Press, 1965) pp. 116-17.
8. *Variorum Plays,* p. 488.
9. Ibid., p. 510.
10. Nathan, op. cit., p. 120.
11. *Essays and Introductions,* pp. 215-6.
12. Ellman, op. cit., p. 166.
13. *Letters,* pp. 471-2.
14. Ibid., p. 758.
15. *Collected Plays,* p. 259.
16. Ibid., p. 256.
17. Ibid., p. 270.
18. *Variorum Plays,* p. 456.
19. Ibid., pp. 474-6.
20. *Collected Plays,* p. 252.
21. *Variorum Plays,* pp. 644-5.
22. *Collected Plays,* p. 271.
23. *Variorum Plays,* p. 932.
24. *Collected Plays,* pp. 254-5.
25. W. B. Yeats, *Mythologies* (London: Macmillan, 1959) pp. 288-9.
26. *Collected Plays,* p. 267.
27. Ibid., p. 276.
28. *Variorum Plays,* p. 566.
29. W. B. Yeats, *The Collected Poems of W. B. Yeats* (London: Macmillan, 1952) p. 398.
30. W. B. Yeats, *A Vision* (London: Macmillan, 1962) p. 81.
31. *Collected Plays,* p. 291.

32. Ibid., p. 292.
33. Ibid.
34. Ibid.
35. Ibid., p. 219.
36. *A Vision*, p. 196.
37. Regardie, op. cit., pp. 245-63.
38. *Collected Plays*, p. 211.
39. Ibid., p. 239.
40. Ibid., p. 256.
41. Ibid., p. 268.
42. Ibid., p. 256.
43. Ibid., p. 259.
44. Ibid., p. 278.
45. Ibid., pp. 283-4.
46. Ibid., p. 697.
47. Ibid., p. 209.
48. Ibid.
49. Ibid., p. 210.
50. These are the terms used by Yeats to describe Phases 8 and 22 in the diagram on page 81 of *A Vision*.
51. *Larousse Encyclopedia of Mythology* (London: Paul Hamlyn, 1959) p. 244.
52. *Larousse*, p. 244.
53. Curtis B. Bradford, *Yeats at Work* (Carbondale and Edwardsville: Southern Illinois University Press, 1965) p. 180.
54. *Collected Plays*, p. 209.
55. Ibid., p. 217.
56. *Larousse*, p. 244.
57. *Collected Plays*, p. 248.
58. Ibid., p. 258.
59. T. G. E. Powell, *The Celts* (London: Thames & Hudson, 1963) pp. 117-8.
60. Ibid., p. 118.
61. Ibid., pp. 121-2.
62. *Variorum Plays*, p. 1010.
63. *Collected Plays*, p. 699.
64. Powell, op. cit., p. 123.
65. *Collected Plays*, p. 281.
66. Ibid., p. 292.

67. Ibid., pp. 262-3.
68. Joseph Campbell, *The Masks of God: Occidental Mythology* (New York: Viking Press, 1964) pp. 163-4.
69. *A Vision*, p. 60.
70. Ibid., pp. 178-9.
71. Ibid., p. 178.
72. Ibid., p. 61.
73. Ibid.
74. Ibid., p. 63.
75. Ibid., pp. 63-4
76. *Collected Plays*, p. 698.
77. *A Vision*, p. 63.
78. *Collected Plays*, p. 704.
79. Ibid., p. 705.

4 The Rag-and-Bone Shop of the Heart

1. *Collected Poems*, p. 392.
2. *Autobiographies*, pp. 102-3.
3. W. B. Yeats, *The Variorum Edition of the Poems of W. B. Yeats*, ed. Russell K. Alspach (New York: Macmillan, 1957) p. 803.
4. *Letters*, p. 913.
5. *Collected Poems*, p. 113.
6. *Autobiographies*, p. 123.
7. *Collected Poems*, p. 139.
8. *Collected Plays*, p. 218.
9. Ibid., p. 220.
10. Ellman, op. cit., p. 103.
11. Ibid.
12. *Collected Poems*, p. 121.
13. *Collected Plays*, p. 243.
14. *Explorations*, pp. 83-4.
15. Daniel J. Murphy, "The Reception of Synge's *Playboy* in Ireland and America: 1907-1912", *Bulletin of the New York Public Library*, vol. 64, no. 10, p. 521.
16. Ibid., p. 523.
17. Ibid., p. 524.
18. *Collected Plays*, p. 234.

19. Ibid., p. 227.
20. Ibid., p. 225.
21. David H. Greene and Edward M. Stephens, *J. M. Synge 1871-1909* (New York: Macmillan, 1959) p. 248.
22. Ellman, op. cit., pp. 159-60.
23. Ibid., p. 166.
24. Ibid.
25. *Collected Poems*, p. 203.
26. Hone, op. cit., p. 303.
27. Iseult was the daughter of Maud Gonne and the French journalist Lucien Millevoye, with whom Maud had an affair in the nineties. Cf. *Memoirs*, pp. 132-3.
28. For a description of this last meeting see Hone, op. cit., p. 470.
29. *Collected Plays*, p. 702.

5 Players and Painted Stage

1. *Collected Poems*, p. 392.
2. *Explorations*, pp. 171-2.
3. Ibid., p. 172.
4. Ibid.
5. *Essays and Introductions*, p. 18.
6. *Letters*, p. 374.
7. *Explorations*, p. 219.
8. *Letters*, p. 374.
9. *Essays and Introductions*, p. 16.
10. Ibid., p. 18.
11. Ibid., pp. 18-19.
12. George Moore, *Ave* (New York: Boni & Liveright, 1923) pp. 32-3.
13. Clifford Bax, *Florence Farr, Bernard Shaw and W. B. Yeats* (Dublin: Cuala Press, 1941) p. 19.
14. Ibid., p. 20.
15. Gerard Fay, *The Abbey Theatre* (London: Hollis & Carter, 1958) pp. 70-71.
16. *Essays and Introductions*, p. 22.
17. Ibid.
18. *Variorum Plays*, p. 1009.

19. *Autobiographies,* p. 449.
20. *Essays and Introductions,* p. 528.
21. Gerard Fay, op. cit., p. 30.
22. *Explorations,* pp. 173-4.
23. *Letters,* p. 369.
24. W. G. Fay and Catherine Carswell, *The Fays of the Abbey Theatre* (New York: Harcourt, Brace & Co., 1935) p. 112.
25. Ibid., p. 165.
26. *Variorum Plays,* p. 1009.
27. Ibid., p. 526.
28. Ibid.
29. Lady Gregory, op. cit., p. 79.
30. *Variorum Plays,* p. 1304.
31. *Letters,* p. 609.
32. Ibid., p. 611.
33. Ibid., pp. 610-11.
34. Ibid., p. 611.
35. *A Vision,* p. 34.
36. *Variorum Plays,* p. 1009.
37. Ibid., p. 851.
38. *Letters,* p. 760.
39. Ibid., pp. 761-2.
40. *Variorum Plays,* p. 1308.
41. Ibid., p. 567.
42. Ibid., p. 1009.
43. Ibid., pp. 1009-10.
44. Ibid., p. 1010.
45. *Collected Plays,* p. 694.
46. *Essays and Introductions,* pp. 527-8.
47. *Explorations,* p. 109.
48. *Letters,* p. 367.
49. Ibid., p. 370.
50. Ibid., p. 441.
51. Ibid., p. 367.
52. Ibid., p. 370.
53. *Explorations,* p. 86.
54. Ibid., p. 87.
55. *Essays and Introductions,* p. 529.
56. Ibid., p. 528.

57. *Letters,* pp. 424-5.
58. *Autobiographies,* p. 524.
59. Ibid., pp. 524-5.
60. *Explorations,* pp. 248-9.
61. Ibid., p. 249.
62. *Essays and Introductions,* pp. 231-2.
63. *Explorations,* pp. 86-7.
64. *Autobiographies,* p. 526.
65. Ibid.
66. Ibid.
67. Ibid., pp. 526-7.
68. Denis Bablet, *Edward Gordon Craig* (London: Heinemann, 1966) p. 110.
69. *Essays and Introductions,* p. 226.
70. Bablet, op. cit., p. 109.
71. *Essays and Introductions,* pp. 226-30.
72. Ibid., p. 224.
73. Ibid., pp. 230-31.
74. Ibid., p. 222.
75. *Letters,* p. 609.
76. Ibid., pp. 609-10.
77. Ibid., p. 611.
78. *Variorum Plays,* p. 571.
79. *Collected Plays,* p. 694.
80. Ibid.
81. *Letters,* p. 371.
82. Ibid., pp. 308-9.
83. Ibid., p. 309.
84. Edward Gordon Craig, *Index to the Story of my Days* (London: Hulton Press, 1957) p. 239.
85. Ibid.
86. *Letters,* p. 380.
87. Ibid., pp. 385-6.
88. Ibid., p. 366.
89. *Essays and Introductions,* pp. 100-01.
90. Ibid., p. 101.
91. *Variorum Plays,* p. 1290.
92. *Explorations,* p. 88.
93. Lady Gregory, op. cit., pp. 107-8.
94. Ibid., p. 107.

95. *Letters*, pp. 425-6.
96. Ibid., p. 427.
97. *Variorum Plays*, p. 1306.
98. Lady Gregory, op. cit., p. 45.
99. *Variorum Plays*, p. 421.
100. Ibid., p. 454.
101. *Explorations*, p. 179.
102. Ibid., pp. 179-80.
103. *Letters*, p. 546.
104. Bablet, op. cit., pp. 125-6.
105. *Letters*, p. 546.
106. *Variorum Plays*, p. 1301.
107. Ibid., p. 396.
108. Ibid., p. 644.
109. *Letters*, p. 554.
110. *Variorum Plays*, pp. 644-5.
111. *Letters*, p. 577.
112. *Explorations*, p. 173.
113. *Essays and Introductions*, p. 225.
114. *Letters*, p. 445.
115. *Variorum Plays*, pp. 415-16.
116. *Essays and Introductions*, p. 221.
117. *Letters*, p. 612.
118. *Collected Plays*, p. 694.
119. *Collected Poems*, p. 122.

6 The Sudden Cry of a Hawk

1. *Collected Poems*, p. 57.
2. Ibid.
3. *Collected Plays*, p. 214.
4. *Collected Poems*, p. 392.
5. *Collected Plays*, p. 284.
6. Ibid., pp. 241-3.
7. Ibid., p. 264.
8. *Essays and Introductions*, p. 63.
9. Ibid., p. 216.
10. Ibid.
11. *Variorum Poems*, p. 806.

12. Ibid., p. 808.
13. *Variorum Plays,* p. 571.
14. *Essays and Introductions,* p. 55.
15. Ibid.
16. Ibid., p. 54.
17. Ibid., p. 57.
18. *Collected Poems,* p. 57.
19. *Collected Plays,* p. 208.
20. Ibid.
21. *Essays and Introductions,* p. 221.
22. *Collected Plays,* p. 704.
23. Ibid., p. 208.
24. Ibid.
25. Ibid., p. 220.
26. Ibid., p. 255.
27. Ibid., p. 209.
28. Ibid.
29. Oliver St. John Gogarty, *It Isn't This Time Of Year At All* (New York: Doubleday, 1954) p. 245.
30. *Collected Plays,* p. 209.
31. Ibid.
32. Ibid.
33. Ibid., p. 210.
34. Ibid.
35. Ibid., pp. 210-11.
36. *Collected Poems,* p. 280.
37. *Collected Plays,* p. 211.
38. Ibid., p. 290.
39. Ibid., p. 211.
40. Ibid.
41. *Collected Poems,* p. 347.
42. Ibid.
43. *Collected Plays,* p. 211.
44. Ibid.
45. Ibid.
46. Ibid., p. 257.
47. Ibid., p. 212.
48. Ibid.
49. Ibid.
50. Ibid.

51. *Letters,* pp. 293-4.
52. *Essays and Introductions,* pp. 238-45.
53. *Collected Poems,* p. 203.
54. Ibid., p. 113.
55. Ibid., p. 204.
56. *Collected Plays,* p. 212.
57. *Mythologies,* pp. 184-90.
58. *Collected Plays,* pp. 212-13.
59. Ibid., p. 213.
60. Ibid.
61. Ibid.
62. Ibid.
63. Ibid.
64. *Mythologies,* pp. 213-24.
65. *Collected Poems,* pp. 49-50.
66. *Collected Plays,* p. 214.
67. Ibid.
68. Ibid.
69. Ibid.
70. *Collected Poems,* pp. 210-11.
71. *Collected Plays,* pp. 214-15.
72. *Letters,* pp. 471-2.
73. *Collected Plays,* p. 215.
74. Ibid.
75. Ibid.
76. Ibid.
77. Ibid., pp. 215-6.
78. Ibid., p. 216.
79. Ibid.
80. Ibid.
81. Ibid.
82. Ibid.
83. Ibid., p. 217.
84. Ibid.
85. Ibid., p. 262.
86. Ibid., p. 217.
87. Ibid.
88. Ibid.
89. Ibid.
90. Ibid.

91. Ibid., pp. 217-8.
92. Ibid., p. 218.
93. Ibid.
94. Ibid.
95. Ibid.
96. Ibid., p. 219.
97. Ibid.
98. Ibid.
99. Ibid., pp. 219-20.

7 *A High, Wide, Foxy Man*

1. *Valorium Plays*, pp. 569-70.
2. *Collected Plays*, p. 242.
3. *Letters*, p. 307.
4. *Collected Plays*, p. 224.
5. Ibid., p. 229.
6. Ibid., p. 238.
7. *Letters*, p. 307.
8. Ibid., p. 457.
9. *Collected Plays*, p. 225.
10. Ibid., p. 228.
11. Ibid.
12. Ibid., p. 234.
13. Ibid., p. 235.
14. Ibid., pp. 237-8.
15. Ibid., p. 239.
16. Ibid.
17. Ibid.
18. Ibid., p. 240.
19. Ibid., p. 242.
20. Ibid.
21. Ibid.
22. Ibid.
23. Ibid.
24. Ibid., pp. 242-3.

8 *Between a Fool and a Blind Man*

1. *Variorum Plays*, p. 932.

2. *Essays and Introductions*, p. 215.
3. *Collected Plays*, p. 271.
4. Ibid., p. 247.
5. *Letters*, p. 324.
6. *Collected Poems*, pp. 66-7.
7. *Collected Plays*, p. 247.
8. Ibid., pp. 247-8.
9. Ibid., p. 248.
10. Ibid.
11. Ibid.
12. Ibid.
13. Ibid.
14. Ibid.
15. Ibid.
16. Ibid.
17 Ibid.
18. Ibid., pp. 248-9.
19. Ibid., p. 249.
20. Ibid., p. 248.
21. Ibid., p. 249.
22. Ibid.
23. Ibid.
24. Ibid.
25. Ibid.
26. Ibid.
27. Ibid.
28. Ibid.
29. Ibid., pp. 249-50.
30. Ibid., p. 250.
31. Ibid.
32. Ibid.
33. Ibid.
34. Ibid.
35. Ibid.
36. Ibid.
37. Ibid.
38. Ibid., p. 251.
39. Lady Gregory, *Cuchulain of Muirthemne*, p. 214.
40. *Collected Plays*, p. 251.
41. Ibid.

42. Ibid.
43. Ibid.
44. Ibid.
45. Ibid., p. 252.
46. Ibid.
47. Ibid.
48. Ibid., p. 253.
49. Ibid.
50. Ibid.
51. Ibid. pp. 253-4.
52. Ibid. p. 254.
53. Ibid.
54. Ibid., pp. 254-5.
55. Ibid. p. 255.
56. Ibid.
57. Ibid.
58. Ibid.
59. Ibid., pp. 255-6.
60. *Letters*, p. 425.
61. *Collected Plays*, p. 256.
62. Ibid.
63. Ibid.
64. Ibid.
65. Ibid.
66. *Collected Poems*, p. 398.
67. *Collected Plays*, p. 258.
68. Ibid.
69 Ibid., pp. 258-9.
70. *Collected Poems*, p. 348.
71. *Collected Plays*, p. 259.
72. Ibid.
73. Ibid.
74. Friedrich Nietzsche, *The Philosophy of Nietzsche* (New York: Modern Library, 1927) p. 951.
75. *Letters*, p. 758.
76. *Mythologies*, p. 336.
77. *Collected Plays*, p. 259.
78. Ibid., p. 260.
79. Ibid.
80. Ibid.

81. Ibid., p. 261.
82. Ibid.
83. Ibid.
84. Ibid.
85. Ibid., p. 248.
86. Ibid., p. 261.
87. Ibid., p. 262.
88. Ibid.
89. Ibid.
90. Ibid.
91. *Mythologies*, pp. 213-24.
92. *Variorum Poems*, p. 807.
93. *Collected Plays*, p. 262.
94. Ibid., p. 290.
95. *Letters*, pp. 471-2.
96. Ibid.
97. *Collected Plays*, p. 262.
98. Ibid., p. 259.
99. Ibid., p. 263.
100. Ibid.
101. Ibid.
102. Ibid.
103. Ibid.
104. Ibid.
105. Ibid.
106. Ibid.
107. Ibid.
108. Ibid.
109. Ibid., pp. 219-20.
110. Ibid., p. 264.
111. *Collected Poems*, p. 62.
112. *Collected Plays*, p. 265.
113. Ibid., pp. 265-6.
114. Ibid., p. 266.
115. Ibid.
116. Ibid.
117. Ibid.
118. Ibid.
119. Ibid., p. 274.
120. Ibid., p. 266.

121. Ibid.
122. Ibid.
123. Ibid.
124. Ibid., pp. 266-7.
125. Ibid., p. 267.
126. Ibid.
127. Ibid.
128. Ibid.
129. Ibid.
130. Ibid.
131. Ibid.
132. Ibid.
133. Ibid.
134. Ibid., pp. 267-8.
135. Ibid., p. 268.
136. Ibid.
137. Ibid.
138. Ibid.
139. Ibid.
140. Ibid., p. 269.
141. Ibid.
142. Ibid.
143. Ibid.
144. Ibid.
145. Ibid.
146. Ibid.
147. Ibid., pp. 269-70.
148. Ibid., p. 270.
149. Ibid.
150. Ibid.
151. Ibid.
152. Ibid.
153. Ibid.
154. Ibid.
155. Ibid.
156. Ibid., p. 271.
157. Ibid.
158. Ibid.
159. Ibid.
160. Ibid.

161. Ibid., p. 272.
162. Ibid.
163. Ibid.
164. Ibid.
165. Ibid.
166. Ibid.
167. Ibid.
168. Ibid., pp. 272-3.
169. Ibid., p. 273.
170. Ibid.
171. Ibid.
172. Ibid.
173. Ibid.
174. Ibid.
175. Ibid.
176. Ibid., p. 274.
177. Ibid.
178. Ibid., p. 267.
179. Ibid., p. 274.
180. Hyde, *A Literary History of Ireland*, p. 541.
181. *Collected Plays*, p. 266.
182. Ibid., p. 274.
183. Ibid.
184. Ibid., p. 275.
185. Ibid.
186. Ibid., pp. 275-6.
187. Ibid., p. 276.
188. Ibid.
189. Ibid.
190. Ibid.
191. Ibid.
192. Ibid.
193. Ibid., pp. 276-7.
194. Ibid., p. 277.
195. Ibid.
196. Ibid., pp. 277-8.
197. Ibid., p. 278.
198. *Collected Poems*, p. 392.

9 *The Fifteenth Night*

1. *A Vision*, p. 60.
2. Ibid., p. 61.
3. Ibid.
4. *Collected Plays*, p. 281.
5. Ibid.
6. Ibid., pp. 281-2.
7. Ibid., p. 282.
8. Ibid.
9. Ibid.
10. Ibid.
11. Ibid.
12. Ibid.
13. Ibid.
14. Ibid.
15. Ibid.
16. Ibid.
17. *A Vision*, p. 61.
18. *Collected Plays*, p. 282.
19. Ibid., p. 263.
20. Ibid., p. 282.
21. Ibid., p. 283.
22. Ibid.
23. Ibid.
24. Ibid.
25. *Variorum Plays*, p. 808.
26. *Collected Plays*, p. 283.
27. Ibid.
28. *Variorum Plays*, p. 561.
29. *Collected Plays*, p. 285.
30. Ibid.
31. Ibid., pp. 285-6.
32. Ibid., p. 286.
33. Ibid.
34. Ibid.
35. Ibid.
36. Ibid.
37. Ibid., pp. 286-7.
38. Ibid., p. 287.

39. Ibid.
40. Ibid.
41. Ibid.
42. Ibid.
43. Ibid.
44. *A Vision,* p. 63.
45. Ibid., p. 60.
46. *Collected Plays,* p. 287.
47. Ibid., p. 288.
48. Ibid.
49. Ibid.
50. Ibid.
51. Ibid.
52. Ibid.
53. Ibid., pp. 288-9.
54. Ibid., p. 289.
55. Ibid.
56. Ibid.
57. Ibid.
58. Ibid., pp. 289-90.
59. Ibid., p. 290.
60. Ibid.
61. Ibid.
62. Ibid.
63. Ibid.
64. Ibid.
65. Ibid., p. 291.
66. Ibid.
67. Ibid.
68 Ibid.
69. Ibid.
70. *Variorum Plays,* p. 553.
71. Ibid., p. 559.
72. *Collected Plays,* p. 292.
73. Ibid.
74. Ibid.
75. Ibid.
76. Ibid.
77. Ibid.
78. Ibid., pp. 292-3.

79. Ibid., p. 293.
80. Ibid.
81. Ibid.
82. Ibid.
83. Ibid.
84. *Variorum Plays,* p. 559.
85. Ibid.
86. *Collected Plays,* p. 293.
87. Ibid.
88. Ibid., p. 294.
89. Ibid.
90. Ibid.
91. Ibid.
92. Ibid.
93. Ibid., p. 295.
94. Ibid.
95. Ibid.
96. Ibid.
97. Ibid., p. 296.

10 What Stood in the Post Office?

1. *Collected Plays,* p. 693.
2. *Variorum Plays,* p. 572
3. *Essays and Introductions,* p. 529.
4. *Collected Plays,* p. 693.
5. *Letters,* p. 922.
6. *Collected Plays,* p. 693.
7. Ibid.
8. *Variorum Plays,* p. 566.
9. *Collected Plays,* p. 693.
10. Ibid., pp. 693-4.
11. Ibid., p. 694.
12. Ibid.
13. *Letters,* p. 921.
14. *Collected Plays,* p. 694.
15. *Essays and Introductions,* p. 14.
16. *Collected Plays,* p. 694.
17. *Variorum Plays,* p. 1010.

18. *Collected Plays,* p. 694.
19. Ibid., p. 704.
20. Ibid.
21. Ibid., p. 694.
22. Ibid.
23. Ibid.
24. Ibid.
25. Ibid.
26. Ibid.
27. Ibid., p. 276.
28. Ibid., p. 698.
29. Ibid.
30. Ibid.
31. Ibid., p. 699.
32. Ibid.
33. Ibid.
34. Ibid.
35. Ibid.
36. Ibid.
37. Ibid.
38. Ibid., pp. 699-700.
39. Ibid., p. 700.
40. Ibid.
41. Ibid.
42. Ibid.
43. Ibid., pp. 700-01.
44. *A Vision,* p. 182.
45. *Collected Plays,* p. 701.
46. Ibid.
47. Ibid., p. 248.
48. Ibid., p. 701.
49. Ibid.
50. Ibid., p. 273.
51. Ibid., pp. 701-2.
52. Ibid., p. 702.
53. Ibid., p. 272.
54. Ibid., p. 702.
55. Ibid.
56. Ibid.
57. Ibid.

58. Ibid., p. 273.
59. Ibid., p. 702.
60. Ibid., p. 274.
61. Ibid., pp. 702-3.
62. Ibid., p. 703.
63. *A Vision*, p. 63.
64. *Variorum Plays*, p. 1010.
65. *Collected Plays*, p. 640.
66. Ibid., pp. 703-4.
67. Ibid., p. 704.
68. Ibid.
69. Ibid.
70. Ibid.
71. Ibid.
72. Ibid., pp. 704-5.
73. Ibid., p. 705.
74. Ibid.

Select Bibliography

A. PRIMARY

Gregory, Lady A., *Cuchulain of Muirthemne* (London: John Murray, 1902; New York: Oxford University Press, 5th ed., 1970).

Yeats, William Butler, *Autobiographies* (London: Macmillan, 1966; New York: Macmillan, 1966).

— *The Collected Plays of W. B. Yeats* (London: Macmillan, 1962; New York: Macmillan, 1963).

— *The Collected Poems of W. B. Yeats* (London: Macmillan, 1950; New York: Macmillan, 1951).

— and T. Sturge Moore, *Correspondence 1901-1937,* ed. Ursula Bridge (London: Routledge & Kegan Paul, 1953; New York: Oxford University Press, 1953).

— *Essays and Introductions* (London: Macmillan, 1961).

— *Explorations* (London: Macmillan, 1962; New York: Macmillan, 1963).

— *Fairy and Folk Tales of the Irish Peasantry* (London: The Walter Scott Publishing Co., 1888; New York: Thomas Whittaker, 1888).

— *The Letters of W. B. Yeats,* ed. Allan Wade (London: Rupert Hart-Davis, 1954; New York: Macmillan, 1955).

— *Letters to the New Island,* ed. Horace Reynolds (Cambridge, Mass.: Harvard University Press, 1934; London: Oxford University Press, 1970).

— *Memoirs,* ed. Denis Donoghue (London: Macmillan, 1972; New York: Macmillan, 1972).

— *Mythologies* (London: Macmillan, 1959; New York: Macmillan, 1969).

— *Uncollected Prose 1,* ed. John P. Frayne (London: Macmillan, 1970; New York: Columbia University Press, 1970).

- *The Variorum Edition of the Plays of W. B. Yeats,* ed. Russell K. Alspach (New York: Macmillan, 1966; London: Macmillan, 1966).
- *The Variorum Edition of the Poems of W. B. Yeats,* ed. Peter Allt and Russell K. Alspach (New York: Macmillan, 1957; London: Macmillan, 1957).
- *A Vision* (New York: Macmillan; 1956; London: Macmillan, 1962).

B. CRITICAL

Bjersby, Birgit, *The Interpretation of the Cuchulain Legend in the Works of W. B. Yeats* (Upsala: A. B. Lundequista Bokhandeln, 1950).

Bradford, Curtis B., *Yeats at Work* (Carbondale and Edwardsville: Southern Illinois University Press, 1965).

Bushrui, S., *Yeats's Verse Plays, The Revisions 1900-1910* (Oxford: Clarendon, 1965).

Clark, David R., *W. B. Yeats and the Theatre of Desolate Reality* (Dublin: Dolmen Press, 1965).

Ellmann, Richard, *The Identity of Yeats* (New York: Oxford University Press, 1954).

Engelberg, Edward, *The Vast Design, Patterns in W. B. Yeat's Aesthetic* (Toronto: University of Toronto Press, 1964).

Grossman, Allan R., *Poetic Knowledge in the Early Yeats* (Charlottesville: University Press of Virginia, 1969).

Hall, James (ed.), *The Permanence of Yeats* (New York: Macmillan, 1950).

Hoare, Dorothy M., *The Works of Morris and Yeats in Relation to Early Saga Literature* (Cambridge: Cambridge University Press, 1937).

Hoffman, Daniel, *Barbarous Knowledge* (New York: Oxford University Press, 1967).

Jeffares, Alexander Norman, *The Circus Animals* (London: Macmillan, 1970; Stanford: Stanford University Press 1970).

Kermode, John Frank, *The Romantic Image* (London: Routledge & Kegan Paul, 1957).

Lucas, F. L., *The Drama of Chekhov, Synge, Yeats, and Pirandello* (London: Cassell, 1963).

Miller, Liam (ed.), *The Dolmen Press Yeats Centenary Papers MCMLXV* (Dublin: Dolmen Press, 1968).

Moore, John Rees, *Masks of Love and Death* (Ithaca: Cornell University Press, 1971).

Nathan, Leonard E., *The Tragic Drama of William Butler Yeats* (New York: Columbia University Press, 1965).

Rajan, Balachandra, *W. B. Yeats, a Critical Introduction* (London: Hutchinson University Library, 1965).

Reid, Benjamin Lawrence, *William Butler Yeats, the Lyric of Tragedy* (Norman: University of Oklahoma Press, 1961).

Saul, George Brandon, *Prolegomena to the Study of Yeats's Plays* (Philadelphia: University of Philadelphia Press, 1958).

Seiden, Morton Irving, *William Butler Yeats — The Poet as a Mythmaker* (East Lansing: Michigan State University Press, 1962).

Stock, Amy Geraldine, *W. B. Yeats, His Poetry and Thought* (Cambridge: Cambridge University Press, 1961).

Ure, Peter, *Toward A Mythology* (New York: Russell & Russell, 1967).

— *Yeats the Playwright* (London: Routledge & Kegan Paul, 1963).

Vendler, Helen H., *Yeats's Vision and the Later Plays* (Cambridge: Harvard University Press, 1963).

Wilson, F. A. C., *W. B. Yeats and Tradition* (London: Victor Gollancz, 1962).

— *Yeats's Iconography* (London: Victor Gollancz, 1960).

Zwerdling, Alex, *Yeats and the Heroic Ideal* (New York: New York University Press, 1965).

C. HISTORICAL AND BIOGRAPHICAL

Bablet, Denis, *Edward Gordon Craig* (London: Heinemann, 1966).

Bax, Clifford, *Florence Farr, Bernard Shaw and W. B. Yeats* (Dublin: Cuala Press, 1941).

Clarke, Austin, *The Celtic Twilight and the Nineties* (Dublin: Dolmen, 1969).

Craig, Edward Gordon, *Index to the Story of My Days* (London: Hulton Press, 1957).

Crowley, Aleister, *The Confessions of Aleister Crowley*. ed. John Symonds and Kenneth Grant (New York: Bantam Books, 1971).

Ellis-Fermor, Una, *The Irish Dramatic Movement* (London: Methuen, 1939).

Ellmann, Richard, *Eminent Domain* (New York: Oxford University Press, 1967).

— *Yeats: The Man and the Masks* (New York: E. P. Dutton, 1948).

Fay, Gerard, *The Abbey Theatre* (London: Hollis & Carter, 1958).

Fay, W. G., and Catherine Carswell, *The Fays of the Abbey Theatre* (New York: Harcourt, Brace, 1935).

Gogarty, Oliver St. John, *It Isn't This Time Of Year At All* (New York: Doubleday, 1954).

— *William Butler Yeats: A Memoir* (Dublin: Dolmen Press, 1963).

Greene, David H., and Edward M. Stephens, *J. M. Synge 1871-1907* (New York: Macmillan, 1959).

Gregory, Lady A., *Our Irish Theatre* (London: Putnams, 1913).

Henn, T. R., *The Lonely Tower* (London: Methuen, 1950).

Hone, Joseph, *W. B. Yeats 1865-1939* (London: Macmillan, 1962; New York: St. Martin's Press, 1962).

Lieberson, Goddard (ed.), *The Irish Uprising 1916-1922* (New York: CBS Records, 1966).

Jeffares, Alexander Norman, *W. B. Yeats, Man and Poet* (London: Routledge & Kegan Paul, 1949).

Marcus, Phillip L., *Yeats and the Beginning of the Irish Renaissance* (Ithaca: Cornell University Press, 1970).

Moore, George, *Ave* (New York: Boni & Liveright, 1923).

Moore, Virginia, *The Unicorn* (New York: Macmillan, 1954).

Murphy, Daniel J., 'The Reception of Synge's *Playboy* in Ireland and America, 1907-1912', *Bulletin of the New York Public Library*, vol. 64, no. 10.

O'Driscoll, Robert, and Lorna Reynolds (ed.), *Yeats Studies Number 1 — Yeats and the 1890s* (Shannon: Irish University Press, 1971).

Pearse, Padraic H., *Collected Works of Padraic H. Pearse* (Dublin: Phoenix Publishing Co., 1917).

Price, Alan, *Synge and the Anglo-Irish Drama* (London: Methuen, 1961).

Raine, Kathleen Jessie, *Yeats, the Tarot, and the Golden Dawn* (Dublin: Dolmen Press, 1972).

Regardie, Israel, *My Rosicrucian Adventure* (St. Paul: Llewellyn Publications, 1971).

Skelton, Robin, and Ann Saddlemeyer (ed.), *The World of W. B. Yeats* (Seattle: University of Washington Press, 1967).

Williams, Gertrude Marvin, *Madame Blavatsky Priestess of the Occult* (New York: Lancer Books, 1946).

D. SPECIALIZED

Blavatsky, H. P., *The Secret Doctrine* (Los Angeles: Theosophy Co., 1947).

Campbell, Joseph, *The Hero With a Thousand Faces* (New York: Pantheon, 1949).

— *The Masks of God: Occidental Mythology* (New York: Viking Press, 1964).

— *The Masks of God: Primitive Mythology* (New York: Viking Press, 1959).

Crow, W. B., *A History of Magic, Witchcraft and Occultism* (Hollywood: Wiltshire Book Company, 1970).

D'Arbois de Jubainville, Henry, *The Irish Mythological Cycle and Celtic Mythology*, tr. Richard and Irvine Best (New York: Lemma Publishing Corporation, 1970).

Dillon, Myles, *Early Irish Literature* (Chicago: University of Chicago Press, 1948).

— (ed.), *Irish Sagas* (Cork: Mercier Press, 1968).

Eliade, Mircea, *Rites and Symbols of Initiation* (New York: Harper and Row, 1965).

Frazer, Sir J. G., *The Golden Bough* (London: Macmillan, 1957; New York: St. Martin's Press, 1957).

Graves, Robert, *The White Goddess* (London: Faber & Faber, 1959.

Hall, Manly P., *The Secret Teachings of All Ages* (Los Angeles: The Philosophical Research Society, 1971).

Hawkins, Gerald S., *Stonehenge Decoded* (New York: Dell Publishing Co., 1966).

Hyde, Douglas, *The Story of Early Gaelic Literature* (London: T. Fisher Unwin, 1895).

— *A Literary History of Ireland* (London: T. Fisher Unwin, 1910).

Joyce, P. W., *Old Celtic Romances* (London: Longmans, Green, 1914).

Jung, Carl, *The Basic Writings of C. G. Jung*, ed. Violet Staub D. Laszlo (New York: Modern Library, 1959).

— *et al.*, *Man and his Symbols* (New York: Dell Publishing Co., 1968).

Kinsella, Thomas (tr.), *Táin bó Cúailnge* (Dublin: Dolmen Press, 1969).

Larousse Encyclopedia of Mythology (London: Paul Hamlyn, 1959).

Loomis, Roger Sherman, *Celtic Myth and Arthurian Romance* (New York: Haskell House, 1967).

Macculloch, John Arnott, *The Mythology of All Races — Celtic* (bound with Jan Máchal, *Slavic*) *Volume III* (New York: Cooper Square Publishers, 1964).

Mathers, Macgregor S. L., *The Kabbalah Unveiled* (London: Routledge & Kegan Paul, 1951).

Nietzsche, Friedrich, *The Philosophy of Nietzsche* (New York: Modern Library, 1927).

Pound, Ezra, and Ernest Fenollosa, *The Classic Noh Theatre of Japan* (New York: New Directions, 1959).

Powell, T. G. E., *The Celts* (London: Thames & Hudson, 1963).

Rees, Alwyn and Brinley, *Celtic Heritage* (London: Thames & Hudson, 1961).

Regardie, Israel, *The Golden Dawn* (River Falls: Hazel Hills Corporation, 1970).

— *The Middle Pillar* (Saint Paul: Llewellyn Publications, 1970).

Rhys, John, *Lectures on the Origin and Growth of Religion as Illustrated by Celtic Heathendom* (London: Williams & Northgate, 1892).

Seligmann, Kurt, *The History of Magic* (New York: Pantheon Books, 1948).

Waite, A. E., *The Holy Kabbalah* (New York: University Books, n.d.).

— *The Holy Grail* (New York: University Books, 1961).

— *The Pictorial Key to the Tarot* (New York: University Books, 1959).

Waley, Arthur, *The No Plays of Japan* (New York: Grove Press, 1920).

Wilson, Colin, *The Occult* (New York: Random House, 1971).

Zimmer, Heinrick, *The King and the Corpse* (New York: Pantheon Books, 1956).

Index